Vera Zasulich: A Biography

JAY BERGMAN

Vera Zasulich

A BIOGRAPHY

STANFORD UNIVERSITY PRESS

Stanford, California 1983

Stanford University Press
Stanford, California
© 1983 by the Board of Trustees of the
Leland Stanford Junior University
Printed in the United States of America
ISBN 0-8047-1156-9
LC 82-80927

Frontispiece:
Photograph of Vera Zasulich reproduced by
permission of R. Oldenbourg Verlag, Munich

To My Mother and Father

Preface

THE STORY of Vera Zasulich will not alter completely our perceptions of the Russian revolutionary movement. Compared with Lenin or Plekhanov or Martov, Zasulich is a relatively minor figure, and there is nothing in the pages which follow to suggest that this estimation of her significance should be revised. Her attempts at theoretical analysis were mostly amateurish, and her skills as a revolutionary agitator were very nearly nonexistent.

Zasulich's story, nevertheless, deserves to be told. In many ways her life embodied all the important aspects of revolutionary politics in Russia in the late nineteenth and early twentieth centuries: one can see in her youth in microcosm the forces which turned against the state the energy, intelligence, and creativity of a large segment of the educated elite, the very people whose loyalty and knowledge were essential to the survival of the government; one can see in her attempted assassination of Trepov the moral passion and dedication of the intelligentsia, that elusive social category so peculiarly Russian in its penchant for extending ideas to their ultimate conclusions; one can see in her populism and Marxism how radical dogma equating poverty and virtue could fascinate men and women possessed by an altruism which demanded that the affluent and educated help redistribute the material and intellectual resources of society; and one can see in the turbulence of her personality how revolution could often ravage beyond repair the lives of those who adopted it as a profession, leaving as its most immediate consequence tattered friendships, interrupted relationships, and damaged psyches.

But there were other aspects of Zasulich's personality and politics which distinguished her career from others' in the revolutionary movement. I have tried in this biography to emphasize two of them. The first concerns the relationship between Zasulich's personal life and her political and ideological choices. Unlike those who shared her political and ideological commitments, Zasulich came to these commitments as a consequence of impulses reflecting her status after 1869 (and even more so after 1878) as a homeless, lonely, isolated, and impoverished émigré or exile, subject to periods of depression and anxiety that increased in frequency and magnitude as she grew older. As a result, she selected ideologies—first populism and then Marxism—whose promise to benefit classes she considered less fortunate than herself made these ideologies convenient vehicles by which her own problems and predicament could be transcended. Helping others, in short, became a means of helping herself.

Thus, the second aspect of Zasulich's career I have chosen to emphasize is her insistence on the moral virtue of collective action. When she dealt with revolutionary strategy and tactics, she determined that only a Popular Front of revolutionary parties, acting on the basis of common interests and goals, could overthrow autocracy. When she dealt with the structure of revolutionary parties, she concluded that only a party in which authority was distributed collectively could acquire the moral rectitude to justify a revolutionary transformation. And when, as a Marxist, she tried to ascertain the principal virtue of the new society that this revolution would create, she decided that it lay precisely in the capacity of a socialist order to inculcate what she referred to as *"solidarnost'"*: the willingness of the proletariat to sacrifice its class interests for the interests of humanity. Whenever she dealt with the organization, the tactics, the justification, or the consequences of revolutionary action, in every instance her conclusions reflected this pervasive faith in the nobility of collective endeavor. For Zasulich a politics of revolutionary unity was a moral as well as a practical necessity.

Preface

Ironically, though, the individualism implicit in Zasulich's lonely struggle with the problems that plagued her seemed to inspire other revolutionaries far more than the collectivism that was implicit in her ideas; time and again revolutionaries who expressed their affection and respect for her focused on those aspects of her life—the uniqueness of her personality, her disdain for bourgeois comforts, the idiosyncratic quality of her thought, her moral stature as a would-be assassin—that suggest the sanctity and the inviolability of the individual. To this extent, one can discern in her career, with its disparity between the way she lived and the ideas she espoused, a larger antithesis not easily resolved in revolutionary movements (or in politics generally) between the competing claims of individual and collective endeavor to foster moral virtue and social justice. Russian revolutionaries did not resolve this question satisfactorily in the years before the October Revolution, but perhaps a biography of Zasulich can show how a single individual, in her ideas and in her life, could embody both of these claims simultaneously.

One accumulates many debts in the course of writing a book. Professor Firuz Kazemzadeh of Yale University ably supervised this project in its original form of a doctoral dissertation; indeed, it was Professor Kazemzadeh who first suggested Zasulich as a possible subject of a biography. In transforming the dissertation into a manuscript suitable for publication, I benefited greatly from the assistance, encouragement, and criticisms of Professors Abraham Ascher, Deborah Hardy, Char Miller, Philip Pomper, and Reginald Zelnik. I am especially grateful to J. G. Bell, Editor of the Stanford University Press, for giving my work the full benefit of his special knowledge, and to Shirley Taylor, who edited the manuscript with a critical and sensitive awareness of the awkward phrase and the ill-chosen word which did much to clarify meanings and eliminate the worst excesses of my prose.

Three other acknowledgments are in order. Professor Marshall Shatz of the University of Massachusetts at Boston, who at Brandeis University many years ago inspired me to follow his example and pursue a career as a historian of Russia, has continued to help me in ways that reflect both his humanity and his impeccable scholarship. With humor and grace he has corrected my grammar, challenged my assumptions, clarified my thinking, and more than anyone else has helped me sustain a commitment to a career as a historian when the vicissitudes of the job market have driven to despair many others less fortunate in the caliber of their mentors.

My late grandfather; Israel M. Goodelman, I shall always remember for the dogged persistence with which he continued his intellectual labors in spite of almost total blindness. The memory of him sitting at his typewriter, struggling to complete a translation, has strengthened my determination to perpetuate a family tradition of scholarship and intellectual accomplishment.

Finally, my debt to my mother and father is so deep and personal that words cannot adequately express it. It is to them that this book is dedicated with love and affection.

J.B.

Contents

A Note on Transliteration

Transliteration of Russian words follows the Library of Congress system. The only exceptions are to render Trotskii, Tolstoi, and Dostoevskii as Trotsky, Tolstoy, and Dostoevsky, respectively, and the "ks" in, for example, Aleksandra and Aleksandrov as "x"—hence, Alexandra and Alexandrov.

Vera Zasulich: A Biography

ONE

The Early Years

VERA IVANOVNA ZASULICH was born on July 27, 1849,* in the Gzhatsk district of Smolensk province, the fourth of five children of Feoktista Mikhailovna and Ivan Petrovich Zasulich.[1] Not much is known about her parents' background, but the few facts we have place them among the numerous Russian lesser nobility who after decades of inflation, technological stagnation, financial mismanagement, and profligate spending were distinguished by their status rather than by their wealth. The family estate on which Vera was born had originally been only one of several owned by her maternal grandfather, Mikhail Alexandrov, whom Vera's sister Alexandra described in her memoirs as a gentleman of considerable fortune.[2] Alexandrov had eleven children. When he died he bequeathed to his two youngest daughters, Feoktista and Glafira, the estate commonly referred to as Mikhailovka and apportioned the remaining plots of land among his six sons. Mikhailovka was a medium-sized estate consisting of nearly 200 *desiatinas* (540 acres) and some forty serfs, most of whom did not live or work on the property but paid off their obligations with goods or money (*obrok*) acquired elsewhere. With only a few serfs actually working the land, it probably was left largely uncultivated, so that its condition deteriorated with the passage of time.[3]

---

* All dates in this book, except where noted otherwise, are rendered in the Old Style according to the Julian Calendar, which was twelve days behind the Gregorian (or Western) Calendar in the nineteenth century, thirteen days in the twentieth.

For a few years, it seems (Alexandra is not precise on this point), Glafira and Feoktista tried to live comfortably on their serfs' payments along with what remained of their father's inheritance, but sometime before Glafira's death they were obliged to mortgage large parts of the estate to a local municipal council which had been established to reimburse nobles for land they could no longer afford to own. After Glafira died, Feoktista, who was evidently not suited for the job of estate manager and certainly had no control over an unfortunate economic system, appeared destined for a bleak future.[4] In 1842, a relatively impoverished Feoktista married Ivan Petrovich Zasulich, a former army captain of noble birth but little means, the owner of a small estate in the Poretsk district. Between 1843 and 1852 Feoktista bore him five children. Ivan, according to his daughter Alexandra, had won medals for his army service, but he became an alcoholic and spent long periods away from his family on the Poretsk estate.[5] The editor of Vera Zasulich's memoirs infers from them that Ivan was "a man of energy," but since Vera was barely three years old when her father died, her impressions could hardly have been first hand.

Left a widow, Feoktista, apparently to ease the financial burden of educating her children, sent three of her daughters, Ekaterina, Alexandra, and Vera, to live with well-to-do cousins. (Mikhail, the eldest child and only son, was already in military school in Moscow.)[6] The cousins to whom Vera was entrusted lived on a nearby estate called Biakolovo, ten *versts* (roughly six miles) from Mikhailovka.[7] Except for summers with her mother and sisters at Mikhailovka, Vera spent most of her childhood and adolescence at Biakolovo. It was not a happy existence. Vera says in her memoirs: "The older I became, the more I was convinced I was an alien: I did not belong. No one ever caressed me, kissed me, or sat me on his knee; no one ever referred to me in affectionate terms. The servants abused me."[8] Vera seems to have felt that she had no family legitimacy, unloved by both the Mikuliches and the Alexandrovs and not quite a part of either house. At the Mikuliches she felt rebuffed and rejected, ridiculed partly as an intruder and partly for her poverty.

Even so, "decorum" demanded that she be educated by a governess—if only so that she could learn enough to become one herself—and she got her lessons along with her cousins from a governess named Mimina. Like all governesses to the gentry, Mimina was supposed to instill in the female members of the family the manners, habits, and attitudes appropriate for women of their class. Zasulich does not describe her teacher with any fondness: "Mimina was about sixty, with weak eyes, and so obese that she was almost spherical. It was too late for her to find a new position, and she could talk about this with no one except me. She would be a hanger-on until her death. . . . She had spent her entire life in other people's homes raising other people's children."[9] Mimina taught Vera French, German, arithmetic, spelling, and Russian literature, administering a mild whipping if the girl proved the least bit stubborn. Vera does not say that Mimina regarded her as brighter than her girl cousins, but it is clear that Mimina's attitude toward her was different, more confiding. She loved to remind Vera of the apparent similarities in their backgrounds, and would say, "We do not belong here. No one really cares for us."[10]

Vera's dislike of Mimina may well have had something to do with Mimina's presumption, but she also scorned her commonness—her bedtime stories replete with images of coffins, skulls, and ghosts—and as she grew older she came to hate Mimina's excessive religiosity, in which she saw no hint of real compassion. Vera was attracted early to Christ the man, whose suffering, social ostracism, and isolation had perhaps some vague resemblance to her own, but conventional piety never appealed to her, and if her reminiscences are to be believed, by the age of fifteen she no longer believed in the existence of a deity.[11] Mimina's religion seemed to her only a veneer and a sham. Despite these and other failings as an instructor, however, Mimina did inculcate in Vera a respect for books, ideas, and foreign cultures that remained strong throughout her life. She introduced her charge to writers such as Lermontov, Schiller, Nekrasov, and Ryleev, whose fictitious world of heroism, struggle, and moral virtue seemed preferable in every way to Vera's tedious and cold surroundings at Biakolovo. Not least important, it was from Mimina that Zasulich began to learn the languages that she used during her many years of exile in Western Europe.

If Zasulich was acquiring any sense of social consciousness as

she grew up, it was not the result of personal observation. Biakolovo's serfs, like those of Mikhailovka, fulfilled their obligations
by *obrok* payments, and Vera saw mainly the household servants,
who were well treated and never beaten or abused. She says in
her memoirs, "I did not see any of the atrocities of serfdom. I
never heard of any at Biakolovo."[12] In these years her worries
about injustice were all very self-centered: "It seemed to me that
I was being forced to accept a plan for my future. I was repelled
by the fate that my social position betokened. It was referred to
casually at Biakolovo. I was to be a governess. I could tolerate
anything but that."[13] She could imagine years of teaching children who, like the children at Biakolovo, would look down on
her. Certainly Mimina, with her petty cruelties and utter depen-
dence upon her employers, was not an appealing embodiment
of a profession unlikely even in the best of circumstances to
satisfy adolescent yearnings for heroism and struggle. But there
was little choice under the conditions of the time. Women could
not enroll in the universities, perform state service without special permission, or, if married, work without the approval of
their husbands (nor could they initiate divorce proceedings).
The male chauvinism of nineteenth-century Russia still largely
followed the *Domostroi* (or Domestic Regulations) of early Mus-
covy, which prescribed that husbands should regularly beat their
wives and keep them without authority.[14]

In her memoirs Zasulich says:

Even before my revolutionary dreams, even before I was sent to boarding school, I made elaborate plans to keep from becoming a governess.
Of course it would have been much easier if I had been a boy; then I
could have done what I wanted. . . . And then, the distant specter of
revolution appeared, making me the equal of any boy; I too could
dream of "action," of "exploits," and of the "great struggle." . . . I too
could join those "who perished for the great cause of love."*

Certainly for many women of Zasulich's time a commitment to
revolution was in part an escape from the stifling fate their sex
imposed on them, and one of the attractions of revolutionary
circles in St. Petersburg in the 1860's, and of the revolutionary

---

* V. I. Zasulich, *Vospominaniia* (Moscow, 1931), p. 15. The last phrase, from
Nekrasov, was no doubt familiar to most contemporary readers of her memoirs.

intelligentsia in general, was their effort to treat men and women as equals. Sexual differences were indeed quite irrelevant, they believed, and sexual inequality was an impediment to the overriding quest for "moral wholeness." Zasulich's peculiar social position as a poor relation scorned for her poverty had already brought her to the point of resentment for her own unfair lot in life, but it was her experiences in Moscow a few years later that brought her in touch for the first time with people who had any thoughts about social injustice on a large scale.

As early as 1858, when Vera was nine, Feoktista Mikhailovna had talked of sending her daughters to school in Moscow or St. Petersburg when and if she could afford to do so.[15] Finally, she was able to send, first, Ekaterina, and then Alexandra to a *pension* in Moscow for the polishing needed to pass the state examinations required for governesses. Sometime in the summer or fall of 1866 Vera joined Alexandra at the pension. Vera was no more enthusiastic about becoming a governess than Alexandra was, and they both found life at the establishment rather grim. Classes were conducted entirely in French or German and students who responded in Russian risked the obloquy of having to eat dinner standing up; only music was taught besides the two languages and all the instruction was superficial.[16] Vera was now more determined than ever to escape the dreaded profession.

But Vera's experiences in Moscow in 1866–67 extended well beyond the narrow confines of her schooling and opened a new avenue. It was in Moscow that she first read Lavrov, Chernyshevskii, and John Stuart Mill, the patron saints of the revolutionary intelligentsia; there that she was first exposed to utilitarianism, positivism, socialism, and the other European ideologies of the time. And for the first time she began to see the possibility of realizing through revolutionary action her vague notions of heroism and struggle. The year in Moscow brought a fusion of hazy ideals and practical action: "That year," Zasulich says, "the seventeenth of my life, was filled with the most feverish internal activity; I finally took my fate into my own hands."[17]

Vera's oldest sister Ekaterina was already a member of the student revolutionary society of Moscow, radicalized originally by the inadequate reforms of Alexander II, and it was through her that Vera, and Alexandra also, were drawn into the movement. At Ekaterina's, Vera met Anna and Liudmila Kolachevskaia, two sisters who had belonged to the clandestine group whose leader, Karakozov, had tried to assassinate the Tsar on April 4, 1866. They subsequently introduced her to their brother Andrei, a member of a similar group led by Nikolai Ishutin. A short time later, also in a social setting, she met the sisters of Leonid Obolenskii and Osip Motkov. These two young men had been among the hundred or so men and women arrested in St. Petersburg and Moscow following the attempt on the life of the Tsar.[18] All these new acquaintances seem to have been made in the summer or early fall of 1866, very soon after Zasulich arrived in Moscow. On October 1, sentences were meted out to those convicted in a secret trial, and on October 3 Karakozov was hanged.

Nothing is known about Zasulich's relationship with Anna and Liudmila Kolachevskaia and their brother, or with the sisters of Obolenskii and Motkov. Assuming that Zasulich's dating is correct in memoirs written nearly a half-century later, the revolutionaries she met through these young people probably belonged to the more "moderate" wing of the revolutionary movement, those who preferred agitation and propaganda to terrorism. By then, the real extremists were in jail. Osip Motkov, of peasant origins himself, headed a moderate faction in the Ishutin group which believed in the "slow but sure road" of education and enlightenment; according to Motkov, "The present regime will change when ideas are spread throughout all levels of society. Until that time we must hold back others and ourselves from unleashing a revolution."[19] Thus, although Zasulich claims that she became a socialist at seventeen, it seems clear that if she got her socialism from discussions with the Moscow radicals she met during her stay at the pension in 1866–67, it amounted to little more than a commitment to eliminating poverty, injustice, and ignorance by peaceful agitation and propaganda.[20]

This commitment was strengthened by the books she read. One of Zasulich's early heroes was the Decembrist Ryleev, whose mission, as Zasulich interpreted it, was to reduce the material and spiritual impoverishment of the masses. In her memoirs she describes Ryleev's poem "Nalivaiko" as "a holy relic."[21] Ryleev's life, like Christ's, confirmed her growing belief that to help others one must suffer oneself. From Ryleev, Zasulich went on to John Stuart Mill. She read his *Political Economy* in Chernyshevskii's translation, and for years it remained her principal intellectual inspiration: "I first tried to read it when I was in boarding school, but at that time it went very badly. . . . Now I read it the way I studied my lessons; I read one chapter and then recited its contents to myself. Toward the end, when I was reading Mill, I would begin to guess beforehand what objections Chernyshevskii would raise about this or that passage, and when I succeeded I was very pleased with myself."*

Paradoxically, Mill's utilitarian calculus of human needs and social imperatives appealed to the altruist in Zasulich, perhaps because both altruism and utilitarianism are centrally concerned with increasing happiness. In effect, Zasulich transformed an ideology based on self-interest into an ethos based on self-sacrifice. Her utilitarianism was neither Chernyshevskii's belief that society would somehow benefit if its members simply calculated their self-interest rationally nor Pisarev's practice of evaluating everything in terms of its social utility, but the effort of people like herself to increase the general sum of happiness in society by bringing material prosperity and cultural enlightenment to "the people." Utilitarianism and altruism were, in her mind, the same thing.

Another source of inspiration for the young Zasulich was Pyotr Lavrov's *Historical Letters,* which, before their publication in book form in 1870, were serialized in the magazine *Nedel'ia* (The Week). Phrased in the idiom of utilitarianism, replete with calculations of social pleasures and social miseries, this work was the first significant attempt by a member of the Russian intelligentsia to define its role and obligation to society. Pisarev and other nihilists had seen the intelligentsia's role as primarily iconoclastic, a matter of revealing the absurdities and contradictions of life. Lavrov disagreed: for him the intelligentsia had a more

---

* Zasulich, *Vospominaniia,* pp. 58–59. For purposes of comparison it is revealing that when Lenin listened to a reading of this same work, he experienced "boredom" and "indifference." N. Valentinov, *The Early Years of Lenin* (Ann Arbor, 1969), p. 143.

positive function, that of increasing the general sum of enlightenment and material prosperity in society, without which—as he
never tired of repeating—no change in the political structure of
society was possible. Both Pisarev and Lavrov, each with some
justification, claimed the mantle of Mill. But where Pisarev had
concluded from utilitarian calculations that the intelligentsia
could best serve society by providing an incisive critical minority
to speak out on the crucial issues, Lavrov concluded from the
same calculations that this was not enough: "The recognition of
the injustice of what had seemed just is the first step. . . . This
recognition gradually spreads, preparing the ground for people
who are not only conscious of the new principle, but determined
to put it into practice."[22] To Pisarev, man's principal goal was
moral perfection; to Lavrov it was social justice.

Zasulich seems to have been exposed to only one side of this
debate. She read Lavrov's *Historical Letters* (and subsequently
recommended them to friends and associates), but apparently
did not read Pisarev or other nihilist writers.[23] This may have
been a deliberate choice, but it was more likely an uninformed
oversight. Certainly Zasulich, young and unsure, was not ready
for the lengthy self-analysis that Russian nihilism implicitly demanded.

In 1867 Zasulich completed her training at the Moscow pension, and both she and Alexandra passed the official examinations at Moscow University.[24] Through the efforts of the head-
master at the pension, Vera found a job in Serpukhov, a town
not far from Moscow, as an assistant to a justice of the peace.[25]
Since the Judicial Reforms of 1864, the newly established jus-
tices of the peace had been empowered within their geographical jurisdiction to adjudicate all misdemeanors, libel suits, civil
suits, and claims for damages involving small amounts of property.[26] According to the State Council:

The duty of the justice of the peace is the examination of petty cases
occurring almost daily among the majority of the population, a considerable part of which has no knowledge of laws, cannot endure formal-
ism, respects natural equity only, has no time to lose, and seeks above all
a rapid decision in accordance with its notion of justice. The main goal
of the justice of the peace is to satisfy this elemental need of administra-
tion of justice according to conscience.[27]

For the first time in her life, Zasulich was exposed in her daily routine to rural existence at its worst: the peasants who passed through the justice's chambers desperately needed both education and material assistance. It was indeed, as the Soviet historian R. A. Kovnator says, a "school of life" for Zasulich.[28] Zasulich herself commented that her year at Serpukhov reinforced her belief that "living well in the midst of poverty was more a misfortune than a privilege."[29]

When the justice who employed her succumbed to mental illness in the summer of 1868, Zasulich left Serpukhov for St. Petersburg, convinced that only those who shared her background, education, and compassion could alleviate the poverty and ignorance she was certain she would find there. While Zasulich was in Serpukhov, Feoktista had leased her estate and moved to St. Petersburg with her youngest daughter, Sonia. That winter (1868) Sonia died of typhus, and Feoktista, Ekaterina, and Alexandra then moved to a *dacha* in a village near Moscow where for several months they worked in a seamstresses' artel modeled after the one in Chernyshevskii's novel, *What Is to Be Done?* Shortly after Vera (accompanied by Ekaterina) left Serpukhov for St. Petersburg, Feoktista joined them there, but lived with Mikhail. Alexandra, too, moved to St. Petersburg, where she married Pyotr Uspenskii not long after Ekaterina married Lev Nikiforov; all four would be arrested, for different reasons, in 1869.[30] In St. Petersburg, Zasulich worked for a brief time in seamstresses' and bookbinding artels and then got a job in an evening school teaching illiterate workers to read and write. At this stage in her life, Zasulich did not see her pedagogical and philanthropic activities as potentially subversive; only very gradually would she come to realize that one could not do such things in tsarist Russia without confronting the enormous power of the state. Soon after her arrival in St. Petersburg, however, she found herself among revolutionaries whose actions raised questions of political tactics and morality more profound than any she had encountered in Moscow or Serpukhov.

In trying to make sense of Zasulich's relations with Sergei Nechaev, one must bear in mind that she was dealing with an unbalanced, perhaps even pathological, personality. The murder of Ivan Ivanov, a fellow revolutionary, by Nechaev and his followers in late November 1869 was a brutal, despicable act. Nechaev and some of his closest associates (one of them Pyotr Uspenskii, Zasulich's brother-in-law) coldly pronounced a death sentence on Ivanov because they suspected him of betraying them. Then they lured him to a remote section of the park of the Petrovskii Academy in Moscow, and violently, if clumsily, strangled him to death. Nechaev shot him through the back of the head, and after some ineffective efforts to strip the body of evidence, they shoved it—insufficiently weighted—through a hole in the ice of the lake. Most of the conspirators, including Uspenskii, were caught by the end of the year, but Nechaev, who had masterminded the entire affair, was not apprehended until 1872.* He was ultimately convicted of murder and incarcerated in the Ravelin fortress, where he died of scurvy in 1882.[31]

The murder of Ivanov was a serious setback for the revolutionary movement, causing many of its supporters to draw back in despair as they realized how easily it could attract the most twisted and sinister elements of society. In the end the movement survived, but its margin of survival was exceptionally slim. Ivanov's murder could have sparked a chain of homicidal recriminations resulting in the disintegration of radical politics in Russia; this did not happen. But Ivanov's murder caused many to recoil from Nechaev's belief, shared by other revolutionaries in the 1860's, that there are no ties stronger than complicity in crime to bind together a revolutionary circle.

Zasulich's relationship to Nechaev is difficult to determine precisely.† Sometime after her arrival in St. Petersburg in 1868,

* Uspenskii was arrested after a search of his apartment—unrelated to the discovery of Ivanov's body—turned up material that connected him with the Nechaev group. He confessed and in the trial in 1871 received the harshest sentence—fifteen years at hard labor in the mines in Siberia. He was murdered by fellow prisoners in December 1881. Philip Pomper, *Sergei Nechaev* (New Brunswick, 1979), pp. 117–18, 121.

† In 1883 Zasulich was asked by Plekhanov and Deich to write an account of the Nechaev Affair, but because she was living abroad as a fugitive from the Russian police, she deliberately omitted from her account most of the details of her own participation. Her account was first published as "Nechaevskoe delo" in L. G. Deich, ed., *Gruppa 'Osvobozhdenie Truda': Iz arkhivov G. V. Plekhanova, V. I. Zasulich i L. G. Deicha* (Moscow-Leningrad, 1923–28), vol. 2, pp. 22–72, and reprinted in 1931 in her *Vospominaniia*, pp. 17–57. To complicate matters, Alex-

Zasulich began attending classes at the Andreevskii teachers' college on Vasilevskii Island, where she learned a phonetic method of teaching reading. One day her teacher invited her and several other students to his apartment, where they discussed the books that were to be studied in the course. Sergei Nechaev was among those present. Nechaev, the son of a craftsman-waiter and a seamstress in the textile town of Ivanovo, was an ambitious, clever, somewhat theatrical, and very egoistic young man who was at this period teaching part-time at the Sergievskii Academy and beginning to plot a revolutionary career. After the meeting, Nechaev introduced himself to Zasulich and invited her to accompany him to the Academy.[32] In her memoirs Zasulich does not indicate how she responded, nor does she reveal how much contact, if any, she had with Nechaev between this first meeting and the next incident she described, which occurred in January 1869.

Besides being a part-time teacher at the Sergievskii Academy, Nachaev occasionally attended lectures at St. Petersburg University. In both places he was already, by January 1869, widely known as the leader of a group of students who had as their goal the overthrow of the tsarist government, an effort that was to commence, according to Nechaev, on February 19, 1870, the ninth anniversary of the emancipation of the serfs.[33] Students now, unlike those of the early part of the 1860's, often had to worry about unemployment. In the absence of industrialization, neither the *zemstva* nor the other professions created by Alexander's reforms could employ the many students whose families had been ruined economically by the abolition of serfdom. The revolutionary life was therefore more and more tempting, and Nechaev's elaborate plans had the added attraction of offering a full-time occupation.

Zasulich's January encounter with Nechaev was, she later said, "my first serious conversation about revolution, my first step toward the cause."[34] She met Nechaev while visiting her friend

---

andra Uspenskaia's recollections often contradict her sister's, and generally read like an apologia for Nechaev, whom Alexandra refers to as "a simple boy . . . smart, very energetic, with his entire soul devoted to the cause." See Alexandra Uspenskaia, "Vospominaniia shestidesiatnitsy," *Byloe*, no. 18 (1922), p. 33.

Anna Tomilova, in whose house Nechaev's sister Anna was rent-
ing a room. Nechaev described to her in detail—some of it fictitious—his elaborate plans for inciting a revolution among the
peasants. When he finished, he asked Zasulich if she would give
him her address. Zasulich did so, but apparently with some hesitation, for she told him: "I really know very little and want very
much to do something for the cause. I don't believe that what
you are doing will produce a revolution, but I don't know any
other way. I'm not doing anything myself just now, and I would
be happy to help in any way I could." Then, according to Zasulich's account, Nechaev stood up, abruptly walked into another
room, and returned a few minutes later to declare that he was in
love with her. Flustered and surprised, Zasulich replied that,
though she could not return his love, she greatly valued his
friendship. Nechaev then silently bowed and left the room.[35]

Alexandra says in her memoirs that Nechaev's declaration of
love was sincere, despite his manifest conviction, as expressed
by him and Bakunin in their "Revolutionary Catechism," that
women were stupid and foolish and wanted nothing more than
to be manipulated by men.[36] Vera was skeptical. She thought
Nechaev was only using the proposal as a way of getting her to
accompany him to Switzerland, where her knowledge of French
and German would be invaluable to him. In her memoirs she
does not say what answer she made to him at the time.[37] She
implies that they spent that night alone together, but sexual
contact cannot be inferred from Nechaev's subsequent claim
(according to Alexandra) that she was "healthy in all respects,"[38]
since among Russian revolutionaries this meant simply that a
person lacked a police record. Nechaev had few scruples—later
on he tried to procure the inheritance of Alexander Herzen by
seducing Herzen's daughter Nathalie—and was certainly not
above using a declaration of love as a way of getting Zasulich's
support.

At any rate, the following morning Nechaev treated Zasulich
"as if nothing had happened," and informed her enigmatically
that while he was gone she might receive letters addressed to
other people. When she asked him how she should deliver these
letters, he replied simply, "You'll see when you get them."[39] A
few weeks later, Nechaev was questioned by the police and

threatened with arrest if he continued to participate in meetings called by protesting students. The day after Nechaev's interrogation, Zasulich, staying the night at Tomilova's, awoke with a start to find Nechaev standing by her bed. He handed her a package and told her to hide it and then immediately left "without explaining anything or saying another word." Zasulich never saw him again.* With the events that came after—Nechaev's trip to Switzerland to meet Bakunin, and the murder of Ivanov in the fall of 1869 not long after his return—she had no direct connection, but she did serve Nechaev briefly as a go-between.

Zasulich was of course young and politically naïve, though well-intentioned. As Samuel Baron, Plekhanov's biographer, observes, it is most doubtful that she was aware of Nechaev's Machiavellianism.[40] If she was really fond of Nechaev, as apparently she was, it may well have been because he seemed to her a true representative of the *narod,* the class to whose well-being she hoped to dedicate her life, but to which she had no claim herself—and indeed little actual knowledge of. Nechaev's origins were certainly a far cry from her own (though not so humble as he liked to make out) and his education was rather makeshift (Zasulich could easily have discerned the inaccuracy of his frequent quotations from Kant's *Critique of Pure Reason*). His desire for self-improvement, his talk of revolution, his persuasive, brusque manner all aroused her interest and compassion: "To serve the revolution—I could imagine no greater pleasure than this. Before I had only dreamed about it, but now [Nechaev] was saying that he wanted to recruit me, otherwise he would not have said anything. . . . And what did I know of 'the people'? I knew only the house servants at Biakolovo and the members of my seamstress collective, while he himself was a worker by birth."[41] Indeed, the very strangeness of Nechaev's behavior, the abrupt entrances and exits, the mysterious letters and packages, the unexplained directives and declarations of

---

* Zasulich, *Vospominaniia*, p. 63. After Nechaev's disappearance Tomilova told Zasulich that if the police found the package, over one hundred people could be incriminated. Zasulich hid the package without examining it, and only the ineptitude of the police kept them from discovering it when they searched her apartment a few months later. F. A. Gallinin, *Protsess Very Zasulich: sud i posle suda* (St. Petersburg, n.d.), pp. 50–51.

love, may all have served to confirm the fearful distance between the masses and the educated elite. Perhaps by agreeing to help Nechaev, Zasulich felt that she could be of service in the struggle to bridge the gap.

Early in February, very soon after Nechaev's midnight appearance, Zasulich received in the post an envelope containing a brief letter and a note. The letter, from an anonymous student, said that the enclosed note had been thrown out to him from a passing carriage by a prisoner who was in the custody of the police and that the prisoner had asked him to deliver it to the designated address. The note was from Nechaev. In typically cryptic fashion it said: "They are taking me to a fortress. Tell this to our comrades. Let our cause continue."[42] By the time Zasulich received this letter, Nechaev had, in fact, already been interrogated and released by the police in St. Petersburg and was in Moscow. A short time after this, Zasulich received another letter from Nechaev, saying—in a typical embroidery which Zasulich did not question—that he had escaped from the Peter and Paul fortress and was now in Switzerland. Letters continued to arrive from Nechaev in the following weeks enclosing others addressed to revolutionary confederates outlining plans and describing his talks with Bakunin in Switzerland. All these Zasulich dutifully passed on.[43]

Though Zasulich's faith in Nechaev, and his clever use of her, did not make her a part of the inner circle, she continued, somewhat irregularly, to attend meetings of the Nechaev group in St. Petersburg, at which the works of Belinskii, Louis Blanc, Chernyshevskii, and Nekrasov were discussed.[44] Though Zasulich spoke at these meetings of the need "to deliver Russia from the Tsar," she denied that she harbored "evil thoughts" about him when the police interrogated her in 1871.[45] Her later statement was undoubtedly false. But her actions during this period—as opposed to her rhetoric—suggest that her revolutionary commitment did not extend beyond a readiness to perform occasional menial services.

The police, who rarely made fine distinctions, considered her a radical. After gendarmes searched her apartment in April 1869 (and somehow overlooked the package that Nechaev had given her), they returned several times to warn her that, though

ures in her childhood, the hostility directed against her at Biako-lovo, the absence of strong ties to any geographical entity, and the demand that she adopt Mimina's profession may have con-tributed to her sense of isolation and alienation—feelings that need not have produced a revolutionary commitment. In Zasu-lich's case, however, they served as fertile soil in which other ideas and resentments could take root.

Years later, in Moscow and St. Petersburg, the social altruism that these feelings of alienation had produced was not only tolerated but encouraged by Zasulich's sisters. More important, this altruism found corroboration in political ideology, and ulti-mately in political commitment. To want to help the people, to hope to elevate their level of education and enlightenment, to desire an end to poverty and material deprivation, to regret the existence of social and economic inequality—all these impulses which had inflamed her imagination at Biakolovo now could be legitimized intellectually by ideology and enshrined as ethical principles by the moral virtue of the revolutionaries in her mi-lieu who seemed to share them. The Nechaev Affair was a set-back, but no more.

By 1869, all Zasulich needed to solidify her revolutionary commitment was to experience injustice and humiliation analo-gous to what she lamented in the lives of others. The tsarist government obliged her by arresting her without any explana-tion or formal determination of her guilt. During six years of prison and administrative exile, she became convinced that so-cial justice in Russia could only be achieved by the violent trans-formation of the state. She was not yet clear whether this trans-formation could only be the work of a small minority or whether it required the active participation of the masses; nor had she thought seriously about the new society a revolution would cre-ate, or which institutions might best serve her vague commit-

---

superficial collaboration. Years later, in a conversation with Lev Deich sometime after the February Revolution, Zasulich talked of such a resemblance and con-cluded that although Lenin was by far more intelligent than Nechaev, they both had a certain "steadfastness" and "strength of character." Letter of L. G. Deich, May 24, 1924, p. 11. Arkhiv V. M. Zenzinova, Bakhmetoff Collection, Columbia University, New York.

ment to equality of opportunity and wealth. But by 1869 Zasulich was in every other respect a revolutionary, committed to revolution as a political objective, a moral principle, and a profession whose many dangers would permeate every aspect of her life.

TWO

The Trepov Shooting

FOLLOWING her arrest at the end of April 1869, Zasulich was sent to Litovsk prison. In early 1870, for no apparent reason, she was transferred to the Peter and Paul fortress, where she was confined for another year.[1] Then in March 1871, after appearing as a witness in the trial of the Nechaevists, she was abruptly released.[2] Several days later, still in St. Petersburg, she was arrested again and ordered to proceed under police guard to Kresttsy in the province of Novgorod, and report there regularly to the police. In Kresttsy, her two guards gave her several rubles and a box of chocolates (some accounts say also a dress), and left. Lacking any connections in Kresttsy, and failing in her efforts to find work there, Zasulich for several months lived the life of a vagabond, dependent upon the charity of townspeople who were kind enough to offer her food and shelter.[3]

From the time of Zasulich's first arrest her mother had submitted numerous petitions to the authorities in St. Petersburg asking for explanation of the reason for her imprisonment. After Zasulich was exiled to Kresttsy, her mother continued her efforts—asking either for a rescinding of the exile or at least for permission for her daughter to live in the city of Tver with her sister and brother-in-law, Ekaterina and Lev Nikiforov. In June 1871, the authorities agreed to let Zasulich go to Tver.[4] There, for a year or so she enjoyed security and companionship. But the Third Section had not lost sight of her. In the summer of 1872 a police search of the house where she lived with the Nikiforovs uncovered manuscripts and letters implicating Nikiforov in the illegal activities of a group of local seminarians. Though they had no proof of a connection between Zasulich and the seminarians, they arrested her, and after extensive interrogation, exiled her to the more distant town of Soligalich in Kostroma province.[5] The period in Soligalich was uneventful and apparently bleak, for Zasulich says nothing about it in her memoirs. But in December 1873 she was transferred to the city of Kharkov. During her twenty-one months in Kharkov—she was not permitted to leave the city until September 1875—she tried to put her time to good use by taking a course in midwifery at Kharkov University, but because of the stigma of administrative exile, she could not practice her newly acquired profession, and once again she barely managed to survive.[6]

In his memoirs, Henri Rochefort, the French socialist and *communard* who helped Zasulich find shelter in Switzerland at the end of the 1870's, says that at times in the years of her exile Zasulich subsisted literally on bread and water, too poor to afford anything more nourishing.[7] Poverty on such a scale was no doubt embittering in itself as a denial of human dignity, but the irrationality of the government's treatment of Zasulich was far more infuriating to her. Periods of near starvation, after the more tolerable months that she spent with the Nikiforovs, resentment at the government's continuing suspicion, and the inability to lead any sort of useful life in the years 1869–75—all this showed how badly the system needed changing. The pettiness and pointlessness of the government's treatment of Zasulich were evidence, at the least, of bureaucratic muddleheadedness. If arresting Zasulich in 1869 made some sense given the growing menace of student protest, there was no excuse for holding her so long without charge, then releasing her and immediately arresting her again—or for permitting her to learn but not to practice a profession.

Not surprisingly, Zasulich emerged from these experiences convinced more strongly than ever that any improvements she desired in her own life or in those of the Russian people would have to be preceded by the destruction of the state. Immediately upon her release from exile in September 1875, Zasulich went to Kiev, where she contacted revolutionaries active in an organization called Iuzhnye Buntari (Southern Rebels). There, for the remainder of 1875 and during the year that followed, she participated in a revolutionary circle, assumed an "illegal" existence, and engaged in activities of a sort that could justifiably precipitate her arrest.[8]

For Zasulich, imprisonment and exile did more than merely solidify a commitment to revolution. Her experiences in the early 1870's also made her unusually sensitive to anyone whose suffering she considered comparable to her own. Her lawyer, Alexandrov, described these critical experiences at her trial in 1878:

The years of youth are justly regarded as the best years of one's life. It is easy to imagine how Zasulich passed [these years], what happiness she felt, what rosy dreams she dreamed behind the prison wall and in the fortified chambers of the Litovsk castle and the Peter and Paul fortress. . . . For two years she saw neither family nor friends. She saw no human being except the warden who brought her meals and the guard who looked from time to time through the slit in the door. She heard nothing except the sound of doors being opened and closed, the clank of rifles of guards being relieved, and the monotonous music of the fortress clock. Instead of friendship, love, and genuine contact with the world she had only the consciousness that behind the wall, to the right and to the left, were fellow sufferers, the victims of an equally miserable fate. Indeed, during these years of nascent sympathies, Zasulich clung to and strengthened in her soul one sympathy—a selfless love for everyone who, like herself, had to bear the miserable existence of a political suspect. The political offender, whoever he might be, became a dear friend to her, the companion of her youth, the comrade-in-learning. The prison was her alma mater, which strengthened this friendship and this camaraderie.[9]

Alexandrov's conclusion erroneously suggests that all his client's political upbringing was confined to these two years of wrongful imprisonment, but it does accurately describe Zasulich's conviction that those who suffer the same punishment are bound together by indissoluble bonds. From there it is but a short step to the conclusion, so decisive in Zasulich's career, that victims of injustice are right in opposing not merely their own oppressors but all those who have inflicted injustice upon others.

This was not the only lesson Zasulich drew from her imprisonment and exile. She also learned that imprisonment and exile were a metaphor for Russian society itself (an analogy that predates by some seventy years its same expression in Alexander Solzhenitsyn's *Gulag Archipelago*). In an essay published in *Zaria* in 1901, Zasulich describes in minute detail life among the prisoners in the Schlüsselberg fortress, and, obviously drawing upon her own experiences, reflects that the things one misses most in prison are not good health, tasty food, or pleasant surroundings but rather the intangibles of companionship, camaraderie, and friendship. She had made a similar comparison in a letter to her sister Alexandra written in June 1871, after going from Kresttsy to Tver, observing that a prisoner or someone in transit from one place of exile to another was apt to treasure companionship even more than the material necessities of life.[10] On the basis of her own experience Zasulich had concluded that man's humanity consists precisely in his capacity to establish ties with other human beings, and that imprisonment degrades one because it makes such ties impossible to maintain. Imprisonment and exile were intended not merely to prevent political unrest but also to destroy moral virtue. All too often men and women emerged from years of isolation in prison or exile without any capacity left to establish ties with other human beings, and as a result were thereafter scarcely more virtuous in their behavior than animals, incapable of camaraderie, friendship, or love. But indeed, Zasulich declares in the 1901 essay, Schlüsselberg fortress is really only a microcosm of Russia itself. The bars that imprison the Russian people are invisible, but they are no less real than those in the Schlüsselberg fortress because the Russian government refuses to allow the existence of voluntary associations and organizations through which this yearning for companionship and solidarity can be expressed.[11]

Thus, for Zasulich the greatest crime of autocracy is not that it is cruel or inefficient or that it denies its people political freedom. Rather, its crime is that it robs individuals of the capacity to share the human experience: by dividing Russia into prison corridors, by denying people the opportunity "to speak to one another through prison walls," autocracy engenders in its subjects an egoism which deteriorates into political impotence and psychological quirks.[12] Thus set apart from others, each person can tell himself, "It is not your affair to worry about the affairs of others."[13] In other words, this egoism or lack of sociability (in the broadest sense) implied the absence of the very qualities that most clearly confirm the humanity of man.

The revolutionaries whom Zasulich met in Kiev in 1875 were mostly of her own generation, many of them, like herself, recent converts to revolutionary politics. Including in its ranks such figures as Deich, Kolenkina, Stefanovich, Frolenko, Kovalev- skaia, Bokhanovskii, and Chubarov, the Kievan group consti- tuted a major nexus of the revolutionary chain in southern Rus- sia, and it helped to preserve the revolutionary movement between the "movement to the people" in 1874 and the estab- lishment of Zemlia i Volia in St. Petersburg in 1876. In the brief period of its existence, this Kievan group produced little of theo- retical value, but its activities, most notably the so-called Chigi- rin affair, made its members celebrated in revolutionary circles throughout Russia, and from its ranks would come much of the talent which later infused Zemlia i Volia with a special brand of dedication and commitment.

As Deich described it, Iuzhnye Buntari was more an informal circle of like-minded individuals than an organization with an explicit hierarchy and division of labor. When Zasulich applied to join the circle in 1875, it had about fifteen members, almost half of them women, most of whom shared a house near the university owned by the parents of one of the members, Vla- dimir Debagorii-Mokrievich, whom Deich describes as *primus inter pares* in his relations with the other members of the group.[14] Zasulich herself lived elsewhere, also in communal fashion with nine others, but some distance from the center of activity. Deich, writing years later, remembered that this community of revolu- tionaries and assorted hangers-on endured the rigors of revolu- tionary secrecy with a minimum of friction, but one wonders whether his memory had suffered lapses with the passage of time.

Deich says that the members of Zasulich's commune—which included Iakob Stefanovich and Lydia Barisheva, the sister of the populist theorist Vorontsov—spent much of their time in animated conversation, discussing a variety of issues with the passion and total seriousness of purpose common among Rus- sian revolutionaries in the late nineteenth century. The intensity of the discussions reflected the recent crisis in revolutionary tactics following the failures of the early 1870's. When, in the summer of 1874, revolutionaries from St. Petersburg and Moscow fanned out into the Russian countryside, driven in many instances by a conscious or a subconscious desire to expiate their sins of education and affluence, they brought with them many preconceptions about the Russian peasantry that they subsequently realized were inaccurate. Those who expected the peasants to accept them as brothers were forced by the undisguised hostility they encountered to question their faith in a revolutionary alliance of peasants and students. Those who, like Lavrov, emphasized the importance of educating and enlightening the peasants were impelled by the ignorance and suspicion they encountered to revise their conviction that urban intellectuals and students were capable of performing what now seemed to them to be a superhuman task. And many of those who, like Bakunin, considered the peasants "inherently" revolutionary, requiring only a catalyst to create a gigantic conflagration, came to the sobering conclusion that the peasantry were not really revolutionary at all, or were at any rate not the incendiary material that could instantly destroy the Russian autocracy.[15]

Accordingly, in March 1876, several members of Iuzhnye Buntari (but not Zasulich) decided that only a strategy which somehow took into account the peasants' traditional devotion to the Tsar could stir the Russian masses to revolt. That such a strategy might entail deception of the peasants as well as the government indicates the desperation in revolutionary circles engendered by these recent failures in the countryside. A rumor circulating in the Chigirin District near Kiev that the Tsar would soon encourage peasants to seize the land of the nobility inspired Deich, Stefanovich, and Bokhanovskii to consider forging a manifesto ostensibly signed by the Tsar calling upon the peasants to seize the nobles' land and create a clandestine militia for a subsequent insurrection against the government.[16] To keep the risk of exposure of the plot at a minimum, Zasulich and several other Buntari were purposely not informed of the details.[17] Debagorii-Mokrievich and some others who knew about the plan were against it because they thought it immoral and also because they feared it might backfire and strengthen the peasants' faith in the Tsar. But Deich and his supporters went ahead. A manifesto was forged and disseminated, a peasant militia was formed, and the hoax remained undetected for nearly a year. The police finally learned what was happening, however, and arrested most of those directly involved in the plot.[18]

Perhaps the most revealing aspect of this rather clumsy episode is the debate about revolutionary tactics and morality that preceded it. Clearly, the failure of "going to the people" in 1874 had forced Russian revolutionaries, not yet terrorists, to improvise in their search for a new faith and a new strategy to supplant the old shibboleths about the peasants. Several Buntari even enlisted in the armies of Bosnia and Herzegovina when these Balkan peoples rebelled against Turkish rule in 1875. Although one should not impute pan-Slavic motives to those Buntari sympathetic to the plight of Slavs in Eastern Europe, the fact that many members of the group would, for a time, abandon their efforts to foment revolution in one country in order to support a nationalist insurrection in another bespeaks a genuine uncertainty about the efficacy and value of revolutionary politics in Russia.[19]

In his reminiscences of Iuzhnye Buntari, Deich notes that, in their interminable discussions and debates, he and Zasulich often tried to illustrate to Debagorii-Mokrievich and others how Marxist laws of economic development were applicable everywhere, and most especially in Russia, which was therefore destined to experience a capitalist stage in her evolution.[20] The implication is that he and Zasulich were already, in 1876, Marxists. But since the two would experience considerable soul-searching before they would declare themselves such in the early 1880's, Deich's memoirs in this regard must be considered suspect.* Deich's descriptions of the theoretical confusion and the weigh-

* See Zasulich's letter to Marx of February 16, 1881, reprinted in *K. Marks, F. Engel's i revoliutsionnaia Rossiia* (Moscow, 1967), p. 434. If Zasulich felt constrained in 1881 to request Marx's guidance regarding the future of the commune (and of industrialization in Russia generally), it is difficult to believe that she should have been so certain in 1875–76 about something that so perplexed her in 1881. Zasulich's conversion to Marxism was far more gradual than Deich's chronology and analysis suggest, and it would not be complete—or as nearly complete as it would ever be—until some nine years after Marx replied to Zasulich's letter, cited above, in March 1881.

ing of alternatives to the simplistic notion that peasants are by nature revolutionary, requiring only a signal from the intelligentsia to revolt, are more to the point. Deich describes how, after a time, the Buntari finally agreed that even if their attempts to incite rebellions were unsuccessful, the propaganda value of the attempts was great enough to justify the risks they entailed. Of course Deich and Stefanovich could always pursue their own ideas, as they did in the Chigirin affair, since the structure of the circle was loose and there were no party rules. Zasulich believed that even among those who persisted in their "Bakuninist" assumptions, the commitment to them was more rhetorical than real, and it appears that the Buntari spent a great deal of their time agonizing over problems of ideology and tactics.[21]

They were not pure theorists, however. Their thinking, by and large, was far too muddled—and they occasionally stirred themselves to revolutionary action. Frolenko mentions "mounted detachments" which traveled from village to village preaching to the peasants that they should act in their own self-interest and rise in revolution against the state.[22] And Deich says that the police kept their distance from the Buntari because they feared that they would respond with gunfire. He also mentions that if a member of the group was arrested and imprisoned, the other members of the organization felt obliged to attempt to rescue him.[23]

Zasulich entered into the revolutionary side with enthusiasm. Mikhail Frolenko says that she strapped a pistol to her belt and went along (apparently with some clumsiness) with her fellow Buntari in the "cavalry detachments." Also, she and Frolenko lived together briefly in a scheme that was meant to expand the political consciousness of the peasantry. Though never more, apparently, than fellow revolutionaries, they supplied themselves with false passports and lived for a time as husband and wife in the Ukrainian town of Tsibulenka, where they wore peasant dress and adorned their dwelling with portraits of the Tsar and his family. The idea was that by posing as peasants themselves, they could spread the message more effectively among the downtrodden. But Zasulich's unmistakable Moscow accent betrayed her true origins, and she was so inept at cooking and housekeeping that they were obliged to scrap their plans to sell tea for an income so that they could devote most of their time to politics. Ultimately, the suspicions of peasants and government officials alike brought an end to the arrangement. Frolenko went back to the commune in Kiev with Debagorii-Mokrievich and Zasulich went to live with Maria Kolenkina in the village of Krilov.[24] There, in February 1876, she helped plan (but did not participate in) Deich's successful attempt to get another revolutionary, Semen Lurie, out of prison in Kiev. When Deich himself was arrested, Zasulich again assisted in the planning, but not in the execution, of his escape.[25]

By and large, the fourteen months that Zasulich spent in and around Kiev were among the most exciting and gratifying periods of her life, a time when she at last gained the respect and admiration of men who considered her sex irrelevant to her fundamental worth as a human being. A passage in an article she wrote in 1892 in which she reflected upon the role of women in revolutionary movements has the ring of autobiographical truth:

In the 1870's women ceased to be exceptional phenomena. Ordinary women—an entire network of such women—attained a good fortune rarely achieved in history: the possibility of acting in the capacity not of aspiring wives and mothers, but in total independence as the equals of men in all social and political activity. And however great were the sufferings that the government vengefully inflicted upon them for their actions, they did not envy anyone. They were very happy.[26]

In fact, it was as a result of working together in Iuzhnye Buntari that Zasulich and Deich became lovers, and subsequently lived together as husband and wife in everything but name whenever the circumstances permitted it—up until 1884, when Deich was arrested in Germany, extradited, and banished to Siberia for trying to smuggle seditious literature into Russia.[27]

There was one sordid incident during these months that Zasulich spent with the Buntari in Kiev, and her connection with it is an indication of how far she had already traveled on the revolutionary road. Always fearful of police infiltrating their organization, the Buntari may have been impelled as well by their own defeats to deal especially harshly with anyone they suspected of betraying them. In 1876 their suspicions fixed on N. E. Gorinovich, one of the group. Many Buntari were certain—though they had no proof—that Gorinovich had revealed to the police during an investigation in 1875 their identities and the nature of their activities. It was decided that Gorinovich must be dealt with: the plan called for Deich and several others to seize Gorinovich, beat him to death with a ball and chain, and then pour acid on his face. Somehow, Gorinovich survived this horrible scheme, but at the cost of blindness and disfigurement, which not surprisingly made him more than happy to render the suspicions of the Buntari self-fulfilling by telling the police all that he knew of them.[28]

Zasulich did not take part in the brutal attack but knew of it and evidently approved of it, even though proof of Gorinovich's guilt was lacking.[29] It is interesting that in her later condemnations, written in 1883 and after, of Nechaev and the murder of Ivanov, she does not refer to the equally reprehensible treatment of Gorinovich by a group of which she was an active member. We are obliged to conclude that Zasulich evidently accepted, at least for a time, the view increasingly popular in revolutionary circles in the 1870's that terrorism was justified as a defensive measure against police agents and informers within revolutionary circles.[30] It may be that it was only as the full import of Gorinovich's blinding and disfigurement became clear to her that she began to realize that terrorism could only be justified as a gesture of moral conscience and as a means to avenge unpunished acts of official brutality. For the time being, she apparently was not revolted either by the need for doing away with Gorinovich or by the act itself but concurred in the revolutionary logic of condemning suspected traitors on the strength of entirely circumstantial evidence. The most that can be said in her defense is that she did not remain at that level and on later occasions generally defended individuals who in her view were being unfairly accused of revolutionary treason or ideological deviance.*

Gorinovich's revelations to the police subsequent to the attack on him by his fellow Buntari effectively destroyed the circle in

---

* In 1918, for example, Zasulich defended Stefanovich against recent charges that in the 1880's he had betrayed to the police certain members of Narodnaia Volia. See V. I. Zasulich, "Pravdivyi issledovatel' stariny," *Byloe*, no. 13 (1918), pp. 178–81. After Zasulich's death in 1919, evidence was uncovered suggesting, though not proving conclusively, that the allegations against Stefanovich were, in fact, correct.

Kiev. The various members scattered to different locations in southern Russia. Zasulich and Kolenkina lived together for a short time in Kharkov, and in December 1876 moved north to St. Petersburg with the intention of joining the recently established Zemlia i Volia (Land and Liberty).[31] The two women, partly out of anger at Stefanovich and Deich for their secrecy about the Chigirin affair, were ready for a new venture.

Although Zemlia i Volia was dedicated to mass agitation, O. V. Aptekman, one of the founders of the group and many years later its principal historian, was perspicacious enough at the time of its creation to see beyond the euphemisms about "disorganization" (meaning defensive terrorism) and detect a potential for conflict between those who believed in mass agitation and others in the group who were attracted by conspiracy and terrorism.[32] Zasulich, perhaps recognizing her own confusion about revolutionary tactics, contented herself with working for Zemlia i Volia as a typesetter while vaguely contemplating with Kolenkina the possibility of avenging the suffering of those still in prison for having "gone to the people" in 1874.[33] Little else is known of Zasulich's activities in St. Petersburg except that from time to time she visited the Nikiforovs at their residence in Penza, a village some distance southeast of Moscow. These visits would be of little significance were it not for the fact that it was in the company of her sister and brother-in-law that Zasulich first read in *Golos* in July 1877 of the flogging of Arkhip Bogoliubov in the St. Petersburg House of Preliminary Detention, an event whose repercussions were to lift her from obscurity and make her a figure of international reputation.[34]

What was this young woman like? What were her character, appearance, and personality? Descriptions of Zasulich by fellow revolutionaries who knew her after the shooting of Trepov are naturally tinged with a certain amount of fascinated interest, but even those observers comment on how thoroughly unprepossessing she seemed, and how slight was her resemblance to a daring activist. Zasulich's close friend and fellow revolutionary, Sergei Kravchinskii, described her in 1882 as follows:

She has nothing about her of the heroine of a pseudo-Radical tragedy, nor of the ethereal and ecstatic young girl. She is a strong, robust woman, and although of middle height, seems at first to be tall. She is not beautiful. Her eyes are very fine, large, well-shaped, with long lashes, and of grey colour, which become dark when she is excited. Ordinarily thoughtful and somewhat sad, these eyes shine forth brilliantly when she is enthusiastic, which not infrequently happens, or sparkle when she jests, which happens very often. The slightest change of mind is reflected in the expressive eyes. The rest of her face is very commonplace. Her nose somewhat long, thin lips, large head, adorned with almost black hair.[35]

Deich, too, commented on the spontaneous quality of Zasulich's responses, and how, when she was with people with whom she felt comfortable, her whole manner could be miraculously transformed, "and her eyes could sparkle with unusual sincerity and simplicity."[36] Plekhanov's wife, Rosaliia, also was struck by the eyes: despite the "awkward" and "cumbersome" quality of Zasulich's figure, her eyes "shone with intellect and good-natured jest," and she says, "as I listened attentively to the words and stories of our new friend, I yielded more and more to the charm and fascination of her personality."[37]

Virtually all observers of Zasulich also agree that whatever innate beauty she possessed was effectively obscured by what Liubov Axelrod (no relation to Pavel) once called "her complete and absolute indifference to her own appearance." Axelrod thought this was an expression of Zasulich's desire to assert her individuality and independence,[38] but one must remember that, for most of her life, Zasulich was very poor and, furthermore, too preoccupied with other matters to think much about how she looked. Rosaliia Plekhanova's description of Zasulich's customary garb gives a vivid picture: "She wore a shapeless grey dress. . . . It was a piece of linen from the center of which had been cut a hole for her head and from the sides of which had been cut a hole for her arms. This piece of linen, thrown over our new acquaintance, was held by a narrow belt, and its edges hung loosely all around. On her head was something resembling not a hat, but rather a pie, made of crumpled grey material. On her feet were clumsy wide boots which she had made herself."[39] As she grew older, Zasulich's sloppiness of dress became even more noticeable, if in some ways endearing to those who admired her, and her habits even more casual. Mikhail Frolenko, visiting Zasulich in 1911 when she lived in semi-retirement in the House of Writers in St. Petersburg, was not surprised to find her room in chaos, littered with dirty drinking glasses and plates with scraps of uneaten food.[40] One of the most amusing and striking pictures is Leon Trotsky's description of her struggling to complete an article for publication: "She wrote very slowly, suffering truly all the torments of creation; she put down one sentence at a time, pacing up and down her room, shuffling in her slippers, chain-smoking cigarettes she had rolled herself, throwing butts in all corners of the room, on the window sills, on the tables, scattering ash over her blouse, her arms, her manuscripts, her cup of tea, and incidentally also over her interlocutor."[41]

Zasulich never lost the timidity and reserve she had acquired in childhood. All her intimate friends noted this and realized how difficult it was for her to establish and maintain superficial relationships with large numbers of people. She kept aloof, as Kravchinskii commented: "She admits very few into her intimacy. I do not speak of that superficial intimacy which is simply the result of esteem and reciprocal confidence, and among us is the rule, but of that other intimacy which consists in the exchange of the most secret thoughts. . . . She lives very much within herself."[42] To Kravchinskii, this tendency toward introspection, sometimes pronounced, seemed typically Russian:

She is very subject to the special malady of the Russians, that of probing in her own mind, sounding its depths, pitilessly dissecting it, searching for defects, often imaginary, and always exaggerated. Hence those gloomy moods which from time to time assail her, like King Saul, and subjugate her for days and days, nothing being able to drive them away. At these times she becomes abstracted, shuns all society, and for hours paces her room completely buried in thought, or flies from the house to seek relief where alone she can find it, in Nature, eternal, impassable, and imposing, which she loves and interprets with the profound feeling of a truly poetical mind.[43]

Even after becoming a recognized revolutionary, Zasulich was slow to speak out, and Deich said she never really lost the tendency, first observed in Iuzhnye Buntari, "to follow in practical matters a course of action already agreed upon by those whom she trusted and liked."[44] Friends and adversaries alike were often deceived by her reserve and external appearance, confusing shyness for cowardice, reserve for hostility, and an unwillingness to express her own opinions for evidence that she had none of her own. But Deich praised her for having a mind "as fresh, original, and witty" as her clothing was slovenly and her physical appearance undistinguished.

Zasulich was an individual one could easily underestimate, and though one should not idealize her on this account, one should also not make the mistake so common even among those who loved and respected her of confusing external appearances for internal realities. The work of Zasulich's later years shows that she had not only a respectable, if often undisciplined, intellect but also a capacity to discern instinctively the moral character of an individual which made her unique among the revolutionaries in her milieu. Kravchinskii writes in *Underground Russia* of "that almost infallible moral instinct which is peculiar to her, of that faculty of discernment in the most perplexing and subtle questions, of good and evil, of the permitted and the forbidden, which she possesses, without being able, sometimes, to give a positive reason for her opinion."[45] Zasulich, though not a theorist like Plekhanov or Marx, was able to apply to ideological questions a keenly developed sense of ethical imperatives that made her thinking refreshingly, if at times confusingly, original. And though she lacked skill as a theorist, polemicist, or organizer, she had an acute sensitivity to moral subtleties that attracted respect and admiration.*

Over the years, under the burden of personal and political problems, Zasulich's naturally melancholic and introspective turn of mind became more pronounced. Kravchinskii, writing in 1883, speaks of occasional bouts of depression. In the late 1870's, however, Zasulich still had a certain gaiety of temperament and was full of enthusiasm for learning, filling in the many gaps in her knowledge which remained from her education at the Moscow pension. Unlike other Buntari who considered book learning an impediment to communicating inflammatory rheto-

---

* According to L. S. Fedorchenko, in the 1880's and 1890's, Zasulich's views were "the highest law" on moral questions for many of those she had helped convert to Social Democracy—a reflection, in part, of the moral rectitude that her example as a would-be assassin seemed to evoke. L. S. Fedorchenko, "Vera Zasulich," *Katorga i ssylka*, no. 2(23), (1926), p. 204.

ric to the peasants, Zasulich retained a reverence for books and
ideas, and spent many hours, often to the point of exhaustion,
grappling with the issues that her reading sometimes raised. A
revolutionary, but also, in some respects, a typical Russian *intelligent,* Zasulich liked nothing more than to indulge her curiosity
about new realms of intellectual endeavor; indeed, the moral
passion typical of the Russian intelligentsia which, for whatever
reason, she was unable to muster in public support of her political convictions seems to have been channeled into an intense, if
sometimes sporadic, investigation of a wide variety of subjects.

All things considered, Zasulich was an unlikely candidate for
the role of an assassin: her political thought was too muddled,
her interest in abstract ideas was too consuming of her time and
energy, and her personality was too prone to episodes of melan-
cholia and introspection. Few of those who knew her could have
predicted that the sensitivity to moral subtleties which could
completely immobilize her when the issue was complex could
also galvanize her into action when the moral imperative was
clear. But this is precisely what enabled Zasulich to do what she
did in January 1878. In her mind, the immorality of Bogoliubov's flogging called for decisive and unequivocal retribution.

Arkhip Bogoliubov, a student at St. Petersburg University,
had been arrested at the demonstration of workers and students
near the Kazan Cathedral on December 6, 1876. Although he
had been active in revolutionary circles as a propagandist, he
had not taken any part in the demonstration but was merely an
onlooker who was swept in by the police along with others. He
was tried in court in January 1877 and sentenced to fifteen years
of hard labor. He appealed and was sent to the House of Preliminary Detention while the appeal was pending. In July 1877,
when he was flogged, the House of Detention contained mostly
people like him who had been accused of political crimes, including many who would later be tried in the so-called "Trial of
the 193."[46]

When Trepov, as the Governor of St. Petersburg, visited the
House of Detention on the thirteenth of July, he had already
acquired a reputation for brutality. As the chief of police in
Warsaw in 1861, he had ordered his men to respond with gun-

fire to demonstrations of protesting students, a decision which prompted an attempt on his life; in 1869, he had ordered the arrest of those involved in student protests in St. Petersburg.* Trepov was a martinet by temperament, poorly educated, arrogant, and extraordinarily protective of his administrative prerogatives, but not especially cruel or sadistic; he did, however, expect—and usually received—instant and absolute compliance with his commands. Because his personality was repulsive to conservatives and his politics abhorrent to liberals, he had numerous enemies inside and outside the government, and their hostility was exacerbated in many cases by the personal friendship Trepov maintained with Alexander II.[47]

While inspecting the prison yard of the House of Detention, Trepov encountered two prisoners taking their morning walk, one of whom was Arkhip Bogoliubov. The first time Trepov passed them, Bogoliubov had the effrontery to try to speak to him, but was severely rebuked. When Trepov passed the two men again a short time later, Bogoliubov failed to tip his cap. Trepov ordered him to remove it. In the next instant, Bogoliubov's cap flew off his head, perhaps as he tried to move away, but to the prisoners viewing the altercation from their cells, it appeared that Bogoliubov's cap flew off because Trepov had struck him. The prisoners immediately began to cause a commotion, shouting epithets at Trepov through the windows, pushing mugs, books, and other objects through the bars. Enraged by Bogoliubov's insolence and the reactions of the inmates, Trepov subsequently ordered that Bogoliubov be flogged and that the birch rods to be used in the flogging be displayed prominently before the other inmates in the prison. The punishment was carried out shortly thereafter, and to avoid the outbreak of further disturbances, Bogoliubov was transferred to Litovsk prison, where he became insane and died a few years later.[48]

Trepov's subsequent protests notwithstanding, it seems indisputable that, under Russian law, the flogging of Bogoliubov was

* Since Zasulich was among those arrested, one wonders whether her animus against Trepov antedated Bogoliubov's flogging. In her trial in 1878 her connections with Nechaev were mentioned, but no attempt was made to ascertain whether Trepov's actions in 1869 predisposed her to want to shoot him. F. A. Gallinin, *Protsess Very Zasulich: sud i posle suda*, pp. 50–52.

illegal. In his reminiscences of the Zasulich Affair, A. F. Koni, at the time of the flogging a prosecutor in the Ministry of Justice, notes that according to the Judicial Reforms of 1864, the flogging of a prisoner was permitted only if he had committed "a breach of discipline" upon departure or arrival at the location of his final imprisonment. Moreover, after reminding the Minister of Justice, Count Pahlen, of this proviso, Koni also pointed out to him that Bogoliubov had in fact been tried and convicted without a preliminary investigation, and therefore should not have been imprisoned at all. It is a reflection of the prevailing atmosphere in the Ministry of Justice that for reminding Pahlen of these provisos Koni was denied the promotion his seniority demanded, and was appointed instead President of the St. Petersburg Circuit Court, in which capacity he would ratify Zasulich's acquittal in 1878.*

News of Bogoliubov's flogging traveled quickly, despite the government's attempts to censor the most lurid accounts. It in no way exculpates Trepov to note that much of what was reported about the flogging was exaggerated, and that much of the animus against Trepov was the result of inaccurate and incomplete information. When the public first learned of the Bogoliubov incident, it assumed as true the allegations that Trepov had indeed slapped Bogoliubov, that Bogoliubov had been flogged to unconsciousness, that Trepov bore sole responsibility for the flogging, and that a tremendous battle had ensued inside the prison as a result of it.[49] Actually, the facts were otherwise. First, it is unclear even now whether Trepov slapped Bogoliubov; second, Bogoliubov was flogged "only" twenty-five times, and retained consciousness throughout the ordeal; third, the turmoil that ensued in the prison, while certainly raucous, could

---

* Quite disingenuously, however, Trepov told Koni on July 14 that he himself doubted the legality of what he had done the day before, and had agreed to the flogging only after Pahlen himself had ordered it. But since the original request came from Trepov, it seems that, at the very least, he shares with Pahlen moral and legal responsibility for the flogging. That Trepov chose to exonerate himself before Koni also makes his apologia suspect, since Trepov knew Koni to be an opponent of corporal punishment, and very upset about the flogging. Moreover, two weeks after Zasulich's acquittal, Trepov tried to make public a declaration in which he justified the flogging and absolved prison officials of all wrongdoing. A. F. Koni, *Sobranie sochinenii: vospominaniia o dele Very Zasulich* (Moscow, 1966), pp. 50–54.

hardly be described as a riot; finally, and perhaps most important, Trepov ordered the flogging of Bogoliubov only after he,
Trepov, had requested, and received, Pahlen's approval.[50]

Most Russians, however, knew none of this, and though the
events of July 13 were lamentable enough, the story as it was
reported by word of mouth and in the press inspired many on
the left to vow to avenge Bogoliubov's flogging, some of them
sufficiently outraged by what they had learned to contemplate
drastic action. Thus, the local Zemlia i Volia in Kiev authorized a
"committee" consisting of Frolenko, V. A. Osinskii, D. A. Lizogub, I. F. Voloshenko, and S. I. Chubarov to proceed to St.
Petersburg for the specific purpose of assassinating Trepov.[51]
Independently of this committee, Zasulich also decided that she
had to respond to the Bogoliubov incident. Her feelings, as she
later described them, were with Bogoliubov's fellow prisoners:
"As I myself had experienced long, solitary confinement, I could
imagine what a frightful impression the entire affair must have
produced on all the political prisoners. It seemed to me that
such a thing should not pass unnoticed. I wanted to see whether
someone would take up the matter, but everyone was silent. I
was determined to prove that a human being may not be insulted in that way with impunity."[52] Not everyone in Russia, of
course, was outraged by the flogging, and after a momentary
surge of interest in the incident, the reading public turned its
attention back to events in the Balkans, where Russian troops
were advancing slowly toward Constantinople. Nevertheless,
Koni and others in the Ministry of Justice were sufficiently concerned about the possible consequences of Trepov's action to
petition Pahlen to delay the Trial of the 193, which was scheduled to begin in October.[53]

Koni, of course, could not have known that both Zasulich and
the committee sent from Kiev had decided independently of one
another to postpone retribution until sentences had already
been meted out to those convicted in this trial; obviously Zasulich and the committee realized that a provocative response to
the flogging might result in more convictions and harsher sentences for the accused. But the trial took more time than expected, and preparations for the assassination went ahead. Frolenko and another revolutionary, G. A. Popko, rented a room

near Trepov's office so they could learn his daily movements and routine; Zasulich and her roommate, Maria Kolenkina, agreed that, once the Trial of the 193 was over, Kolenkina would shoot Zhelikovskii, the prosecutor in the trial, at precisely the same moment at which Zasulich would shoot Trepov. Presumably, with the two women acting together, timing the two shootings to coincide, the impact would be greater, and a public preoccupied with events in the Balkans would be forced to confront the moral issues implicit in the Bogoliubov flogging and in the Trial of the 193.*

In her memoirs, Zasulich gives the impression that only Kolenkina knew of her intentions and that, except for Kolenkina, she had no assistance. She does not mention the assassination scheme of the Kiev Zemlia i Volia, as if she had no knowledge of it nor they of hers. However, there is considerable evidence to indicate otherwise. Frolenko, for one, contends in his memoirs that, in the fall of 1877, the committee informed Zasulich in general terms of its intentions, and adds that Zasulich, Chubarov, and several others worked together in shadowing Trepov as he made his daily rounds; M. R. Popov confirms in his memoirs in *Byloe* that Zasulich maintained contact with the committee throughout the fall and winter of 1877–78.[54] We also have the testimony of E. G. Karpov that, on January 23, 1878, Zasulich, Kolenkina, Chubarov, and the remaining members of the Kiev committee gathered in his apartment and that everyone who attended knew that Zasulich alone would shoot Trepov the fol-

---

* Zasulich, *Vospominaniia*, p. 131. Zasulich and Kolenkina were equally outraged and may have drawn lots to decide who would shoot whom. Certainly Kolenkina's motives for shooting Zhelikovskii appear to have been dictated by the same moral imperative that inspired Zasulich. Many of the defendants in the Trial of the 193 had suffered woefully from disease and malnutrition in the four years of their "preliminary detention," and the impossibility of their ever being able to call attention to the injustices that were still being inflicted upon them seemed to Kolenkina sufficient reason for her to act as their surrogate. As a prosecutor, Zhelikovskii bore no direct responsibility for these injustices: Kolenkina's choice of him as her victim—unlike Zasulich's selection of Trepov—was a symbolic one. Nevertheless, the belief of both women that they acted as surrogates of those incapable of acting for themselves was strikingly at odds with the common justification of terrorism in the 1870's as a "defensive measure" directed at informers and police infiltrators. A. Iakimova, "Pamiati Marii Aleksandrovny Kolenkinoi-Bogorodskoi," *Katorga i ssylka*, no. 2(31), (1927), pp. 180–84.

lowing day.[55] In addition, a police informer stated in a report to his superior shortly after the shooting that the gun Zasulich shot Trepov with was purchased for her by Chubarov, whom she had known since their days together in student circles in the late 1860's.[56] Finally, Lev Deich maintains in an article in *Golos minuvshago* that Zasulich not only knew of the committee's intentions but was willing to defer to it in avenging Bogoliubov, and acted only when it appeared to her that the members of the committee had lost their nerve.*

If it is true that Zasulich knew about the Zemlia i Volia plan, the matter of timing suggests an additional consideration. Zasulich, by her own account, was outraged by the flogging from the moment she learned of it, yet six months elapsed between the flogging and the shooting of Trepov. But in the late fall of 1877, Zasulich was involved in planning the escape from prison of revolutionaries who had been arrested near Kiev in the Chigirin affair. For the moment that took precedence over avenging Bogoliubov. As the year ended and the Trepov matter still hung fire, Zasulich decided that manpower needed in carrying out the escape in southern Russia was being wasted in St. Petersburg in an enterprise that, so far as she knew, was proceeding very slowly. Frolenko's skills, in particular, were considered essential to any rescue. Therefore Zasulich felt it incumbent upon herself to shoot Trepov alone, not merely in the name of abstract principle, but to free Frolenko and possibly others for the rescue she hoped they could carry out in southern Russia. In other words, though her reasons were mainly as before, she now felt that the assassination had to be done at once and that she must do it.[57] When, on January 23, sentences were announced in the Trial of the 193, Zasulich no longer had any reason to fear that shooting

---

* L. G. Deich, "Pamiati ushedshikh: Vera Ivanovna Zasulich," *Golos minuvshago*, no. 5/12 (1920–21), p. 204. A. F. Mikhailov maintains in his autobiography that Zasulich misinterpreted as indecision the vague answers she received from the committee whenever she asked about its time-table. According to Mikhailov the committee had not lost its nerve, but simply wanted to keep from Zasulich and others not directly involved in its conspiracy all specific (and potentially incriminating) information. Indeed, it had already fixed a date for the assassination when Zasulich, not knowing this, shot Trepov herself. A. F. Mikhailov, "Avtobiografiia," *Entsiklopedicheskii slovar' Russkogo bibliografieheskogo instituta Granat* (Moscow, 192–), vol. 40, p. 267.

Trepov might increase their severity, and thus the last obstacle to the assassination had been removed.

On the morning of January 24 Zasulich awoke to prepare for the shooting. All night long she had dreamed of being forced from her bed into a corridor, where she could not contain an urge to scream incessantly; she had no illusions about what would happen to her and expected to die either immediately after the shooting or at least after trial and conviction.[58] After exchanging what she assumed would be her last words with Kolenkina, Zasulich proceeded to Trepov's office, where she knew that he received petitioners requesting assistance. Claiming to be such a petitioner, Zasulich was told by an adjutant to proceed to a particular room; a few minutes after she arrived there, Trepov and his retinue appeared. Trepov asked her to step forward and state the nature of her request. Zasulich explained that she desired a "certificate of conduct," a document granted by local authorities to those qualified to become private tutors. Trepov wrote something with a pencil, and as he turned to an assistant standing beside him, Zasulich pulled her pistol out from under her shawl, pointed it at Trepov, and pulled the trigger. The gun misfired. Zasulich pulled the trigger again, and this time hit Trepov in the pelvis. The act done, she dropped the gun to the floor. She was seized instantly: "A person appeared before me . . . and two enormous hands, with crooked fingers, were headed directly for my eyes. I shut them as tightly as I could, and he only grazed my cheeks. Blows rained down on me—they rolled me around and continued to beat me . . . However, what surprised me was that I did not feel the slightest pain."[59]

After Trepov, now unconscious, had been removed to a hospital, Zasulich was taken to another room for interrogation. She had to instruct the gendarmes who were holding her how best to tie her in a chair, since only a towel was available for this purpose. When asked to identify herself, she said that her name was "Kozlova." When asked why she had shot Trepov, she replied simply, "For Bogoliubov." She felt curiously detached from everything that was happening: "I considered myself completely invulnerable, a state that I had never experienced before. Nothing at all could confuse me or annoy me or tire me. Whatever was being thought up by those men—I would continue to regard them calmly, from a distance they could not cross."[60] Because Zhelikovskii's servant refused to admit Kolenkina into the prosecutor's residence, Kolenkina was unable to execute her part of the plan.[61]

Though Zasulich's initial explanation of the shooting did not necessarily suggest a political motivation, a routine check of police records quickly revealed her identity, her prison record, and her involvement in student protest movements in the previous decade. In addition, on January 25, the day after the shooting, the Ministry of Justice in St. Petersburg received a telegram from the State Procurator in Odessa describing Zasulich's ties with revolutionaries in southern Russia.[62] Thus, within a few days of the shooting, the Ministry of Justice had every reason to believe that Zasulich's motives had indeed been political, and that therefore, according to the Judicial Reforms of 1864, her case should be tried in an "exceptional" court of the Senate rather than by a jury of her peers.

But the government officials responsible for her case determined otherwise. Once Pahlen and his deputy, A. A. Lopukhin, learned of Zasulich's identity, and of what seemed to them to be the political motivation of her crime, they immediately decided, in violation of Russian law, to send her case to the criminal courts, which meant referring it to a jury for a verdict. They reasoned that by having a jury convict Zasulich, as it most certainly would do, any resentment at the verdict would fall on the jury members rather than on the government. Moreover, Pahlen assured the Tsar: "the jurors would deliver a guilty verdict and thereby teach a sobering lesson to the insane, small coterie of revolutionaries; they would show all the Russian and foreign admirers of Vera Zasulich's 'heroic exploit' that the Russian people bow before the Tsar, revere him, and are always ready to defend his faithful servants."[63]

Even though Trepov was hardly a popular figure, the weight of public opinion would probably be on his side, and because the revolutionary Left had been discredited by recent failures, most notably the Chigirin affair, Pahlen could argue plausibly that the public generally disapproved of terrorist attacks on government officials. Pahlen was also quite aware that a secret trial in the

Senate was no guarantee of conviction, as the numerous acquittals in the Trial of the 193 had revealed.

The Minister of Justice now exerted the full weight of his office against the man who would preside over Zasulich's trial. In the middle of March he invited Koni to his office and told him categorically that, as a servant of the State, he, Koni, had an obligation to do all he could to secure Zasulich's conviction. Koni, who like many of the post-Reform members of the legal profession was not only well trained but had a high sense of justice, refused: the responsibility for determining Zasulich's guilt or innocence, he reminded Pahlen, lay entirely in the hands of the jury, and as President of the Court he was obliged to rule as impartially and judiciously as possible. To his final reminder that "the function of a court is not to render service but to pronounce judgment," Pahlen retorted that everything that Koni said was just "theory."[64]

The trial had been fixed for the last day of March. Pahlen continued his pressure on Koni almost to the last hour. Four days before the trial he requested Koni to formulate his instructions to the jury in such a way that it would have no alternative but to convict Zasulich. Annoyed by Koni's persistent use of words such as *bespristrastie* (impartiality), Pahlen suggested that Koni deliberately commit technical violations of the law in the course of the trial so that if the jury should acquit her, the verdict could be overturned on appeal. In his memoirs Koni recalls that he considered Pahlen's request too reprehensible to deserve a reply.[65] There was also pressure, rather more subtle, from the Tsar, who in March summoned Koni to an official reception at the Winter Palace and took the opportunity to express his hope that Koni "continue to serve successfully."[66]

Koni in his memoirs recalls with sadness the expectations of lasting reform with which he had welcomed Alexander's coronation in 1855. A liberal, but also reverent in his feelings toward the Tsar, Koni was perhaps the individual in the State bureaucracy who best personified the commitment to law and legal procedure which was required if enlightened autocracy were to survive its critics on the political extremes. Though Koni disapproved of what Zasulich had done because her action seemed to him expressive of a "vigilante" mentality, he shared her outrage at the Bogoliubov flogging, and considered the greatest impetus to revolutionary protest to be the insensitive and often unlawful manner in which the government responded to it. Whether or not he was aware of the extent of Zasulich's revolutionary activities before the trial began is not clear, though he says in his memoirs that Lopukhin withheld from him the telegram he had received from Odessa, which would have made a criminal trial clearly illegal.[67] At any rate, both as a matter of principle and for raison d'état, Koni hoped Russia would ultimately evolve into a system in which the rule of law would define the limits of permissible behavior, applied with such impartiality that actions such as Zasulich's would no longer seem necessary. By the late 1870's, however, the gap between the State and the intelligentsia was so immense, political dialogue couched so irrevocably in the lexicon of *kto-kogo* (the Russian equivalent of "us against them"), that a modus vivendi based on a mutual adherence to law was no longer possible.[68]

The Minister of Justice had some difficulty selecting his chief prosecuting attorney. He originally assigned the case to V. I. Zhukovskii, and then, when Zhukovskii begged off for personal reasons, chose S. A. Andreevskii to replace him. However, Andreevskii agreed to prosecute Zasulich only if he could openly acknowledge the illegality of Bogoliubov's flogging. Pahlen naturally found that condition impossible, and in desperation had to settle upon K. I. Kessel, a man whom many prominent figures in the government, most notably Pobedonostsev, considered ill equipped for the task. As punishment for their apparent sympathy for Zasulich, both Zhukovskii and Andreevskii were subsequently forced by Pahlen to submit their resignations.[69]

Zasulich was more fortunate in her choice of counsel. With the help of Kolenkina and Katerina Breshkovskaia, she retained P. A. Alexandrov, an ambitious, conceited, but very forceful lawyer with a distinct gift for oratory. Zasulich made it clear that if he, as he suggested, distorted the facts of the case in such a way as to place her action in a more favorable light, she would dismiss him, and she also turned down his suggestion that she should appear in court dressed more respectably, less like a revolutionary. But she did promise not to bite her fingernails in court—that being a habit which, according to popular superstition, attributed evil thoughts to those who indulged in it.[70]

Meanwhile, both in Russia and abroad, the shooting of Trepov had been interpreted in a variety of ways, some of them absurd. A favorite rumor—which even appeared in *The Times* of London—was that Zasulich was really Bogoliubov's mistress and shot Trepov out of love for the man Trepov had wronged.[71] Another favorite interpretation, especially among socialists in England, made Zasulich a kind of Russian Charlotte Corday, the latest in a long series of revolutionary heroines, linked to her historical antecedents by the bonds of politics and sex. (That Charlotte Corday murdered a revolutionary seemed beside the point.)[72] In Russia, news of Trepov's shooting inspired Zasulich's defenders to impassioned flights of rhetoric. One leaflet circulated by *Vol'naia russkaia tipografiia* (Russian Free Press), written in response to attacks upon Zasulich in the press, described Zasulich as "the fearless girl who did not shrink from the awful bloody deed and her own ruin when no other means remained for the defense of the rights of man." "Take for us the gift of our most reverent admiration, Russian girl with a heroine's soul," it declared, "and posterity will place your name among the martyrs for freedom and the rights of man. This girl is Vera Ivanovna Zasulich."[73] As the date of the trial approached, the contest of words between supporters and opponents of the government, and of the woman who was about to appear before the jury, reached a peak. Nearly everyone agreed, however, that the Zasulich trial was going to be an event of considerable import, and that its verdict would be a judgment of the existing social order.

As it turned out, the trial itself was nothing of the sort. By choice, Alexandrov accepted as jurors mostly petty bureaucrats potentially sympathetic to Zasulich but, at the same time, not likely to respond favorably to any indictment of autocracy itself.[74] Alexandrov never brought out what might have been a telling argument for her acquittal, namely, that since the government had not held Trepov accountable for his actions, it had thereby abrogated for itself the right to hold Zasulich accountable for hers. He did, however, skirt close to questioning the political system that had, so to speak, made Trepov possible, and at one point in his defense commented that an acquittal might soften Russia's reputation as a nation of barbarians.[75] But Alexandrov mostly emphasized the character of the woman he was defending—and the character of the man she had shot. At no point was there anything resembling a confrontation between rival ideologies competing for the favor of the jury.

Koni conducted himself impartially throughout the trial and was totally objective in his instructions to the jury, revealing nothing of his personal predilections. The jurors, however, were highly susceptible to the rhetoric of the defense attorney. They acquitted Zasulich because Alexandrov's oratory convinced them to judge her character, not her actions. By her own admission, Zasulich was guilty of having shot Trepov; whether she was seeking to kill him or wanted only to wound him was a question that neither the prosecution nor the defense answered convincingly. But, in some sense, this was irrelevant to the verdict. Alexandrov's description of the hardships that Zasulich had endured and of her strength of character in the face of poverty and injustice was calculated to arouse the emotions of the jurors, to make them look upon her as a martyr. When he finished his closing speech the spectators burst into thunderous applause. It was clear what the popular verdict was, and the jury agreed. Though Koni privately believed that Zasulich should have been convicted but given a light sentence, the jurors, charged with adjudicating the case in an atmosphere alive with emotion, decided otherwise.*

Thus, the Zasulich trial was neither the countertrial anticipated by the Right and the Left, nor the dispassionate adjudica-

---

* Koni, p. 169. One authority says that a few days after the verdict the Third Section received an anonymous note presumably written by one of the jurors claiming that the jurors had acquitted Zasulich because they feared for their lives and those of court officials if they convicted her. Even if one accepts the note as authentic, however, one can still argue that this is precisely what a juror would tell the police if he wanted to prevent retaliation by the government for the jury's verdict. The fear of assassination was no doubt a reasonable one, but the fact that the jurors seemed by all accounts as captivated by Alexandrov's rhetoric as were the spectators in the courtroom suggests that a fear of assassination was, at most, only a secondary factor in the jury's calculations. See A. A. Kunkl', "Vokrug dela Very Zasulich," *Katorga i ssylka,* no. 38 (1928), pp. 62–63.

tion of guilt or innocence that sober jurists such as Koni had hoped for. Rather, it was nothing more nor less than a judgment of two individuals, Zasulich and Trepov, one of them resoundingly acquitted, the other, in effect, condemned in absentia. That the verdict was perceived as a judgment of the existing social order is understandable given the emotions that the shooting had aroused, but a distinction must be made between the trial itself and the conclusions people drew from its outcome.

When, at ten o'clock on March 31, 1878, Koni declared the Circuit Court of St. Petersburg in session, he could, as one observer later remarked, see "all of St. Petersburg" in the audience.[76] Among the spectators at the trial were the Foreign Minister, A. M. Gorchakov, the Minister of War, D. A. Miliutin, the future Minister of Finance, A. A. Abaza, and other prominent officials in the state bureaucracy. Also present was Fyodor Dostoevsky, who would later incorporate into Dmitrii's trial in *The Brothers Karamazov* much of what he had witnessed at Zasulich's.[77] Trepov, though he had recovered from his wounds, did not attend, pleading an illness possibly more diplomatic than real.

After the preliminary formalities, Koni explained to the jurors in general terms the nature of their task: they must evaluate all the evidence impartially, and render a verdict based only upon what they heard in the courtroom. Their role as jurors, he told them, placed upon them "a great responsibility before society and before the accused, whose fate lies solely in your hands." A secretary then read to the court the formal criminal indictment. Recounting the events of January 24, the indictment accused Zasulich not only of attempting to murder Trepov but of having planned his assassination in advance. (Conviction of these charges could result in long imprisonment, but the indictment did not carry any prescribed sentence.) When asked how she wished to plead, Zasulich acknowledged that she had indeed shot Trepov, but maintained that it was irrelevant to her whether she killed him or merely wounded him.[78]

After witnesses to the shooting had given their testimony, Koni permitted Alexandrov to call certain prisoners in the House of Detention who had witnessed Trepov's encounter with

Bogoliubov and had heard rumors about Bogoliubov's flogging. Koni then asked Zasulich to state in her own words why this incident had prompted her to shoot Trepov. Zasulich recounted how she had read of the flogging in the press, and how she was led to believe that Bogoliubov had been flogged to unconsciousness. At first, Zasulich said, she expected a public outcry to follow the flogging. But when the response was largely one of indifference, she concluded that only the dramatic gesture of assassination could rouse Russia from her lethargy: "I didn't find, I couldn't find any other means to direct attention to this event. . . . I didn't see any other means. . . . It is terrible to raise one's hand against one's fellow man, but I decided that this was what I had to do."[79] Certain that, in the end, she would suffer as much as Trepov, she acted in the hope that her example would somehow preclude further atrocities. She was not seeking revenge so much as trying to elevate the moral consciousness of a nation.

In his prosecution Kessel chose to attack not only Zasulich's justification of the shooting but also her contention that she took no special measures to ensure that the shooting would result in Trepov's death. Zasulich, he argued, fired when Trepov turned sideways not because she wanted to spare Trepov's life but because, with Trepov facing her, he would have had a better chance to disarm her. She hesitated a few seconds before firing not because she only wanted to wound Trepov but simply because she was frightened and confused, and she shot Trepov in the pelvis only because not enough time was available to aim for his heart. Therefore, Zasulich failed to kill Trepov only because the circumstances of the shooting itself prevented her from doing so; it seemed to the prosecutor prima facie evidence of premeditation that, before the shooting, she had purchased a revolver more powerful than one she already owned.[80]

As for the morality of the act, Kessel argued that whatever Trepov had done to Bogoliubov was irrelevant to Zasulich's guilt or innocence. Even if Trepov's treatment of Bogoliubov was reprehensible, Zasulich's response to it was a crime because she acted in a manner contrary to Kant's Categorical Imperative: she did something that could not be expressed as a general law for all society. And no society, Kessel declared, could survive if it allowed its citizens to take upon themselves the obligation to avenge what they considered to be the moral turpitude of others. In exercising what she thought were her own rights, Zasulich actually violated Trepov's:

Having created her own court, Zasulich joined in her own person the roles of prosecutor, defendant, and judge; she, a young woman, thought it was possible to decree a death sentence, which fortunately she did not succeed in carrying out. I do not think for one minute that you will disagree that every public figure, whoever he may be, has the right to a legal trial and not to a trial by Zasulich. I am also sure you will agree that no public life whatever, no social organization, would be possible if public figures . . . found it necessary to bear in mind that, however they acted, nevertheless from one side or the other a revolver might be aimed at them. I think these public figures have the right to that which every other individual is entitled to—the right to life.[81]

Hearing this cogent argument, Zasulich dropped her head noticeably. Kessel's logic was building up a rational and potentially persuasive case against her. The lack of response to it from the audience must have had something to do with the "pale and toneless" way in which Kessel presented it.[82]

Alexandrov began his rebuttal quietly, but gradually his voice took on resonance and strength. His oratorical skills were so far superior to Kessel's that it was not necessary for him to respond to Kessel's arguments; he could ignore them as he liked and build up his case in favor of his client. From the start, the spectators were with him; once, they interrupted him with applause.

Alexandrov began by acknowledging that, in legal terms, what Zasulich had done was a crime. But he maintained that to examine Zasulich's action in isolation from the events that had preceded it would be to assume that the motives that impelled her to act had no bearing upon the morality of the action itself. For this reason, the shooting of Trepov could not even be discussed reasonably without also investigating the flogging of Bogoliubov; the two actions were too closely linked in Zasulich's mind for the jury to decide the case without examining them together.[83] Furthermore, Alexandrov went on, one could not reasonably judge what Zasulich had done in 1878 while ignoring all that had transpired in her life. Recounting with considerable eloquence the hardships of imprisonment and exile, the defense

counsel described how Zasulich was mistreated in the early
1870's by a government against which she bore no special mal-
ice, and how this experience had engendered in her a sympathy
for all those who suffered unjustifiably similar humiliation and
degradation. Thus, when Zasulich learned of the Bogoliubov
flogging, she considered it not only "an affront against the moral
dignity of man," but an event whose circumstances were remark-
ably like those she had experienced herself. For Zasulich, Bogoliubov was "neither her relative, nor a friend, nor even an acquaintance; she had never known or seen him," but "is it
necessary to be a sister, a wife, or a mistress in order to be
indignant at the picture of a morally crushed man, in order to
revolt against a disgraceful mockery of a defenseless human
being?"[84]

Bogoliubov was a political prisoner, and to Zasulich, those
words meant everything:

a political prisoner for Zasulich was not an abstract idea found in a book
or something familiar by rumors or judicial trials—an idea rousing in a
pure soul a feeling of pity, compassion, and heartfelt sympathy. A
political prisoner meant to Zasulich her own self, her bitter past, her
personal history, the story of irretrievably ruined years, the best and
dearest in the life of every man who is not afflicted by a fate similar to
that of Zasulich. A political prisoner was for Zasulich the bitter memory
of her own suffering, of her terrible nervous excitement, constant anxiety, wearisome uncertainty, and never ending thought about the questions: "What crime did I commit? What will happen to me? When will
there be an end to all this?" A political prisoner was her own heart, and
every rough contact with it produced a painful response in her agitated
soul.[85]

As she learned further details of the flogging, her outrage only
increased. In her mind she imagined Bogoliubov as he awaited
punishment for a crime he had never committed:

prostrate on the floor, exposed in disgrace, irons around his hands,
chained, deprived of any chance of resisting, and over this picture the
measured whistle of the birch rods and also the measured counting of
strokes by the noble manager of the punishment; everyone was quiet in
anxious anticipation of the moan; they heard it; they were surprised
that it was not one of physical pain; it was rather the agonizing moan of
a suffocated, humiliated, desecrated, crushed man. The religious rite
was performed; the shameful sacrifice was offered![86]

Thus, because her years in exile had made her nature "ec-static, nervous, pained, and impressionable," when she learned of the Bogoliubov flogging she could not respond to it in a deliberate, coldly rational manner; although considerable time had elapsed between the conception of the assassination and its execution (this was Alexandrov's only allusion to plans for rescuing imprisoned colleagues in the south), her shooting of Trepov was not, in the true sense of the word, premeditated.[87] She bought a more powerful revolver only because it could be more easily concealed; given her objectives, the amount of damage she inflicted upon Trepov personally was unimportant. The crime committed, she made no attempt to escape.[88]

In conclusion Alexandrov emphasized again his client's motives and character, which he hoped would induce the jury, in a spirit of mercy, to acquit her:

Gentlemen of the jury! It is not for the first time in the court of the people's conscience that a woman accused of a bloody crime appears before this dock of crime and oppressive moral suffering. Women have appeared here who have avenged their seducers by killing them. Women have appeared here who have steeped their hands in the blood of their more fortunate rivals. These women left this place acquitted. These verdicts were just, an echo of divine justice, which takes into consideration not only the external side of an action but its inner meaning as well—the real guilt of the accused. These women who did bloody, summary justice fought for and avenged themselves. But for the first time there appears here a woman who had no personal interest in her crime, who linked her crime with the fight for an idea, for the sake of a man who was for her no more than a companion of distress. If these motives for crime prove lighter on a scale of social justice, if for the sake of the general welfare, the triumph of law, and public safety she must be punished, then yes, impose your judicial penalty. Not much more suffering can your sentence add to this broken, crushed life. Without a reproach, without a complaint, and without offense, she will accept your decision, and she will console herself with the fact that perhaps her suffering and her sacrifice will prevent the repetition of the incident that called forth her act. However somberly one looks at this deed, in the motives themselves it is impossible not to see an honest and noble impulse.[89]

When Alexandrov finished, many, including Zasulich, began to sob, overcome by the emotions that his oratory had aroused.

With the restoration of order, Koni again explained to the

jury the questions it must decide; whether the shooting of Trepov was premeditated, whether Zasulich shot him with the intent of depriving him of life, whether she did everything necessary to ensure that her plan would succeed. In his resumé, Koni made no judgment of Zasulich's guilt or innocence, but he attempted to clarify for the jury the legal interpretation that should be placed upon words such as "premeditation," "revenge," and "culpability." Without explicitly contradicting Alexandrov, Koni stated that Zasulich's "agitation" was irrelevant to the issue of premeditation; if she had time enough to reflect upon her crime before she committed it, then her crime was premeditated. On the other hand, without explicitly rebuking Kessel, Koni allowed that the motives and character of the defendant were points that the jury could properly include in its deliberations. Moreover, Koni noted—as was his legal obligation—that even if the jury found Zasulich guilty of any or all charges, it could exercise leniency in determining its verdict.* Finally, Koni reminded the jurors that everything he said to them was meant only as advice, and that, in the end, "only the voice of your conscience" should determine the verdict.[90]

The jury went off to deliberate. Notwithstanding Alexandrov's brilliant oratory, virtually all the spectators in the courtroom—and even Koni himself—expected a conviction. At seven o'clock in the evening, after being out only ten minutes, the jury returned. As the foreman handed Koni the paper on which were written the three charges against her, a "deathly silence" settled over the courtroom. The charges were read aloud; the foreman began to reply "Not Guilty." Before he could finish, pandemonium erupted. Koni described the scene in his memoirs:

It is impossible for one who was not present to imagine the outburst of sounds that drowned out the foreman's voice and the movement that like an electrical shock sped through the entire room. The cries of unrestrained joy, hysterical sobbing, desperate applause, the tread of

* Unlike the Anglo-American system of jurisprudence, that established in Russia in 1864 permitted juries to acquit defendants they considered guilty, or even defendants who had made a confession, provided that the jurors made their decision on the basis of "conscience." Samuel Kucherov, *Courts, Lawyers, and Trials under the Last Three Tsars* (New York, 1953), p. 65.

feet, cries of "Bravo! Hurrah! Good girl! Vera! Verochka! Verochka!" merged in one roar both moan and howl. Many crossed themselves;
in the upper, more democratic sections for the public people embraced; even in the places reserved for the judges there was enthusiastic applause.[91]

Among those applauding in the galleries was the Foreign Minister, Prince Gorchakov. Dostoevsky, not known for radical
sympathies, remarked to the man sitting next to him that
"punishment of this girl would have been inappropriate and
superfluous."[92] Fearful that any attempt to establish order would
only make the tumult worse, Koni refused to permit the bailiffs
to suppress the demonstration. Outside the courtroom, where a
crowd of approximately one thousand had gathered since early
morning to await the verdict, word of the acquittal brought an
excited reaction and even seemed to please the gendarmes who
were stationed there. Koni, anticipating that the government
might rearrest Zasulich if she were engulfed by the crowd, tried
to get the police to escort her to the House of Detention next
door to the courtroom and release her there through a side door
far removed from any demonstrators; but the police, possibly
acting on orders from their superiors, ignored the plea and
simply directed her through a front door to the waiting crowd.[93]

What happened next revealed the passions that the trial had
aroused. So that "everyone could see Vera Ivanovna," a man
lifted her and set her upon his shoulders. To cries of "Long live
Zasulich" the crowd began to march triumphantly through the
streets of St. Petersburg. Along the way, through the intervention either of the police or of a sympathetic bystander, a carriage
was found for Zasulich, and thus she continued with her entou-
rage down the Voskresenskii Prospekt.[94]

Suddenly, as the crowd approached an intersection, police
surrounded Zasulich's carriage. They explained to her that they
merely wanted to transfer her to another one, but her followers,
fearing the worst, immediately closed in to protect her.[95] In the
turmoil that ensued, three shots rang out and two people fell to
the ground, one of them wounded slightly in the scalp, the other
fatally wounded in the head; the third bullet glanced off the
helmet of a gendarme. A ballistics investigation of the incident
later established that all three bullets had been fired from the

pistol found on the body of the dead man, subsequently identified as G. P. Sidoratskii, a student at the St. Petersburg Medical Academy. Although many, including Zasulich, were convinced that Sidoratskii was shot by the police, the most plausible explanation of what happened is that Sidoratskii drew his pistol when it seemed to him that the police were about to arrest Zasulich, shot a demonstrator by mistake, and thinking that he had killed him, shot himself. The fact that all the bullets issued to the police that morning were returned intact after the incident seems to bear out this theory.[96]

Not surprisingly, Sidoratskii was quickly enshrined in revolutionary martyrology. The police wanted to bury him secretly, but details of their plan leaked to the press, and a requiem mass on April 5 in the Vladimir Church became a protest against police brutality.[97] Writing anonymously in the clandestine journal *Obshchina* (The Community), young Georgii Plekhanov declared that, in the Sidoratskii incident, "the fury of the police knew no limits," and proclaimed that the incident marked the first time shots had been fired in a political demonstration in Russia since the Decembrist revolt in 1825.[98] Articles no less passionate in their rhetoric appeared in journals such as *Golos* (The Voice), *Severnyi vestnik* (Northern Courier), and *Russkoe obozrenie* (Russian Survey).

Despite Koni's fears of a rearrest—and the crowd's assumption of the same—the police probably were, as they said, trying to protect Zasulich, and disperse the crowd, and did not intend to make an arrest at that time. After the incident, an order for arrest *was* issued, but Zasulich was already in hiding. Immediately following the shooting, her carriage had sped away in the confusion, and once again she assumed an "illegal existence," moving from place to place to elude the authorities. In a defiant letter dated April 3 and published on April 5 in *Severnyi vestnik* she declared that although she would have endured any punishment the court might have prescribed for her, she refused to submit to extra-legal persecution, and would therefore remain in hiding until she could move freely again in public without fear of arrest.[99] As it happened, Zasulich finally escaped to Western Europe, where (with the exception of brief, clandestine trips to Russia in 1879 and 1899) she would remain until the general amnesty proclaimed in 1905 made it possible for her to live permanently in Russia again.

Thus, whatever moral capital the government might have gained from the trial was irrevocably lost in its dénouement. If Zasulich had been left alone by the authorities, and Koni applauded by his superiors for his impartiality, the acquittal might have been received as a vindication of the Russian legal system and proof that Russia was evolving at last in the direction of a *Rechtsstaat*. But because the government reacted to the acquittal in ways that made its pretensions to judicial procedure seem hypocritical, it made Zasulich the martyr she would have been if the jury had convicted her, and imprinted her trial in people's consciousness as evidence of its own brutality and hypocrisy.

To Koni's dismay, the Zasulich trial and its aftermath epitomized to opponents of enlightened autocracy on both the left and the right the moral bankruptcy of a political system based upon the supremacy of law, for if the Left found objectionable the government's refusal to abide by the verdict of the court, the Right considered the verdict evidence enough that the courts themselves should be curtailed or abolished. In reactionary journals such as Mikhail Katkov's *Moskovskie vedomosti* (Moscow News), the verdict was a "scandal" and a "disgrace"; in liberal and radical ones such as *Golos* and *Severnyi vestnik* it was a triumph of moral conscience and a repudiation of autocracy; journals such as *Novoe vremia* (New Times) were roundly criticized for characterizing the acquittal as a vindication of the 1864 Reforms.[100] The Minister of War, Dmitrii Miliutin, described this polarization in his diary: "The entire public split into two camps. . . . Any such case creates rumors and stirs up protest in society, on the one hand against our new legal procedures and especially against the institution of juries, and on the other hand against the arbitrariness and despotism of the administrative authorities."[101]

In the universities, where sympathy for Zasulich was considerable, though not unanimous, students held meetings and collected money "for Verochka"; one student, who would later become a terrorist himself, even hung Zasulich's portrait on his wall in place of a religious icon.[102] Straining in his prose to reflect what he saw as the moral polarities of the situation, Plekhanov wrote in *Obshchina* that, if Trepov represented "law, authority, power, cowardice, and falsehood," Zasulich symbolized by comparison "the human condition and the sanctity of a heroic exploit."[103] In a similar vein, the journalist G. K. Gradovskii penned an article for *Golos* in which he described how, as he observed the proceedings in court, "it seemed to me that not Zasulich, but I myself, and with me society as a whole, were on trial, and that the defense was delivering an accusatory speech which deprived us of any hope of acquittal. And when the word of acquittal resounded, muffled by the outburst of enthusiasm, again it seemed to me that not Zasulich but I myself was acquitted, and that everything would be all right after many failures and much distress."[104] Leo Tolstoy stated simply, and perhaps prophetically, that "the Zasulich Affair is not a joke but rather like a harbinger of revolution."[105]

In Europe, for the most part, news of Zasulich's acquittal provoked much the same sorts of responses as in Russia. Liberals and radicals applauded it, monarchists and reactionaries condemned it, and nearly everyone who knew anything at all about it found it a welcome diversion from the much greater problems of the day. As Gustave Valbert put it in the *Revue des deux mondes* that May: "For forty-eight hours Europe forgot everything about peace, war, M. Bismarck, Lord Beaconsfield, Prince Gorchakov—so as to occupy itself with nothing except Vera Zasulich and the strange judicial adventure of which this unknown woman was the heroine."[106] Reports of the trial, mostly approving the verdict, appeared in German, French, English, Polish, and Austrian newspapers. Some of the French journalists were so carried away by what they saw as an extension into Russia of the ethos of the French Revolution that they labeled Alexandrov "another Camille Desmoulins" (after the famous Dantonist orator) and the trial itself the Russian equivalent of the fall of the Bastille.[107] Engels, in England, hailed Zasulich as a "heroic citizen."[108] Turgenev, in Germany, was importuned to write an article about her by readers of his novel *Virgin Soil*, who claimed to see a close resemblance between Zasulich and Marianna, the heroine of the book.* According to Kropotkin, who was in Paris when he learned of the verdict, "the devotion of Vera Zasulich produced a profound impression on the workers of Western Europe."[109] And A. E. Brailovskii says that the verdict even inspired parents in England to name their children "Vera."[110]

There was occasional thoughtful reaction. In an article in the English journal, *Contemporary Review,* a Russian émigrée named Elizaveta Bezobrazova discussed the complex nature of Zasulich's act and the dilemma that arose when appeals to moral conscience and to higher laws of nature were weighed against society's right to self-preservation:

When the agents of the Government have no respect for law, and resort to illegal means to ensure public security, one cannot expect to find such respect in the hearts of their victims, and violence on one side produces violence on the other. Nevertheless, society . . . ought to be more cautious in approving such applications of lynch-law. There are no political or personal motives that can justify murder, and if we are justly proud of having struck out the penalty of death from our code, how can we deliver that fearful power into the hands of private men, and applaud their using it? Granting that General Trepov has deserved his fate, and that Russia has found a heroine in Vera Zasulich, the latter ought still to have been punished, to wear her martyr's crown. To let her go free is to lessen the worth of her deed, and to proclaim that murder is now always forbidden by law, but may be admitted under certain circumstances.[111]

By and large, however, this dilemma was ignored. With its easy polarities of heroine and villain, suffering and revenge, moral purity and barbarism, the trial did not easily lend itself to an objective analysis of the political and ethical questions it suggested. Not without its comical repercussions, the trial even inspired a theater company in Naples to reenact it on the stage; when the dramatic moment arrived for Zasulich's fate to be

---

* R. A. Kovnator, "V. I. Zasulich: k istorii russkoi kritiki," Introduction to V. I. Zasulich, *Stat'i o russkoi literature* (Moscow, 1960), p. 6. *Virgin Soil,* Turgenev's last novel, drafted in 1870 but not published until 1877, deals with the "going to the people" movement and Marianna does resemble Zasulich in a number of ways, but Zasulich was only one of numerous young noblewomen who joined the revolutionary movement in the early 1870's. Schapiro in his recent biography of Turgenev thinks it likely that Zasulich's trial prompted Turgenev's prose poem "Threshold," dated May 1878. See Leonard Schapiro, *Turgenev: His Life and Times* (New York, 1978), p. 287.

decided, the actor impersonating Koni would appear on a balcony, resplendent in a red cape, and declare her innocence with a "benevolent bow."[112]

Meanwhile, in St. Petersburg, the government found nothing humorous about the response to the verdict, and moved to reassert the authority that the acquittal had seemed to undermine. On the very night of the trial the Tsar convened the Council of Ministers in special session to discuss what measures should be taken to quell the spreading tide of anti-government fervor. At this meeting, the chairman, P. A. Valuev, accused Koni of having ensured Zasulich's acquittal by not being sufficiently partial to the prosecution. Koni himself was not present at the meeting and his sole defender was Dmitrii Miliutin, from whom he subsequently learned that Pahlen had failed to explain to the ministers that in his behavior at the trial Koni had merely performed the role that the law prescribed for him. It was also at this meeting that the Tsar approved Pahlen's request that Zasulich be apprehended and imprisoned.[113]

Encouraged by its supporters in the press, the government adopted the position recommended by Pobedonostsev, who, in a letter to the Tsarevich, expressed the opinion common in reactionary and conservative circles that "in the Zasulich case the government displayed inadmissible, unpardonable weakness which can have fatal results. . . . Either the government must wake up and defend itself or it will perish."[114] Accordingly, on April 6, the day after *Severnyi vestnik* published Zasulich's declaration of defiance, the Minister of the Interior, A. E. Timashev, banned further publication of the journal, and the police intensified its search for the missing woman.[115]

As has been noted already, Andreevskii and Zhukovskii were forced to resign. Koni, too, was threatened with dismissal by Pahlen, who on April 5 tried to get him to confess his "guilt" in a declaration to the Tsar.* On April 21 Pahlen submitted to the State Council a bill that would disbar lawyers who had defended clients subsequently judged to be guilty.[116] In a decision which

---

* Koni, pp. 202–3. Years later, "narrow and superficial minds" embittered by Zasulich's acquittal would attribute to Koni responsibility for the October Revolution. Elizaveta Narishkin-Kurakin, *Under Three Tsars: The Memoirs of a Lady in Waiting* (New York, 1931), p. 56.

revealed how thoroughly the Tsar's ministers wanted to dispel (though in fact probably only strengthened) the appearance of political weakness, the government also jailed for seven days and then fired the manager of the House of Detention for having released Zasulich when she returned there after the trial to collect her belongings.[117] Seven weeks after the trial the Senate declared it invalid, and referred the case to the Novgorod Circuit Court for retrial.[118] On May 9 a law was passed which removed from the jurisdiction of the jury most cases involving acts of violence against government officials; on August 9 such cases were reserved exclusively for the courts-martial.[119] Finally, after Zasulich had escaped successfully to Switzerland, the new Minister of Justice, D. N. Nabokov, petitioned the Tsar to seek her extradition, presumably so she could be retried and convicted; the Tsar refused Nabokov's request solely because his ministers convinced him that a retrial would precipitate further disorders and damage Russia's image abroad.[120] Virtually the only sensible action in all these misguided actions was the Tsar's dismissal of Pahlen for his "negligent handling of the Zasulich Affair."[121]

In its significance the Zasulich trial fully deserved the lofty adjectives applied to it in its immediate aftermath; Kravchinskii, Mikhailovskii, Mikhailov, Sinegub, Plekhanov, Osinskii, and Klements were just a few of the many revolutionaries for whom the shooting and acquittal were truly an emotional catharsis and an inspiration to renew revolutionary struggle against the government.[122] Moreover, because Zasulich's motives were so widely misunderstood, and because the arguments employed in her defense were so thoroughly ignored, the trial to some extent legitimized political terrorism. Perceived as the repudiation of autocracy that neither Zasulich nor Alexandrov ever intended, her acquittal placed an imprimatur of legitimacy upon acts of violence committed for political purposes. Indeed, when Zasulich was acquitted and the same day forced to go underground to evade rearrest, simple logic suggested that to eradicate the evils of society one had to destroy those in positions of authority who bore responsibility for what the Trepovs within the government were allowed to do. In the words of Vera Figner, herself a revolutionary terrorist, "it began to seem ridiculous to punish the servant who had done the will of him who had sent him, and to leave the master untouched."[123] Extended to its logical conclusion, such reasoning seemed to necessitate the assassination of the Tsar.

Thus, the Zasulich trial revitalized the revolutionary movement and inspired its more extremist wing to turn to terrorism as a means by which to change the status quo. In May terrorists in Kiev—one of them, at least, inspired by Zasulich—shot and killed a police official, Baron Geiking.[124] On August 4 Sergei Kravchinskii stabbed to death in broad daylight General Mezentsev, the Chief of the Third Section and a figure notorious in revolutionary circles for his mistreatment of political prisoners; Kravchinskii, too, would claim later that his action had been inspired by Zasulich's.[125] In the clandestine *Listok Zemli i Voli* (Newspaper of Land and Liberty), Alexander Mikhailov and Nikolai Morozov began printing editorials proclaiming the efficacy of political assassination, and Morozov was so certain that Zasulich agreed with him that, without her knowledge or consent, he formally inducted her into Zemlia i Volia a few months later.[126] In a short time the journal attracted to it revolutionaries eager to organize a purely terrorist organization, and the "Death or Freedom" group that was formed as a result included many of those who would subsequently plot the assassination of the Tsar. By 1879 a faction within the revolutionary movement was so intent upon devoting its energies to terrorism that it seceded from Zemlia i Volia to form the so-called Narodnaia Volia (People's Will).

Less than three years after Zasulich's acquittal, Narodnaia Volia succeeded in assassinating Alexander II. Had Zasulich not shot Trepov, revolutionaries probably would have turned to terrorism anyway, impelled by their failures in fomenting peasant revolution to see in it a quick (and illusory) solution to their problems. Still, the shooting of Trepov and the events that occurred directly as a result of it helped to give terrorism a legitimacy in Russia that it generally did not acquire in Western Europe. As a result, one found in Russia in the late 1870's considerable sympathy for terrorism in liberal circles and even within the government, which was a sign of decay far more threatening to the government than any terrorist action itself.

Ironically, among those most distressed by this was Zasulich herself. When, in April 1879, A. K. Soloviev tried but failed to kill the Tsar, Zasulich, in despair, considered herself personally responsible, and wrote in anguished tones to Lev Deich that "it is impossible for me to endure a [terrorist] movement which my case had such influence in initiating."* Olga Liubatovich, who lived near Zasulich in Switzerland at the time, confirmed this in an article in *Byloe* years later: "as a result of Soloviev's attempt, V. I. Zasulich refused to see anyone for three entire days, and was beset by a severe depression; she saw no justification for such a thing. It seemed to me at the time that every violent act . . . affected her nerves because she consciously and perhaps subconsciously attributed to herself the first step in this trend of activity, obviously tending toward an active struggle with the government."[127] Largely because she did not approve of its espousal of political terrorism, Zasulich would subsequently refuse to join Narodnaia Volia, preferring instead the company of those who shared her commitment to agitation among the peasantry.

Indeed, in subsequent decades Zasulich would expend a good deal of energy attempting to disabuse revolutionaries of the arguments advanced for political terrorism. In articles written many years after her acquittal, Zasulich would argue that, as a weapon of political struggle, terrorism had no practical advantages: it was too divisive, too exhausting, and too convenient an excuse for government repression to be of use to a revolutionary party. In fact, terrorism was so alluring an alternative to tedious work among the masses, and yet so all-encompassing in the commitment it demanded of those who indulged in it, that it could easily become a psychological obsession. As Zasulich wrote in 1892: "The example of terrorist exploits can impress only those already possessing revolutionary spirit. . . . But terrorist acts cannot make a movement more powerful, no matter how popular they may be. However great the delight it sometimes arouses,

---

* Letter, Zasulich to Deich, April 4, 1879, reprinted in V. I. Nevskii, ed., *Istoriko-revoliutsionnyi sbornik* (Leningrad, 1924), vol. 2, pp. 348–49. Henri Rochefort notes in his memoirs that, throughout the years that he knew her, Zasulich unfailingly referred to the Trepov shooting as a "crime." Rochefort, "Vera Zasulich i narodovol'tsy," *Golos minuvshago*, no. 5/12 (1920–21), p. 87.

in order to carry out terrorist acts all of one's energies must be
expended, and a particular frame of mind almost always results:
either one of great vanity or one in which life has lost all its
attractiveness."[128]

Zasulich was not simply opposed to random shootings of officials uninvolved in the machinery of repression but also emphasized the effects of terrorism upon the terrorists themselves,
insisting that terrorism served no purpose great enough to justify its adverse effects. Terrorism, she wrote in 1892, creates
political passivity among the vast majority of those who cannot
partake in it. Because terrorism, by its conspiratorial nature, is
effective in inverse proportion to the number of people who
practice it, its use as a political tactic effectively nullifies the
potential power of both the masses and the revolutionaries who
would otherwise be actively participating in political struggle
against autocracy. If, using Zasulich's metaphor, autocracy is like
an army with generals at the top and conscripted soldiers at the
bottom, any revolutionary group that resorts to terrorism becomes an army consisting solely of generals (that is, of terrorists), and thus hopelessly inferior in the forces it could amass on
any battlefield.[129] It came as no surprise to her—she proclaimed
in 1902—that double agents in the service of the police were, for
this reason, actually encouraging revolutionaries to commit terrorist acts.[130]

Quite apart from these pragmatic objections to terrorism,
which Zasulich maintained she had formulated in the months
immediately following her acquittal, it seemed clear to her that
terrorism was not an appropriate means of defending one's personal honor or dignity, or the honor and dignity of a revolutionary party; taken together with Zasulich's belief in 1878 that she
was acting as Bogoliubov's surrogate, these perceptions yield the
conclusion that terrorism, in Zasulich's formulation of its moral
limits, can be used only to advance the interests of someone
other than the terrorist himself.* Terrorism, in other words, can

* V. I. Zasulich, "Po povodu sovremennykh sobytii," *Iskra*, no. 3 (April 1901),
reprinted as "Vystrel Karpovicha" in Zasulich, *Sbornik statei* (St. Petersburg,
1907), vol. 2, pp. 389–400. In this same article Zasulich states that terrorism
cannot properly be used on behalf of comrades imprisoned or even persecuted
by the government. However, she does not explicitly rule out terrorism on
behalf of individuals like Bogoliubov who are not known personally by the
terrorist and who are not in prison because of revolutionary activity. In 1902, for

only be an act of selflessness. Used for any other purpose, it leads not to spiritual redemption or political power, but rather to the vanity, the morbidity, and the self-absorption that she described in her article in 1892. Fundamentally, Zasulich viewed the issue of terrorism through the prism of noblesse oblige and social altruism, which enabled her to consider what she had done in 1878 more defensible than other forms of terrorism precisely because her action entailed an element of self-sacrifice. The same ethos of sacrifice which contributed to her becoming a revolutionary demanded as well that she shoot Trepov and that she offer no resistance to arrest.

For Zasulich terrorism was justifiable only as a gesture of moral conscience and as a means by which to publicize particular acts of brutality against individuals incapable of defending themselves. When, on January 24, 1878, Zasulich shot the Governor of St. Petersburg, she did so not to inspire the overthrow of autocracy, nor even, one suspects, to force specific changes in Russian law. Rather, she shot Trepov because she found his amorality repugnant and productive of an outrage which she could not ignore. On balance, shooting Trepov probably did her cause more harm than good; by legitimizing political terrorism, her acquittal helped divert revolutionary endeavor in a direction which culminated three years later in disaster. Alexander's assassination did not destroy autocracy, but it very nearly extinguished the revolutionary movement.

Having done so much to trigger this sequence of events, Zasulich was utterly powerless to stop it, since the acquittal, the attempt to reverse it, and the crescendo of terrorist violence that followed it were events with a dynamic that she could not control. With the passage of time, however, one could, as passions cooled, reflect upon the shooting as Zasulich explained it, and deduce the moral equation it seemed to proclaim: if, on the one hand, no government can tolerate assassinations of public offi-

---

example, she applauded the attempt of a Jewish worker, Hirsh Lekkert, to assassinate the Governor of Vil'na, who had ordered the flogging of a worker under circumstances similar to Trepov's flogging of Bogoliubov; despite Lekkert's mea culpa in court disavowing any political motivation, Lenin criticized Zasulich's approval of the shooting, as well as the shooting itself, as the worst kind of revolutionary self-indulgence. See his letter to Plekhanov of July 2, 1902, in L. G. Deich, ed., *Gruppa 'Osvobozhdenie Truda,'* vol. 6, p. 125.

cials no matter how repellent their behavior, on the other hand, private citizens have just as great an obligation to call attention—if necessary, through violence—to intolerable violations of human rights. To some, the Trepov shooting may seem to have been an act of political naïveté: that Trepov's brutality was symptomatic of a lawlessness much larger than his own revealed perhaps a lack of realism in Zasulich's choice of whom she would shoot. But Zasulich's limited justification of terrorism as well as her willingness to endure the legal consequences of her actions elevate the Trepov shooting to a moral plane approached by few other acts of terrorism in Russian history.

THREE

From Populism to Marxism

As HER CARRIAGE sped away on the evening of her acquittal, Zasulich realized that she would again have to assume an illegal existence. Moving from house to house in St. Petersburg with the assistance of M. N. Glagol and Lev Tikhomirov, she successfully eluded the police. Finally, after three weeks she was able to establish residence in a room above the clinic of an orthopedic surgeon sympathetic to revolutionary causes.* Here, in relative safety, Zasulich could contemplate her future; in practical terms her alternatives were limited to remaining underground inside Russia or escaping to comparative freedom in Western Europe. Her decision to go abroad was not made without considerable anguish. On the one hand, as Breshkovskaia warned her, life in exile would leave Zasulich to play the role of a "retired heroine," valued mostly as a symbol of the past; moreover, her distance from Russia would make her opinions increasingly irrelevant to the specific controversies that would arise there in the future.[1] On the other hand, Zasulich was understandably attracted to any haven beyond the reach of the police, and the personal freedom she would enjoy in Western

---

* Zasulich, *Vospominaniia*, pp. 71–73; M. N. Glagol, "Protsess pervoi russkoi terroristki," *Golos minuvshago*, nos. 7–9 (July–September 1918), pp. 158–61. This surgeon, a Dr. Weimar who had previously assisted Kropotkin in escaping from prison, was subsequently arrested because a gun he had sold to Dmitrii Klements found its way to Narodnaia Volia. When many Narodovol'tsy were arrested in April 1879, Dr. Weimar was arrested as well and sent to Siberia, where he became a drug addict and died in 1885. Adam Ulam, *In the Name of the People* (New York, 1977), p. 316.

Europe might compensate the loss of whatever influence she might exert from St. Petersburg. Indeed, in exile she would be free to indulge her interest in foreign cultures, and could avail herself of the resources of Western libraries in composing any articles she might want to smuggle back to Russia.

In May this second alternative became especially alluring as she learned of the Senate's decision to nullify her trial. Since the Senate ordered as well that she be tried again, Zasulich realized that, if captured, she faced not merely certain conviction and imprisonment, but a humiliation far worse than anything she might endure as an expatriate in Western Europe. Her trial had been such an emotionally unsettling experience for her that she doubted if she could stand a repetition. Moreover, while in hiding, she had had long conversations with Dmitrii Klements, a revolutionary and former member of the Chaikovskii Circle, whose invitation to travel with him to Switzerland reawakened her longtime passion for mountain hikes and country life.[2]

Accordingly, at the end of May, Zasulich and Klements left for Western Europe. With the assistance of A. M. Zundelevich, whose responsibility in Zemlia i Volia consisted of spiriting revolutionaries across the Russian border, the pair succeeded in reaching Switzerland in five days. To preserve her anonymity Zasulich rented a room in Geneva under the name "Mme. Stoudenevskii." It is an indication of the interest her acquittal had aroused that, when her escape became known in St. Petersburg, the rumor spread that, to ensure her safety, the Tsar's brother, the Grand Duke Nicholas, had provided her with an auburn wig and a carriage.[3]

Almost immediately after her arrival in Geneva, Zasulich found herself, much to her dismay, an object of attention for many European radicals. For example, she received an invitation from German anarchists requesting that she send a letter to the German Social Democratic Party announcing her opposition to its program. At Klements's urging, and also because she thought it was foolish "to write about things of which I am ignorant," she politely refused.[4] For the same reason, she announced that she would not attend a demonstration in Paris planned by French anarchists to celebrate her arrival in the West; in this instance she felt her presence would constitute an implicit endorsement of their ideology.[5] It is not surprising, given her shyness and propensity to self-effacement, that Zasulich refused such invitations. But that she refused them also because she considered herself insufficiently knowledgeable about radical politics in Western Europe indicates that, in 1878, she was not yet committed to revolution as an international principle. In her view it was the Russian government—rather than any international system such as capitalism—that was responsible for the injustices which, in the aftermath of her acquittal, caused her to reaffirm her revolutionary commitment.

As she explored the rugged beauty of the Alps, often accompanied by Klements and his wife, Anna Epstein, Zasulich quickly recovered from the severe depression that her acquittal had inexplicably produced. Free from the demands of French and German anarchists, she could experience on these expeditions a genuine euphoria:

In those deserted mountains virtually untouched by human hands . . . I felt I was in another kind of world, and my intense feeling of freedom grew stronger; I was liberated from everything that oppressed me— from people, but most of all from myself. All my painful thoughts and unresolved questions disappeared. It was not that I looked at them differently; while I was there I simply gave up thinking altogether. "Later there will be time," I thought, and for the moment I abandoned myself entirely to the impressions of that other world.[6]

Throughout her life Zasulich would welcome any opportunity to spend time alone in a completely rural environment, and this was especially true in the months immediately following her acquittal. At the same time, however, she discussed with Klements the "burning issues" of the day that most perplexed them, and his advice, which she valued highly, helped to harden her opposition to all forms of conspiratorial politics.[7] From Switzerland Zasulich viewed with considerable trepidation the growing popularity of political terrorism, and was so disturbed by what seemed to her to be its tactical futility that she determined in April 1879 to return to Russia as quickly as possible to argue against it within Zemlia i Volia.[8]

If Zasulich had returned to Russia in April, her prestige alone might have been sufficient to prevent or at least to delay the formation of Narodnaia Volia, many of the members of which had worked closely with her in Iuzhnye Buntari and considered the Trepov shooting the epitome of revolutionary dedication. Indeed, her prestige was so immense as a result of the acquittal that, according to Deich, one frequently heard in revolutionary circles the opinion that "if Zasulich opposes terrorism it must be wrong."[9] But after long and often emotional discussions, Zasulich was convinced by Kravchinskii and several others whose political judgment she respected that, if she returned to Russia, she would almost certainly be arrested.[10] Particularly after Soloviev's attempt on the life of Tsar Alexander in April, the police were tightening their surveillance of the borders. Thus it was not until the end of the summer that Zasulich, again with Zundelevich's assistance, made her way back into Russia.[11] By then, however, the dispute about terrorism within Zemlia i Volia had become so intense that, despite a modus vivendi achieved in early summer, the organization was on the verge of disintegration. In September 1879, shortly after Zasulich's return to Russia, Zemlia i Volia was officially dissolved, and its assets divided between those who supported terrorism as a regrettable necessity and those who opposed it on both tactical and ethical grounds.

A great deal of ink has been expended explaining the causes and the consequences of this schism. O. V. Aptekman, for example, attributed the break to differences of temperament, style, and personality, and was so bewildered by the events immediately preceding it that he could not decide which faction was primarily responsible for the dissension that ensued.[12] Deich thought the split was an inevitable result of genuine tactical and ideological disagreements of which the debate about terrorism was only the most obvious and divisive expression.[13] Both views were partly right: the personal antagonisms and temperamental differences that Aptekman refers to seem only to have exacerbated conflicts of a substantive nature no less real because they were obscured by a veneer of petty politics.

Ever since the failures in the early 1870's to rouse the rural masses to insurrection, a few perceptive members of the revolutionary movement had been seeking new ways of attaining their objectives, searching desperately for some deus ex machina with which to achieve their populist utopia of semi-autonomous communes. Somewhat reluctantly, they had to recognize that the only function of the commune even remotely "socialist" or egalitarian was its practice of periodically redistributing peasants' land. This recognition in the late 1870's brought on a "crisis" in Russian populism so profound that the solutions proposed in response to it were numerous enough to destroy what little consensus still existed within Zemlia i Volia.[14] The multitude of solutions (and pseudo-solutions) brought to the surface all the other differences, petty and profound, political and personal, that had previously been submerged beneath the facade of revolutionary unity. Without the prospect of success to bind them together, the leaders of Zemlia i Volia, men such as Plekhanov, Zheliabov, and Tikhomirov, struck off to seek their own solutions—terrorism, Marxism, or even a repudiation of revolutionary politics altogether. For a few, the intellectual crisis they experienced was so traumatic that they exhibited symptoms of psychological derangement.[15]

The principal issue in the debate was political terrorism. A meeting of the various factions was set for June 1879 in Voronezh. A few days before, those in Zemlia i Volia who favored terrorism, including Mikhailov, Tikhomirov, and Zheliabov, gathered in Lipetsk, a resort near Kiev, to discuss how the resources of the organization might be redistributed to favor political assassinations. In protest, they said, against the government's attitude that agitation in the countryside was subversive (though this seemed to contradict their assertion that such agitation was politically unproductive), the leaders of this gathering issued a manifesto explaining their commitment to "political warfare":

In view of the existing social conditions in Russia, we see that no activity aimed at the good of the people is possible, given the despotism and violence which here reign supreme. There is no freedom of speech or freedom of the press, which would allow us to act by means of persuasion. And so any man who wants to go in for progressive social work must, before anything else, put an end to the existing regime. To fight against this regime is impossible without arms. And so we will fight with the means employed by William Tell until we achieve those free institutions which will make it possible to discuss without hindrance all social and political problems, and solve them through free representatives of the people. . . . Seeing that the government in this fight against us resorts not only to banishment, prison, and death, but also confiscates our goods, we consider that we have the right to repay it in the same coin by confiscating its own means on behalf of the revolution.[16]

Because terrorism by its very nature required a highly disciplined and clandestine organization, the Lipetsk manifesto also demanded that the very loose, "umbrella-like" structure of Zemlia i Volia be tightened so as to drive away all those not totally committed to a terrorist campaign.

Thus, the lines of the split were already established when Zemlia i Volia convened in Voronezh. The compromise whereby one-third of the budget would be used for terrorism and the remaining two-thirds for peaceful agitation was inherently unworkable, and both the terrorists and the anti-terrorists seemed to assume that it was no more than a temporary expedient. Still, no one except Plekhanov was ready for a final break just yet. If the *derevenshchiki* (or "country people," as the advocates of peaceful agitation were then referred to) hoped to preserve party unity because they believed that the budget allotment would work to their advantage, those who favored terrorism worked for the identical objective because they predicted it would not. Indeed, in the next few months the terrorist faction absorbed a larger and larger percentage of the money Zemlia i Volia had accumulated. On August 26 the executive committee of the organization, which by now consisted entirely of terrorists, formally condemned the Tsar to death. On September 12 it seceded from Zemlia i Volia and proclaimed itself Narodnaia Volia, "a secret society entirely autonomous in its activities." The *derevenshchiki*, however, retained the printing press in their possession, and made plans to publish a journal that they would entitle *Chernyi peredel* (Black Repartition). Only five issues were eventually published, but the name was also used to define as an organization the group of twenty-one individuals who at one time or another actively participated in the issuing of the journal. A formal agreement reached in October affirmed that neither the terrorists nor the *derevenshchiki* would use the name Zemlia i Volia.[17]

To the extent that it functioned as a genuine organization, Chernyi Peredel managed in the short period of its existence to serve as a Cassandra that shadowed Narodnaia Volia, ridiculing its view that regicide alone could overturn a political order that drew for its legitimacy upon sentiments that ran very deep in Russian culture and society; much like the Mensheviks of a later generation, the Chernoperedel'tsy believed that, for tactical reasons as well as moral ones, "the emancipation of the people must be a matter for the people themselves."[18] Although some Chernoperedel'tsy thought that terrorism, applied selectively, might advance the revolutionary cause, the group remained unyielding in its belief that terrorism, if it was to be used at all, had to be subordinated to the creation of a mass revolutionary movement.[19] In sum, the Chernoperedel'tsy favored a revival of agitation among the peasants, a policy which prompted Zasulich to enlist in the organization when she returned from exile in August 1879. Despite its numerical inferiority, Chernyi Peredel was not entirely ineffectual in perpetuating populist notions during the heyday of Narodnaia Volia, and its emphasis on mass agitation as the only means of establishing a society of semi-autonomous communes places the group squarely within a tradition in Russian populism beginning with the Chaikovskii Circle in the early 1870's.

But Chernyi Peredel was more than merely a movement of Russian populism. From its ranks would come Deich, Zasulich, Axelrod, and Plekhanov, who in 1883 established the Emancipation of Labor Group, the first definable organization of Russian Marxism. Given their beliefs, it is not difficult to understand why they would do so. As populists, the Chernoperedel'tsy emphasized above all the need for economic change: well before most of them became Marxists, they considered the transformation of political institutions contingent upon the development of an economic order based on the abolition of private property; terrorism directed against the government was distasteful to them in large part because it attacked the symptoms rather than the causes of peasant poverty and misery. Even if political terrorism were successful, it would merely substitute one set of exploiters for another, in this case liberal landowners who could mask their repression of the peasant behind the platitudes of constitutional government. The only way to make life more bearable for the peasants—so argued the Chernoperedel'tsy through Plekhanov, their spokesman—was to do everything possible to alter the system of property relations in Russia. And to do so was impossible so long as one's time and energy were dissipated in a program of political assassinations.[20]

To be sure, Plekhanov and the other Chernoperedel'tsy still believed in 1879 that economic forces were working to strengthen the commune, and that capitalism could be avoided in Russia.[21] In this respect, the Chernoperedel'tsy were not yet Marxists, for however sincerely they believed in class struggle and economic determinism, they still considered the peasant, rather than the proletariat, the principal agent of historical change. But with the passage of time, the more perspicacious among them would come to see that these perceptions were mistaken and that capitalism, if not exactly a virtue, was, in any event, inevitable. Indeed, if Marx was right when he said that capitalism was a prerequisite of communism, and that communism would be more humane than any society since the primitive egalitarianism of the ancients, then the capitalist system which populists condemned for the cruelties it perpetrated in the present could be tolerated, even praised, for the social justice it would engender in the future.

By this chain of reasoning, a transition from populism to Marxism was not terribly difficult. Because they accepted economic determinism at the same time that they proclaimed themselves to be populists, the Chernoperedel'tsy could become Marxists merely by substituting a capitalist for a communal order as that which this determinism would produce. Having accepted Marxist laws of change as valid, Plekhanov and his followers needed only to accept Marx's view of their outcome. Ironically, Marx, and later Engels, would complicate matters by revising their views on the peasant commune and its chances for survival in Russia, but by the time these revisions became known to the Chernoperedel'tsy, most of them (but not Zasulich) were too far along in their conversion to reverse directions. Having given to the Chernoperedel'tsy the intellectual baggage to make the journey from another ideology to their own, not even Marx and Engels could prevent the majority of them from reaching their final destination.[22]

Moreover, in its emphasis upon mass action, in its claim that only a revolution involving workers, peasants, and students could prove successful, Chernyi Peredel fastened upon a theme which would reappear later on in Russian Marxism as it was adapted to the agrarian and backward nature of Russian society. In Chernyi Peredel, with its hostility to clandestine and elitist methods, one sees in embryo a fundamental thesis of Menshevism; in its efforts to forge coalitions of workers and peasants one sees a faint precursor of Lenin's attempts in 1917 to broaden the base of Russian socialism to include classes other than the urban proletariat. Of course, in the late 1870's the distinction between worker and peasant was so minor as to be virtually nonexistent, since the workers of that generation retained the mentality and traditions of the peasantry, and in many cases returned to their villages as often as possible. Nevertheless, the mere fact that Chernyi Peredel—more so than Narodnaia Volia—considered the factories fertile soil for propaganda indicates a readiness to bend ideology to one's advantage reminiscent of Lenin's efforts several decades in the future: just as Chernyi Peredel included workers in its original constituency of peasants, so, too, would Lenin incorporate the peasants in his original constituency of workers. Writing in February 1879, Plekhanov displayed on the question of agitation in the factories the flexibility for which Chernyi Peredel is justly remembered:

Our large industrial centers bring together tens and sometimes even hundreds of thousands of workers. In the vast majority of cases these men are the same peasants as those in the villages. . . . Their cause is the same; their struggle can and must be the same. Moreover, the towns attract the very flower of the village population, younger people, the more enterprising ones . . . there they are kept far away from the pernicious influence of the more conservative and timid elements of the peasant family. . . . Because of this they will constitute a precious ally for the peasants when the social revolution breaks out.[23]

Both in Russia and as émigrés in Western Europe, the Chernoperedel'tsy were dominated intellectually by Plekhanov, the future "Father of Russian Marxism," as his biographer, Samuel Baron, quite appropriately describes him. Born in 1856, trained as an engineer in the St. Petersburg Mining Institute, Plekhanov made his debut as a revolutionary in December 1876 in the Kazan Cathedral demonstration, at which he displayed for the first time the intellectual ability that would later make him perhaps the finest Marxist theorist of his day, superior even to Engels in the brilliance and originality of his thought. Unfortunately, Plekhanov's virtues as a thinker were surpassed only by his failings as a person; among his contemporaries he was remembered more fondly by those who did not know him than by those who did. Arrogant, often pompous, usually unemotional to the point of apparent callousness, but also possessing a temper that could explode at the most trivial provocation, Plekhanov could easily dominate individuals like Zasulich who were by nature deferential and self-effacing. Indeed, revolutionaries more strong-willed than Zasulich who came to Switzerland to pay their respects to Plekhanov often returned to Russia disillusioned and disappointed by what they found, and even Zasulich, usually so tolerant of others' idiosyncracies, could at times be moved to complain about his overbearing manner.[24] Although Plekhanov also was capable of great generosity, and paid for Zasulich's medical expenses whenever his meager income from copywork and translations would permit, his effect on Zasulich was to increase her own doubts about her intellectual prowess, and to cause her to defer to him even when she felt that he was wrong.

But despite these serious flaws in his character, Plekhanov proved to be an excellent leader of Chernyi Peredel. From 1879 to 1881, when terrorist exploits increasingly captured the imagination of the educated public, Plekhanov shrewdly evoked the Russian worker as a refreshing alternative for those disillusioned by the apathy of the peasants but also perceptive enough to recognize the futility of terrorism. Although populists of every stripe could be found who considered workers likely participants in a peasant revolution, the role Plekhanov envisioned for them was immeasurably greater than that assigned to them even by Narodnaia Volia, which, in its propensity for conspiracy, after a time considered workers more the beneficiaries than the agents of their own emancipation.[25] Along with Pavel Axelrod, who in 1879 had tried to revive the South Russian Union of Workers, Plekhanov argued that, because "agitation in the factories is increasing daily," revolutionaries should recognize the new opportunity available to them, and do everything in their power to ensure that workers' discontent be channeled in an appropriate direction.[26] Regardless of what many populists may have thought of him in the past, the worker was now sufficiently aroused so that he should be included in any revolutionary program devoted to "the principle of the social revolution. . . . Today it is difficult to find a factory, a workshop, or even a craftsman's shop which does not contain some socialist workers."[27]

Although at this point in his intellectual evolution Plekhanov still considered the workers "urban peasants" lacking the traditions, habits, and mentality of a distinctive social class, he was sufficiently free from the dogmas of Russian populism to recognize the workers' revolutionary potential. Not until the early 1880's would Plekhanov realize why "urban peasants" should be more politically conscious than their rural counterparts: this was true, he would argue, because in factories workers could communicate and organize more easily than could peasants tilling separate plots of land. Still, when Chernyi Peredel was formed in 1879, Plekhanov's ideas were already in flux, and Axelrod's far more extensive practical experience in organizing workers in Odessa lent to Plekhanov's arguments, which tended toward the abstract and theoretical, the empirical corroboration they required. Indeed, in many instances in the future, Plekhanov's penchant for the theoretical combined with Axelrod's perception of empirical truths and Zasulich's intuitive grasp of moral imperatives to produce a synthesis of talent that gave the organizations they belonged to a significance far in excess of their numbers.

Unfortunately, we know virtually nothing about what, if anything, Zasulich contributed to Chernyi Peredel after she returned to Russia in 1879; her name appears in the relevant documents only as one of those forced to emigrate again in January 1880 as a result of a police investigation barely four months after the group had been created.[28] One can only emphasize that Zasulich's assumptions were severely tested at this time by the popularity of Narodnaia Volia, and speculate that her own confusion may explain this absence of evidence indicating activity on behalf of Chernyi Peredel. Indeed, when she returned to Switzerland, this time for a stay of fourteen years, her doubts and vacillation became more pronounced as she read in *Otechestvennye zapiski* (Notes of the Fatherland) installments of

V. P. Vorontsov's "The Fate of Capitalism in Russia."[29] In these articles, published as a book in 1882, Vorontsov argued essentially that Russia's lack of an adequate internal market and the continued vitality of the peasant commune in Russia precluded any possibility that capitalism could ever supplant the agrarian economy that existed there.[30] According to Deich some years after the fact, although Kravchinskii and Stefanovich agreed with Vorontsov's conclusions, he and Zasulich considered them fallacious—an assertion which, if correct, would mean that the two of them had already repudiated the fundamental assumptions of populism.[31] But there is reason to believe that Zasulich's views, at least, were more uncertain and confused than Deich's reminiscences would suggest. Significantly, she was disturbed enough by the issues Vorontsov had raised to send Marx a letter requesting his opinion on the survival of the commune, an issue she considered nothing less than "a matter of life and death."[32]

In this letter, after pointing out to Marx his fame in Russian revolutionary circles, Zasulich stated that she hoped his reply would resolve a dispute about the commune (*obshchina*) in which both sides looked to *Capital* for the answer. On the one hand, Zasulich wrote, there were those who claimed that:

if this rural obshchina were relieved of the excessive demands of the state treasury, payments to the landlords, and the arbitrary rule of the authorities, it could develop in a socialist direction; that is, it could gradually organize its production and its distribution of products on collective principles. In this case the socialist-revolutionary would be obliged to devote all his energy to the emancipation of the obshchina and its development.

On the other hand, Zasulich continued, there were those who argued:

If the obshchina is doomed to destruction, then the socialist, as such, must only be occupied with more or less well-founded calculations that will determine in how many decades the Russian peasant's land will pass into the hands of the bourgeoisie, in how many centuries, perhaps, capitalism will attain in Russia the degree of development it has achieved in Western Europe. Then it will be necessary for him to conduct propaganda only among the urban workers who, because of the decomposition of the obshchina, are being thrown onto the streets of the large towns in search of earnings.

Recently we hear the opinion that the rural obshchina is an archaic form which history and scientific socialism—in short everything that is indisputable—doom to destruction. People who advocate this call themselves "Marxists." And their strongest argument is often: "Marx says so."

"But by what means do you conclude this from *Capital*? In it he does not discuss the agrarian question and he is not speaking about Russia," one objects.

"He would have said this if he had spoken about our country," answer your disciples—perhaps somewhat too boldly.[33]

Her conclusion summed up gracefully: "You will understand, therefore, Citizen, the extent to which your opinion on this question interests us and what a great service you would render us if you stated your views on the possible fate of our rural obshchina and on the theory that, owing to historical inevitability, all the countries of the world must pass through all the phases of capitalist production."[34]

Marx's reply has been discussed at length, but for Zasulich's biographer, the letter that prompted it deserves attention as an indication of Zasulich's thinking at an unusually critical point in her life. Most of this letter has been quoted here in translation because it constitutes virtually the only document we possess in which Zasulich states her indecision and uncertainty explicitly. Absent in the letter, for example, is any firm commitment to either side of the controversy she describes. The two points of view are presented quite impartially, and Zasulich carefully refers to "Marxists" in the third person, as if to emphasize that she herself is not one of them. Asking Marx to resolve a matter she considered to be of "life and death" significance indicates that she obviously esteemed him both as a thinker and as a social analyst, but her refusal in the letter to label herself explicitly as his disciple suggests that she had not repudiated everything she had previously believed, and considered the entire matter of the commune an open question.

Yet, the very fact that Zasulich asked someone else to settle a dispute involving the commune indicates that the old maxims of Russian populism were no longer entirely convincing. In 1881 Zasulich was unsure of her political convictions, detached enough from the arguments of Vorontsov to seek corroboration or rebuttal from Marx, but not quite willing to commit herself to

Marx's ideology. If Zasulich was no longer a populist, she was not yet a Marxist, and it is significant that she gives no indication in her letter to Marx that she would necessarily agree with his response.

Ironically, Marx's reply seemed to cast doubt on the basic scheme of Marxist ideology, and its effect may very well have been to *delay* Zasulich's conversion to Marxism. In this letter, Marx stated, in effect, that the general laws of economic development set forth in the first volume of *Capital* need not necessarily apply to Russia and that institutions peculiar to Russian society could lead it in a direction different from that of every other nation:

> In the process under way in the West, the squeezing out of the small landholder involves the transformation of one form of private property into another. In the case of the Russian peasant, however, the issue would involve the transformation of communal property into private property. Thus the analysis presented in *Capital* presents no special arguments for or against the peasant commune's vitality, but investigations that I have carried out on the basis of materials extracted from primary sources have convinced me that *the commune constitutes the point of support of a social regeneration of Russia.* However, before it can begin to play this role, the poisonous influences that attack it from all sides must be eliminated, and its normal, free development ensured.[35]

Unfortunately, Marx failed to explain how these "poisonous influences" might be eliminated, or to elucidate the circumstances in which "the normal, free development" of the commune might be ensured. Even with its qualifying clauses, however, the letter seemed to contradict much of what Marx had written in his lifetime, and perhaps this explains why he wrote four preliminary drafts before composing a final one, and also why he wrote the letter only with the stipulation that Zasulich agree beforehand not to publish it. Because she abided by his wishes, the letter was known only to a few until the Bolshevik theorist, David Riazanov, decided to publish it in 1924.*

---

* These drafts can be found in David Riazanov, ed., *Arkhiv K. Marksa i F. Engel'sa* (Moscow, 1924), vol. 1, pp. 265–86. Another interpretation of Marx's stipulation is that he and Engels planned to include a new introduction in an edition of *The Communist Manifesto* which they hoped to publish in a few months that would address more directly the entire question of the peasant commune.

To be sure, there was a strain in Marx's thinking that made his letter to Zasulich not entirely without precedent in the corpus of his writings. As early as 1850 Marx had argued in an address to the Communist League that, although capitalism was not yet fully mature in Germany, socialists there should not shrink from seizing power should the opportunity arise.[36] Similarly, in the 1870's, as the exploits of revolutionaries like Zasulich forced Marx to abandon his long-standing Russophobia, he wrote in a letter to *Otechestvennye zapiski*:

In order to form a well-grounded judgment on Russia's economic development, I studied the Russian language and, over a number of years, I followed official and other publications that dealt with this question. I arrived at the following conclusion: if Russia continues along the road which she has followed since 1861, she will forego the finest opportunity that history has ever placed before a nation, and will undergo all of the fateful misfortunes of capitalist development.[37]

In return, as if in response to Marx's interest, Russian revolutionaries of all varieties eagerly devoured virtually everything Marx had written. In 1869 *The Communist Manifesto* had been translated into Russian, perhaps by Bakunin; in 1872 Daniel'son had done the same for the first volume of *Capital*. By the late 1870's, Marxist ideas were far more accessible to Russian revolutionaries than in the previous decade, when only those who knew Western languages could read Marx's writings. Although Lavrov, Chernyshevskii, and other Russian radicals in the 1860's had adopted some Marxist concepts and categories, not until the late 1870's were Marx's works disseminated widely enough to make possible discussions like those which originally prompted Zasulich to correspond with him.

Moreover, with the formation of Zemlia i Volia in 1876, and even more so with the formation of Narodnaia Volia three years later, it seemed to Marx that Russia was the only country in Europe where the forces of reaction were effectively challenged.

Iu. Z. Polevoi, *Zarozhdenie Marksizma v Rossii* (Moscow, 1959), p. 163. Polevoi's interpretation and Deich's second one (see n. 32) are not mutually exclusive if one accepts as true the strong possibility that between Marx's letter to Zasulich and the publication of the new introduction a year later Marx's doubts and vacillation on the commune were largely dissipated—a view corroborated by the tone and emphasis of this new introduction.

Despondent over the suppression of the Paris Commune and the dissolution of the First International, but also gratified by the attention Russian radicals devoted to his writings, Marx understandably questioned the inevitability of capitalism and came to believe that the destruction of the Tsar could lead directly to the establishment of socialism. Incredibly, in 1880 he even attacked the Chernoperedel'tsy—that is, the individuals who would become his disciples—for what he considered their "tedious doctrinnairism" and unwillingness to return to Russia to fight alongside Narodnaia Volia for the overthrow of autocracy.[38] As the tide of revolution inexorably ebbed in Western Europe, Marx turned eastward in the last years of his life, finding there a party doing everything it could to precipitate a revolution on the basis of principles he had recently endorsed. All this helps to make more understandable the unorthodox character of Marx's letter to Zasulich.

Unfortunately, neither Marx's letter to *Otechestvennye zapiski* nor his disparaging remarks about Chernyi Peredel were known to Zasulich when she wrote to him in February 1881; with the sole exception of an open letter Engels sent to Tkachev in 1875, none of what Marx and Engels had said about Russia was intended for public consumption—quite possibly because both men recognized the difficulties in squaring their recent statements about the commune and the noninevitability of capitalism with earlier ones.[39] One can therefore imagine Zasulich's confusion and surprise when she received Marx's reply of March 8. Ignorant of recent changes in Marx's thinking, Zasulich must have read his letter and concluded that, in his qualified embrace of the commune, Marx was perhaps just as reluctant as she was to make definitive predictions about Russia's subsequent development. To complicate matters, on March 1 Narodnaia Volia had finally succeeded in assassinating Alexander II. Although, as Zasulich had predicted, the assassination was a political dead end which only brought about the disintegration of Narodnaia Volia, for a brief moment her emotions got the better of her judgment. Deich, in a letter to Plekhanov, who was in Paris, declared that he, Zasulich, and Stefanovich were so confident that the "grandiose event" would precipitate the granting of civil liberties and a constitution that they contemplated returning to Russia in the near future.[40] Deich and Zasulich ignored Plekhanov's cold-blooded assessment of the consequences of the assassination, and only the lack of money prevented them from joining Stefanovich when he returned to Russia that summer.[41] Impressed by the magnitude of the terrorists' achievement, for the first and only time in her life Zasulich responded favorably to an act of political terrorism. Coming as it did when her opinions on other issues were so unclear, the assassination of Alexander II was for Zasulich a means of escape from loneliness and uncertainty, as well as an event that might serve to catalyze a successful revolution. Over the next year or so, as the miscalculations of Narodnaia Volia became too obvious to ignore, and as the police arrested nearly everyone connected with the assassination, Zasulich gradually returned to her original position, more convinced than ever of its correctness. Still, for a short period her judgment had gone completely askew as the prospect of returning home from exile, even more than the prospect of a peasant insurrection, rendered all other issues insignificant in comparison.

Resigned now to remaining in Geneva for the foreseeable future, Zasulich resumed the process of resolving the theoretical problems that had prompted her letter to Marx. Her reluctance to express her thoughts in writing makes necessary a textual analysis of the few documents which reveal the evolution of her views. In an open letter to the German Social Democratic Party composed in February 1882, she appealed as a fellow socialist to her German colleagues to assist in the effort sponsored by Chernyi Peredel and the remnants of Narodnaia Volia to send money to Russian revolutionaries imprisoned or in exile in Siberia. She wrote that the strength of the "socialist, democratic-political party of Russian revolutionaries" (by which she meant the combined forces of the two organizations, which were then negotiating a reunion) lay "in the voluntary energy of its members, the sympathy of the best people of the country, the suppressed dissatisfaction, and, finally, the conspiratorial skills which our party has acquired in its ten-year struggle."[42] Nevertheless, Zasulich continued, the financial assistance German socialists could provide would be invaluable in strengthening the party for the struggles ahead:

It is clear to everyone that already the day is not far when Russian absolutism in one way or another will disappear. After this event undoubtedly a general movement will follow, the animated activity of all elements of society. Then our emerging bourgeoisie will appear on the scene and direct all its energies toward ensuring for itself the fruits of victory. At that time the social-revolutionary party will need all the forces on which it can rely so that, with the aid of extensive agitation and the dissemination of socialist ideas, it can create the basis for a massive organization of peasants and workers which alone can successfully counteract the efforts of the bourgeoisie.[43]

The course of events Zasulich sketches in this letter is extremely revealing. First of all, she predicts the imminent destruction of Russian absolutism, which indicates that the optimism created by the Tsar's assassination had not entirely dissipated. Second, she seems not to perceive any difference between a "social-revolutionary" and a "social-democratic" party, and uses the two terms interchangeably to describe the party which she says will lead the peasants and workers against the bourgeoisie. Third, she implies—in contradiction to Marxist theory—that this bourgeoisie could be dispatched by revolutionaries without the necessity of a dialectic to create the objective preconditions of its collapse. In this letter, in other words, what remained of Zasulich's populism seems to have been reinforced, not refuted, by her correspondence with Marx, and the letter of February 1882, like the one of February 1881, seems to leave her no closer to an understanding, much less an acceptance, of Marxism.

At this same time, Marx and Engels once again seemed to be retarding rather than accelerating their pupil's progress. Despite the disintegration of Narodnaia Volia, both men believed a Russian revolution to be imminent; in an introduction to a Russian edition of *The Communist Manifesto*, prepared by Plekhanov for publication in February 1882, they wrote:

In Russia, alongside a feverishly rapid development of capitalist knavery, and a just emerging bourgeois agriculture, we find more than half the land owned communally by the peasants. The question arises: can the Russian peasant commune—that, to be sure, is a widely decomposed form of primitive communal ownership of the land—evolve directly to a higher form—to communist common property—or does it have to pass through the process of decomposition through which it passes in the historic development of the West?

The only possible answer to this, at the present time, is the following: if the Russian revolution is a signal for proletarian revolution in the West, so that the two can supplement each other, then modern Russian communal ownership can serve as a point of departure for Communist development.[44]

Clearly, in the second paragraph one finds an early version of Lenin's view that Russia, as the "weakest link" in international capitalism, could serve as a catalyst for revolutions in Western Europe; in their enthusiasm, Marx and Engels considered a Russian revolution capable of proceeding directly from feudalism to socialism provided only that revolutions occur in other countries as well.

Zasulich surely read this introduction when it was published, but she wrote nothing herself in the following two years. During those two years Chernyi Peredel was dissolved, the Emancipation of Labor officially established, and its members—including Deich, Plekhanov, Axelrod, and Zasulich—declared their allegiance to Marxism. Unlike the others', however, Zasulich's conversion was incomplete. In 1884, for example, in a letter to Deich she denied the notion central to Marxism that "being" determines "consciousness," insisting that, in the case of Islam, religion, as an expression of "consciousness," was not simply a product of economic relations; so contrary was her argument to Marx's views on religion that it would cause one Soviet historian to conclude that Zasulich could be called a "dialectical materialist" (i.e. a Marxist) only if the term were defined so loosely as to render it meaningless.[45] Whatever the truth of this assertion, it is certainly the case that in the early 1880's Zasulich seemed to follow Marx and Engels as the two men, out of a combination of desperation and hope, came close to claiming that laws of change they had previously characterized as universal really did not apply to Russia.

Indeed, on the next occasion Zasulich expressed herself in print, in 1884 in a preface to her translation of Engels's *The Development of Scientific Socialism,* she espoused a position similar to the one Marx and Engels had espoused in 1882: since the bourgeoisie in Russia was so weak, a socialist revolution could follow fairly soon after the overthrow of autocracy provided only that revolutions also occur in Western Europe. "The days

of capitalism in Western Europe are already numbered," Zasulich predicted, and "the socialist revolution in the West will put
an end to capitalism in Eastern Europe as well."[46] Because Russia
could borrow from the West industrial techniques developed
there through the painful process of trial and error, Russian
capitalism would develop at a rate much faster than that attained
in Western Europe. For this reason, Russia could avoid "those
same consecutive stages of development characteristic of Britain
or France."[47] To claim that economic forces are paramount in
history, Zasulich concluded, does not preclude the possibility
that one country may develop at a rate or in a direction different
from that of all others.[48]

In this preface Zasulich was not simply espousing Marxist orthodoxy, nor was she expressing a point of view similar to
Trotsky's in 1905 (and Lenin's and Trotsky's in 1917), namely,
that Russia could proceed directly from feudalism to socialism.
The socialist revolution Zasulich envisioned would precipitate
not the destruction but the *resurgence* of the peasant commune:
"Given broad preparatory propaganda, the [new] government
could acquire sympathy and the understanding of the mass of
the peasant population, rely in the practical sphere on the remnants of the communal institutions, and so be able to adopt
immediately the broadest measures of the most decisive character."[49] In conclusion Zasulich noted simply that "the commune
would be of the greatest service in Russia."[50] As the economy
evolved toward egalitarian distribution and collective production, the commune would be invaluable both for the socialist
principles it embodied and for the collectivist mentality it per-
petuated.

Although Zasulich's translation of Engels's book was subsequently reprinted four times, her preface, so distinctive in its
praise of the commune, was dropped after the first printing at
the insistence of Plekhanov and Axelrod, who thought it contained arguments at variance with what they believed was the
general thrust of Marxist ideology.[51] Axelrod, however much he
valued Zasulich as a colleague, even advised her in 1888 that she
should turn her attention in the future to literary matters rather
than theoretical ones.[52] But Zasulich persisted in her wanderings
through this ideological labyrinth (one more confusing than it

might have been if Engels had not praised this same introduction as "splendid"),[53] and only in 1890 would she finally reverse
herself on the commune, assert that only the proletariat could
make a socialist revolution, and affirm the view of Plekhanov
and Axelrod that Russia had to experience capitalism before
Russian revolutionaries could make a socialist revolution. As she
declared in her "Revolutionaries of Bourgeois Background,"
written in 1890 for the journal, *Sotsial-demokrat*:

The communist revolution is not completed at one stroke, with one
uprising. Rather, it is a more or less continuous and prolonged process
during which the proletariat grows, educates, and organizes itself. . . .
But [the proletariat] remains an opposition and not a ruling party
because, for socialists to seize power prematurely, when a major part of
the proletariat itself remains unorganized, would mean not victory but
a delay in the ultimate triumph.[54]

Here, at last, is a statement of the Marxism that Zasulich would
profess, with only minor emendations, for the rest of her life. In
its emphasis upon a mass revolution undertaken by the proletariat only after an extended period of maturation, the statement
also expresses the same willingness to wait upon events which
would paralyze Russian Menshevism in 1917.

Thus, in tracing Zasulich's conversion to Marxism, one could
say that she was Marx's disciple before she espoused his ideology. Because her first exposure to Marx came when he and
Engels had reason to question much of what they had written
and argued in the previous thirty years, Zasulich followed Marx
in a direction that seemed to lead not to the proletariat and the
inevitability of capitalism but rather to the commune and a rapid transition to socialism. Only after Axelrod and Plekhanov
pointed out to her the unorthodox character of Marx's pronouncements on the commune did she revert in the 1890's to a
point of view more in harmony with Marx's theory of history.[55]
Living in Geneva in close proximity to European socialists who
tended to have an urban bias against the peasants may have been
another influence on Zasulich's break with populism.

Once completed, however, her conversion, at least in her own
mind, was nearly total. In an interview in London in 1895, Zasulich described the intellectual debt she owed to Marx: "At one
time I had a period of despair and hopelessness. But when I

went abroad and began to study the writings of Marx, that period ended. . . . I am indebted to Marx for clearing up difficulties and for clearing away false ideas. Thanks to [Marx and Engels], we now stand, theoretically, upon the ground of the Social Democracy of today, that is, of scientific socialism."[56] Later, as it became evident that capitalism in Western Europe was growing stronger not weaker, Zasulich would incorporate into her Marxism certain criticisms leveled against it by Eduard Bernstein and other Revisionists. Even as she did so, however, she retained in her political armory the Marxist assumptions she had accepted in approximately 1890, and however much she would confuse and manipulate Marxist categories, at once so rigid and so elastic, in an effort to resolve the special problems of Russian socialism, her belief in these assumptions was strong enough for her to consider the October Revolution in 1917 their ultimate perversion.

Paradoxically, as Zasulich's ideological views became more confused in the early 1880's, her commitment to revolutionary unity became stronger; one might speculate that these trends in her political development were related in the sense that her ideological confusion made it easier for her to believe that the views of others were really not so firm and unchangeable as to justify the conflicts that often followed their expression. Accordingly, in the years of her ideological transformation Zasulich participated energetically in enterprises that she thought would secure the revolutionary unity she desired. First and foremost, she tried to reconstitute Zemlia i Volia after she realized in the summer of 1881 that the assassination of the Tsar would not yield any quick solution to her problems.

Attempts to recreate this organization had begun almost immediately after the original split in September 1879. Upon his return from Odessa to St. Petersburg, Stefanovich put out feelers to Narodnaia Volia expressing interest in a tentative reconciliation; at about the same time, Axelrod and Tikhomirov, representing Chernyi Peredel and Narodnaia Volia, respectively, engaged in preliminary, and ultimately fruitless, negotiations.[57] But because each party believed that the other would shortly collapse or agree to reunion under circumstances where one party would accept the dictates of the other, reunification on the basis of parity was not really possible. The Narodovol'tsy were certain that assassination of the Tsar would precipitate the political changes necessary for an economic transformation; the Chernoperedel'tsy insisted that nothing good would come from assassinating the Tsar, and reiterated their long-standing commitment to agitation among the masses.

However, after the disintegration inside Russia of Chernyi Peredel, and, a year later, the arrest of the Narodovol'tsy involved in the assassination of Alexander, both groups—or what remained of them—had some incentive to attempt a reconciliation; in this instance, failure was an incentive rather than an impediment to revolutionary unity, quite possibly because the police crackdown that followed it was so severe as to make recriminations about what had gone wrong an impermissible luxury. One result was that in the summer of 1881 discussions in Geneva between the two parties led to the creation of a journal called *Vestnik Narodnoi Voli* (Messenger of Narodnaia Volia), to be edited by Plekhanov, Kravchinskii, and Lavrov—Plekhanov because he espoused the views of Chernyi Peredel, Kravchinskii because he favored terrorism but not the centralism of Narodnaia Volia, Lavrov because he rejected terrorism but supported Narodnaia Volia as a force for unity in the revolutionary movement.[58] In addition, the two parties agreed to collaborate on a variety of other matters, including the printing and dissemination of propaganda. Most important, they decided also to establish a Foreign Section of the Krasnyi Krest (Red Cross) of Narodnaia Volia, whose purpose would be to publicize in Western Europe and America the plight of political prisoners inside Russia and to smuggle to Siberia whatever money could be collected in the process.[59]

To preside over this new section the Executive Committee of Narodnaia Volia selected Zasulich and Lavrov. Considering the amount of distrust among warring factions in the revolutionary movement, the choice was a felicitous one. Both were figures of considerable prestige and prominence, and neither was identified closely with a rigid ideology that might color every decision. Virtually everyone on the left in Russia valued the two revolutionaries for their years of service—Lavrov for his work on the journal *Vpered* (Forward), Zasulich, most of all, for shooting Trepov.* Moreover, with Lavrov in Paris and Zasulich in Geneva, the two were well placed to encourage contributions from their political counterparts in Germany and France, the nations with the greatest concentrations of socialists and anarchists, respectively; because the German Social Democrats had largely relocated in Switzerland after Bismarck had effectively outlawed them in 1878, they might be especially receptive to calls for help from Zasulich in Geneva, and the letter she sent to them in February 1882 was written in her capacity as "President" of the Foreign Section of Krasnyi Krest.

Accordingly, on December 27, 1881, a declaration signed by Zasulich and Lavrov appeared in European newspapers appealing to people everywhere to assist the cause of freedom in Russia.[60] This declaration and others that followed it seem to have failed in their purpose, for there exists a letter dated March 1882 from Zasulich to the Executive Committee in which she complains that the European public responded more with curiosity than with sympathy, and that what little money she was able to collect came largely from Russian émigrés, not from European revolutionaries. Despite valiant efforts by Chaikovskii in Great Britain, Zasulich thought an attempted assassination of Queen Victoria precluded whatever chance Chaikovskii and the other representatives of the Foreign Section ever had of soliciting large donations there. She concluded the letter by noting that she had sent a personal note to Garibaldi requesting his assistance in Italy, and was hopeful that his response would be favorable.[61]

The image of Krasnyi Krest one derives from Zasulich's letters and the official statutes elucidating its functions is of an organization autonomous in its daily operations but required to communicate conspiratorially with Narodnaia Volia in transferring

---

* So great was Zasulich's prestige after her acquittal that in 1880 there was talk in émigré circles in Western Europe that she and Marx should co-edit a journal to be published in England and called *The Nihilist*. Its purpose presumably would be to inform revolutionaries in Western Europe of developments in Russia. In their eagerness to solicit Zasulich's services, those promoting the venture forgot that she neither read nor spoke English. Marx initially viewed the project favorably and promised support, but the journal was never published. Franco Venturi, *Roots of Revolution* (New York, 1966), p. 830; S. S. Volk, *Narodnaia Volia: 1879–1882* (Moscow, 1966), pp. 440–41.

funds from the Foreign Section to the sections established simultaneously in Russia. These domestic sections, in turn, were to
channel money collected abroad to revolutionaries imprisoned
or in exile in Siberia, but the lack of any real control over these
sections suggests that their leaders could disburse this money in
whatever way they desired.[62] Indeed, without documentation
about the disbursement of funds, it is impossible to determine
how much of what was collected in Paris and Geneva actually
reached its intended recipients. Despite the best efforts of Zasulich and Lavrov, the Foreign Section never quite fulfilled its
expectations, and in February 1884 the moribund quality of
Narodnaia Volia and the inability to raise sufficient funds to
cover operating expenses forced the Executive Committee to
abolish it entirely. The committee asked Zasulich to become instead a direct agent of Narodnaia Volia, but by this time she was
involved in other matters, and refused the committee's invitation.[63]

It is not difficult to understand why Zasulich expended so
much time and energy on Krasnyi Krest—thereby precipitating
the complaint from Kravchinskii that her work in the Foreign
Section kept her from other, equally pressing obligations.[64] The
opportunity to participate in an enterprise designed to alleviate
the plight of political prisoners in Russia would hardly be lost
upon an individual whose concern for them had prompted her
to try to assassinate the Governor of St. Petersburg. For a decade, her political activity had been greatly inspired by a strong
sense of altruism. Besides that, working in the Foreign Section
for a cause she believed in was to some extent—especially because of the assassination of the Tsar—a distraction from perplexing political and economic questions; on the matter of political prisoners, at least, she had no doubts about the moral
imperative, and the task at hand was sufficiently simple to allow
her to immerse herself in her work without the agonizing indecision that plagued her when she dealt with questions of political
theory and ideology. Finally, the invitation to head the Foreign
Section with Lavrov gave Zasulich a vehicle by which she could
help heal the wounds of fratricidal conflict and bring about a
reunion of Narodnaia Volia and Chernyi Peredel. Because its
purpose seemingly transcended the issues dividing the two par-

ties, Krasnyi Krest might have been the very institution under whose aegis unity and reconciliation would be achieved. In 1881 Zasulich accepted the invitation of the Executive Committee convinced that in doing so she was taking the first step toward accomplishing her most urgent political objective.

Her insistence on the nonpartisan character of Krasnyi Krest clearly reflects this objective. In her letters to the Executive Committee concerning the dissemination of information about political prisoners, Zasulich warned that the brochures Krasnyi Krest would publish must retain "an exclusively narrative quality," and refrain entirely from espousing a point of view that might be interpreted to favor any particular faction of the revolutionary movement.[65] To print information partial to Narodnaia Volia, she maintained, would not only defy the guidelines under which the Foreign Section was originally established, but also imply that its point of view was identical to that of Narodnaia Volia, whose tactics and organization kept most European radicals from assisting the Russian revolutionary movement. Similarly, in her letters to Lavrov, Zasulich argued that the Foreign Section must not do anything that might be perceived as confirmation that it acted in the interests of Narodnaia Volia. In October 1883, for example, she disassociated herself from Lavrov's suggestion that money collected by the Foreign Section be used to defray expenses of Narodnaia Volia or to subsidize the publication of its *Vestnik*; to do so, she claimed, would be to betray the objectives of Krasnyi Krest. Instead, as she told Lavrov, whatever funds were collected should be sent to political prisoners in Siberia and in prison in accordance with the statutes promulgated in 1881. Because "the Red Cross always sought to link in a common effort people of every shade of opinion," it should be as nonpartisan as possible in its activities.[66]

It is noteworthy that Zasulich chose not to protest the unconscionable manner in which the Narodovol'tsy pressured her to divert funds from the Foreign Section for its own parochial purposes. Evidently, by maintaining a position of strict neutrality, Zasulich managed to infuriate many Narodovol'tsy who felt that she should openly express her preference for their views, regardless of whether she agreed with them; indeed, their irritation became known to her when she refused to publish pamphlets bearing the inscription of the Executive Committee on the grounds that to do so would constitute implicit approval of their content.[67] Zasulich's answer to these criticisms was silence, but they obviously distressed her. Instead of replying to them publicly or making any substantive rebuttal, she proposed in a private letter to Lavrov that they quietly resign from the Foreign Section and establish a comparable organization of their own.[68] As leaders of the Foreign Section, they had the authority to say that none of the money collected abroad should be sent to Narodnaia Volia, even acting only as an intermediary, but Zasulich, at least, refused to take this step because she felt that the animosities it would engender would aggravate the ill will that existed already. As she explained to Lavrov, by nature she was "so 'peace loving' a person that the possibility of conflict removes from me all desire to involve myself [in such punitive measures.] For this reason I find it very desirable that I state simply that I am no longer an agent of the Red Cross."[69] In other words, the prospect of conflict was so abhorrent to Zasulich that she preferred to submit her resignation quietly rather than to publicize what she plainly considered to have been a breach of faith by Narodnaia Volia.

Although Lavrov subsequently convinced Zasulich to stay on in the Foreign Section, and the question of withholding money was rendered moot by the abolition of the Foreign Section a few months later, Zasulich's behavior in this matter is one more indication of her profound distaste for political squabbling: she would give up opportunities to advance her objectives rather than embroil herself in conflicts of a personal as well as political nature. In some sense, Zasulich's efforts to establish "revolutionary unity" were merely the political expression of this side of her personal psychology. Not only in political affairs, but also in her dealings with landlords, publishers, editors, and creditors, Zasulich always took the course that lessened the possibility of animosity, even when this meant, as it sometimes did, sacrificing her principles. Not without considerable courage, as her shooting of Trepov clearly shows, Zasulich was also so disturbed by the tensions of conflict that she tried to eliminate it from every aspect of her life. One might even speculate that this abhorrence of conflict was in some way a consequence of the unhappiness

and mortification Zasulich suffered as a child when she had to
live as a poor relation and endure the petty animosities and
jealousies within her mother's family.

It is not surprising, therefore, that, in addition to the work she
did for Krasnyi Krest, Zasulich should have supported other
efforts to revive Zemlia i Volia. Indeed, she was so intent upon
achieving a reunion that Plekhanov complained to Lavrov in
1881 that she and Deich were prepared to bargain away virtually
everything the Chernoperedel'tsy stood for.[70] Although no evidence exists to indicate that Zasulich actually participated in
negotiations between the two parties, it is known that in 1882 she
and Deich convinced Plekhanov to help compose a letter to the
few Narodovol'tsy still at large that they hoped would establish the terms of a full reconciliation.[71] Probably owing to
Plekhanov's hand in its composition, the letter included the as-
sertions that "the political education of the working masses is
essential to the successful seizure of power," and that "no serious
political movement is possible without the participation of the
urban workers"—both themes which Plekhanov had emphasized in his arguments against political terrorism.[72] But the letter
did not express any opposition to the centralism of Narodnaia
Volia, and it termed the destruction of Russian absolutism the
most immediate objective of the revolutionary movement. Prior
to this letter, the Chernoperedel'tsy—and Plekhanov in particular—had maintained that absolutism could not and should not
be overthrown until the masses acquired the political consciousness to accomplish this themselves. Now, by suggesting the im-
minence of the overthrow, they seemed to be revising upward
their estimate of the readiness of the masses for revolution. In
an effort to appease Narodnaia Volia, the letter concluded with
the affirmation that the differences between the two parties
were really fewer and less important than virtually everyone
imagined, and should not be an insurmountable obstacle to reunification.

A Soviet historian, S. S. Volk, has argued that this letter was
conciliatory, even obsequious, in tone because the Chernoperedel'tsy hoped that reunification would enable them to convert
the Narodovol'tsy to Marxism.[73] This argument seems plausible
when applied to Plekhanov, who always opposed reconciliation

except under favorable conditions, but it seems less applicable to Deich, and even less so to Zasulich, whose conversion to Marxism was slower than Plekhanov's and who had expressed interest in reunification well before she revealed a commitment to Marxism. It is probable that, unlike Plekhanov, Zasulich was sincere in what she attested to in this letter, and signed it in the belief that it implied no motive other than the stated one of reconciliation. Unlike Plekhanov, Zasulich was incapable of the Machiavellianism that Volk claims to find in their letter. If Zasulich erred in signing this letter, her error was not that of wishing secretly to convert the Narodovol'tsy to her beliefs, but of betraying her own convictions—and perhaps her integrity as well—to secure a one-sided and wholly spurious reunification.

Her willingness to minimize disagreements even when they involved matters of principle in this instance produced a critical response. Sergei Kravchinskii, whose affection for Zasulich could not be doubted, wrote a long letter to her in April 1882 pointing out the flaws in her "conciliationist" position. Disturbed by what he termed its "mellifluous and indecisive tone," Kravchinskii claimed that those who signed the letter to Narodnaia Volia lacked the intellectual honesty to acknowledge differences of opinion when these differences concerned issues of considerable significance within the revolutionary movement.[74] Why, he asked rhetorically, "do you claim to agree with [the Narodovol'tsy] on almost every issue when your views make clear that you actually disagree with them on practically all these same issues? Why reverse roles and express the hope that agreement will follow because you agree with them when the correctness of your position would indicate that they should agree with you?"[75] As an anarchist, Kravchinskii found especially infuriating the failure of the Chernoperedel'tsy to state their opposition to the centralism of Narodnaia Volia. In Kravchinskii's view, Zasulich's pronouncements were taken so seriously inside Russia that she had a moral obligation to her supporters there to point out the dangers of a centralized party: "As you know, on this question, your words have an enormous, perhaps even a decisive impact as a sign for the enemies of a centralized party. . . . It seems to me that you do not even here have the right (moral, of course) to hurt, by your own intervention, people who on Russian soil are struggling against the misuse of centralization."[76] More in sorrow than in anger Kravchinskii noted—with characteristic exaggeration—that, by acceding to the views of Narodnaia Volia, Zasulich was effectively discrediting the very principles that had made her views, rather than those of Narodnaia Volia, the inspiration of revolutionaries inside Russia.

Perhaps out of fear of losing Kravchinskii's friendship and respect, Zasulich subsequently wrote to him that she shared his dislike of what she called the "guiltily apologetic" tone of the original letter to Narodnaia Volia.[77] But neither Kravchinskii's objections nor her subsequent acknowledgment of their validity caused her to doubt the political wisdom of using this letter as a means of reducing tensions between the two organizations.

In the short run, Zasulich was right. As a result of the letter, a verbal agreement was reached on the merger of the two organizations. But just when it seemed that the merger was about to become a reality, Tikhomirov, by now the most prominent Narodovolets, declared that, in any new party that might emerge, the Chernoperedel'tsy would have to apply for membership on an individual basis and be judged by a panel consisting of former members of Narodnaia Volia. Outraged by what they considered the impudence of revolutionaries younger and less experienced than they, Zasulich and the other Chernoperedel'tsy, their patience exhausted at last, angrily responded to Tikhomirov's ultimatum by declaring their unwillingness to join any group whose conditions for membership were so patently insulting.[78] Tikhomirov, acting as the representative of Narodnaia Volia, realized that he and his colleagues had unnecessarily antagonized the Chernoperedel'tsy, and admonished his fellow Narodovol'tsy to be more understanding of the sensibilities of Plekhanov and his friends. But before his words could have their intended effect, Plekhanov produced a lengthy critique of revolutionary populism entitled "Socialism and Political Struggle," which he deliberately submitted for publication in the *Vestnik* fully cognizant that its editors would be obliged to reject it. Plekhanov had been dubious all along about the wisdom of the conciliation favored by Zasulich and Deich, and the Marxist apostasy he expressed in this article, though undoubtedly sincere, wa⁣s probably intended to destroy whatever possibility still existed for a reunion of the two groups. Moreover, by expressing his views in an ideological tract, rather than as part of a political polemic, Plekhanov possibly hoped to scuttle negotiations without having to bear public responsibility for their collapse.[79]

If this was Plekhanov's objective, his article succeeded admirably. By the summer of 1883 relations between the two groups had deteriorated so greatly that the Narodovol'tsy took to intercepting letters sent to Axelrod by Stefanovich, a recent convert to Narodnaia Volia but suspect to the Narodovol'tsy for the friendly relations he maintained with Axelrod and Deich. Pleased by such transgressions because they gave him further ammunition with which to convince Zasulich and Deich of the futility of reconciliation, Plekhanov stated that this violation of privacy caused him to lose "all respect" for members of Narodnaia Volia, and Zasulich and Deich, finally in agreement with Plekhanov, accused the Narodovol'tsy of "Nechaevist tactics."[80] Accordingly, on September 12, 1883, Plekhanov, Deich, Axelrod, Zasulich, and V. I. Ignatov announced in Geneva the formation of the Gruppa Osvobozhdenie Truda (The Group for the Emancipation of Labor), an organization entirely independent of Narodnaia Volia whose stated goals included the dissemination of Marxist ideas through its publishing arm, the so-called "Library of Contemporary Socialism."[81]

Personal differences between Chernyi Peredel and Narodnaia Volia, rather than any sudden realization of the irreconcilability of populism and Marxism, were responsible for the creation of The Emancipation of Labor Group. Although Plekhanov and Axelrod had been retreating from populist orthodoxy for some time, the decision in September 1883 to form a purely Marxist organization seems to have been a fairly spontaneous, almost reflexive response to what the two men considered the arrogance and duplicity of Narodnaia Volia. Indeed, their invitation to Lavrov (who remained a populist) to collaborate with them on the organization's publications corroborates the view that neither Plekhanov nor Axelrod was terribly concerned at first about the ideological implications of their actions.[82] Far from being the result of protracted and dispassionate deliberation, their public espousal of Marxist principles in 1883 was largely a means by which a decision based on emotion and considerations of power could be given intellectual and ideological legitimacy. Only later, after tempers had cooled, would Plekhanov and Axelrod realize that their break with populism also reflected a genuine transformation of their views.

Significantly, as relations between the two populist organizations deteriorated, Zasulich sought other ways to prevent a final rupture. Notable among these was her effort to discredit the enigmatic Ukrainian nationalist, Mikhail Dragomanov, who stated publicly in 1882 in his journal, *Vol'noe slovo* (Free Word), that the general decline in revolutionary consciousness after the assassination of Alexander II was traceable to the influence of traitors and police agents inside Narodnaia Volia. Dragomanov also claimed that a "courtier mentality" pervasive in revolutionary circles caused many revolutionaries (and thus, by implication, the Chernoperedel'tsy) to act obsequiously in their dealings with Narodnaia Volia.[83] Although containing an element of truth, Dragomanov's first assertion was an oversimplification unsubstantiated except in one instance by references to specific individuals and events.* But his second assertion was close enough to the truth to force the Chernoperedel'tsy, in self-defense, to publish an "Open Letter" to Dragomanov demanding that he either document or retract his allegations.[84] Signed by Axelrod, Deich, Zasulich, Plekhanov, and a fifth member of the group, Bokhanovskii, this letter prompted a correspondence between Zasulich and Dragomanov focusing on the question of traitors in Narodnaia Volia that continued through the fall of 1882. Hopeful at first that a third party could somehow ascertain the validity of Dragomanov's allegations, Zasulich became increasingly annoyed with his unwillingness to discuss the mat-

---

* The single instance of treason Dragomanov referred to involved Grigorii Goldenberg, a gullible and unintelligent individual who committed suicide when he finally realized the consequences of betraying his colleagues to the police. Ironically, Dragomanov's journal itself was infiltrated by foreign agents of the Sviashchina Druzhina (Holy Hosts), a counterrevolutionary organization formed after the assassination of Alexander II to penetrate and destroy all groups opposed to the government, no matter how mild or constructive their criticisms. Avrahm Yarmolinsky, *Road to Revolution* (New York, 1962), pp. 264–68, 302–3.

ter in a reasonable fashion, and finally broke off the correspondence entirely when Dragomanov demanded that this "third party" include in its deliberations what he claimed were the slurs she had leveled against his personal integrity.[85]

For anyone except Zasulich's biographer, perhaps, the entire matter is too petty and insignificant to warrant further exploration. Nevertheless, the episode reveals very clearly Zasulich's desire to protect her fellow revolutionaries—even those whom she disagreed with—from the unsubstantiated charges of someone beyond the pale of revolutionary politics. At the very time when Plekhanov and the Narodovol'tsy were doing their best to break up the revolutionary ties, Zasulich was desperately attempting to preserve them. To attack the Narodovol'tsy as Dragomanov had done was in Zasulich's mind tantamount to attacking the revolutionary movement as a whole, and she felt an obligation to close ranks behind Narodnaia Volia despite her opinion of its tactics. There is, to be sure, nothing unusual in revolutionaries of different stripes defending one another against those who seek, through inflammatory rhetoric, to impugn their integrity. What makes Zasulich's defense unusual is that it came when those whom she defended were treating her badly, and when those whom she respected, namely Plekhanov and Axelrod, were increasingly skeptical of the revolutionary unity that she still considered her paramount objective. But the formation of the Emancipation of Labor marked the end of her efforts; and one suspects that she joined the organization saddened rather than gladdened by its creation, all too aware that its very existence was tangible proof of a political defeat.

For this reason, perhaps, Zasulich never stated explicitly why she joined the Emancipation of Labor. It is noteworthy, however, that, in contrast to Plekhanov, she did not permit her allegiance to Marxism or her participation in the Emancipation of Labor to preclude the continuation of cordial, even intimate friendships with revolutionaries who rejected her ideology, such as Stefanovich, Lavrov, Klements, and Debagorii-Mokrievich. As a consequence, in the 1880's and 1890's revolutionaries of different viewpoints considered Zasulich sufficiently detached from the controversies and feuding that divided them to ask her to perform ceremonial functions for the revolutionary move-

ment as a whole, such as writing obituaries of Engels, Kravchinskii, and Mikhailovskii, all of whom she had considered her
friends.

It would be wrong to underestimate the significance of Zasulich's decision to join the Emancipation of Labor. Her participation in its activities, however slight it may have been in the beginning, clearly reflected a growing awareness that she was no
longer a populist, and if her Marxism in the 1880's was hardly of
an orthodox variety, she seemed unconcerned about the difference. On the other hand, her commitment to the Group did not
mean that she would allow her ideology to define the limits of
her personal relationships or to extinguish the vision of revolutionary unity which informed so much of her thinking and motivated so many of her actions. A revolutionary first and a Marxist
second, Zasulich joined the Group mostly because the failure of
political terrorism and her failure to achieve revolutionary unity
left her with no other alternative.

A few months after the creation of the Emancipation of Labor
Group Zasulich suffered what was perhaps the greatest sorrow
of her life. In February 1884 Lev Deich was arrested in Germany for illegally transmitting seditious literature from Switzerland to Russia. He was subsequently turned over to the Okhrana
and eventually exiled to Western Siberia, where he remained
until the spring of 1901. Unlike the other members of the
Group, Deich was a good organizer, and Axelrod's description
of his duties reveals how much his arrest crippled the propaganda apparatus of the group:

On Deich's shoulders rested all the material and administrative tasks
associated with the Group. With inexhaustible energy, he established
ties that might, by any chance whatever, be useful to us; he sought out
financial sources, managed the press, carried on correspondence with
different cities containing revolutionary-minded youth, and arranged
distribution of our publications. In sum, he carried out all the administrative and organizational work of the Group.[86]

Although others would be recruited to replace him, none performed his duties as effectively. The Group never quite recovered from Deich's arrest, and the intellectual brilliance of its
publications was exceeded only by the ineffectuality with which
they were smuggled into Russia and distributed there.

For Zasulich, Deich's arrest was most of all a personal loss. Their common-law marriage, initiated when they worked together in Iuzhnye Buntari, seemed to grow stronger in the years that followed their reunion in Switzerland in 1878. In letters written in 1879 Zasulich refers to Deich as "my dear" and "my beloved"; in letters written after his extradition she speaks of the loneliness resulting from the absence of "the closest person" in whom she could confide her innermost feelings.[87] An acquaintance who was with her in Geneva when she learned of Deich's arrest has left this description of her reaction to the news: "For a long time her infectious laughter and inherent good-natured humor disappeared. As is generally known, even earlier she had periods of severe depression—times when she locked everything up inside herself, avoided everyone, obviously yielding to the gloomiest thoughts. But after his arrest such a mood possessed her for a long time, so that the people close to her began to fear that she would commit suicide."[88] With Deich's arrest, the only sexual relationship Zasulich had ever established seemed to her to have ended forever, and although Plekhanov and his wife did what they could to cheer her, they could not fill the void Deich's arrest had obviously created in her life. Because he deemed their content in many places too intimate for anyone except the two of them to know, Deich destroyed many of the letters Zasulich wrote to him during his years in Siberia, and there exists no other source which might describe Zasulich's reaction when Deich informed her in 1895 that he had recently married a fellow political prisoner.

Deich's arrest also had an effect on Zasulich's politics. Because Plekhanov could be so overpowering in his intellectual abilities, only Deich's support, it seems, could impel Zasulich to disregard Plekhanov's opinions when she considered them erroneous; moreover, with Axelrod in Zurich and the other members of the Group too young and inexperienced to do battle with Plekhanov, only Deich and Zasulich were in a position to restrain him when his polemics crossed the thin line separating substantive attacks from ad hominem ones. Deich's arrest left a political vacuum in the Group which, for obvious reasons, Zasulich could not fill alone. Lacking Deich's organizational skill, unable to write as quickly or as incisively as Plekhanov, unsure of her own convictions as she still groped toward the Marxism she would espouse in the 1890's and afterward, Zasulich deferred to Plekhanov on many matters that she probably should have decided herself. Without Deich to give her moral and intellectual support, she acted toward Plekhanov in ways which often bordered on the obsequious, producing in return an affection which was not without a touch of condescension. That Rosaliia Plekhanova reveals this condescension inadvertently in an otherwise admirable description of the relationship between Zasulich and her husband suggests that neither Plekhanov nor his wife was really aware of it:

There grew in [Georgii Valentinovich] a feeling of love and respect for [Vera Ivanovna] which stayed with him all his life. He valued highly her comments on his works, always took into consideration her opinion on all questions of revolutionary tactics and theories, and also attributed great significance to her appraisal of people. . . . In her philosophical and literary education, and in her great independence of mind, V. I. constituted a rarity among the women in our revolutionary movement. Georgii Valentinovich evoked in Vera Ivanovna an interest in philosophy. In this sphere he was simultaneously her teacher and her colleague. As her teacher, G. V. often admired the capacity for abstract thought as well as the brilliance and originality of his pupil.[89]

Throughout the many years of their association, Plekhanov only rarely treated Zasulich with anything less than genuine affection, no matter how cantankerous and demanding he could be with others. But his intellect and personality were so intimidating to a person of Zasulich's disposition that, after 1884, she allowed him to dominate her to a degree that would have been inconceivable if Deich had remained at her side. Her failure in the 1880's to publish anything of lasting value partly reflects this domination.

   Thus, the years of Zasulich's life most critical in the evolution of her thinking were marked as well by personal tragedy; because the loss she suffered deprived her of a source of intellectual support, it also had implications far beyond her personal affairs. Living alone, deprived of the man who in everything but name had been her husband, dominated intellectually by someone whose influence was probably more destructive than constructive, depressed by the difficulty of political endeavor of any kind in a decade that she would later characterize correctly as one of "indifference, sobriety, and *Tolstovshchina*,"[90] Zasulich passed the years of early adulthood, usually the most productive in a person's lifetime, so depressed and lonely that many feared she might carry her self-destructive impulses to their ultimate conclusion. Thwarted both politically and in her personal relationships, Zasulich had to look to some other avenue of her experience if she was to give some genuine meaning to her life.

Perhaps the source of this new gratification was the peculiar brand of Marxism that Zasulich espoused. Because Marx and Engels, despite convincing empirical evidence to the contrary, believed that the destruction of autocracy was fairly imminent and could be followed by a rapid transition to socialism, their ideology—in the form in which Zasulich received it—offered the prospect of success when nothing else in her life seemed capable of providing her with a convincing raison d'être. Terrorism, of course, was abhorrent to her. Populism, even when it did not degenerate into terrorism, had sustained too many defeats in forging links with the peasants for it to remain intellectually and politically acceptable. And repudiating revolution entirely, whether in favor of liberalism or some form of nonpolitical philanthropy, was psychologically and politically impossible given her status as a political exile. As an ideology relatively new to Russia, Marxism had none of the stigma attached to ideologies and tactics whose effectiveness recent events had seriously called into question. Because the future it evoked seemed so cheerful in contrast to the bleak realities of her everyday existence, Marxism—or at least the unorthodox interpretation Marx had given it in the last years of his life—possibly provided a panacea for everything that had gone wrong for her since her acquittal.

Historians who discuss the attraction of Marxism in Russia often refer to the attributes of underdeveloped countries just beginning to industrialize. Marxism, especially in its Leninist variant, is appealing in underdeveloped and non-Western societies as a Western ideology which repudiates the West, as an ideology which rejects capitalism as destructive of human dignity and freedom while implying that other methods of industrialization will yield the same material results. Occasionally, historians also emphasize a combination in Marxism of scientism and religiosity, expressed in the belief that Marxist laws of change are immutable as well as normatively benevolent. In this way, Marxism is attractive because one can readily infer from it the comforting, if quite illogical and even dangerous conclusion that the inevitability of Marxism is assured by its moral virtue while its moral virtue is somehow inherent in its inevitability.[91]

All these considerations, one can say with some confidence, impelled Zasulich toward Marxism. Her interview in 1895 in which she credits Marx with "clarifying difficulties" and "clearing away false ideas" indicates that Marxism, at the very least, was useful as an explanatory tool. But what is irrelevant in Zasulich's case about such discussions of the popularity of Marxism is that Marxism is most often defined as an ideology and as a pseudo-theology, explaining, predicting, absolving, condemning, and justifying human behavior. For Zasulich, Marxism was surely both these things, but it was much else besides. Most of all, Marxism was for Zasulich a usable and convenient vocabulary of politics in which she could express, defend, and justify the ethical imperative of social altruism. Moved more by feelings than by reason, impelled to revolution more by noblesse oblige than by rational calculations of public needs and private desires, Zasulich found in Marxism, just as she had found in populism and utilitarianism, the intellectual "superstructure" (to borrow Marxist terminology) in which her visceral impulses could be given political expression and intellectual legitimacy. To convert from populism to Marxism meant for Zasulich that the object of her altruism would no longer be the peasantry but rather the proletariat, to which she would impute a moral virtue, or at least a capacity for moral virtue, that she would profess to see in no other class in society.

If asked, Zasulich probably could have explained with some lucidity the tenets of philosophical materialism, historical determinism, the laws of dialectics, and the various other components of Marxist doctrine. But far more important than these ideas in Zasulich's decision to become a Marxist and join the Emancipation of Labor was that Russian Marxists such as Plekhanov and Axelrod—quite apart from the friendship and camaraderie they could give her—professed an ideology which promised the redistribution of the material and intellectual resources of society that her ethos of social altruism seemed to demand. This promise in Marxism, even more than the abstract theory that declared the fulfillment of this promise to be inevitable, was what made Marxism attractive to Zasulich.

Finally, one must mention the therapeutic value of Marxism (and of ideology in general) for someone whose personal misfortunes were so closely linked with her political experiences that the two cannot really be separated in ascertaining motives for her ideological conversion. Liubov Axelrod, a longtime friend and admirer of Zasulich, wrote in her *Vospominaniia* that Zasulich's decision to become a Marxist required as much courage as it did to shoot Trepov.[92] To profess an ideology as yet empirically untested in Russia, professed by barely a handful of individuals, was not easy. For Zasulich, however, the very absence of empirical corroboration may have made Marxism a miraculous focus for restoring meaning to her life when the social altruism she had previously expressed in a populist vocabulary required some other, more reassuring vehicle of expression. Marxism— and everything associated with her conversion to it—promised friendship, camaraderie, intellectual legitimacy, and a vocabulary for the expression of her feelings. But most of all it held out hope for Zasulich in the form of a utopian vision eradicating, or at least significantly alleviating, the psychological consequences of personal misfortune and political failure. Described in such terms, Zasulich's commitment to Marxism seems, under the circumstances, to have been the only one she could conceivably have made.

FOUR

The Emancipation of Labor Group

THE FIRST YEARS of the Emancipation of Labor Group were not easy. The handful of individuals who composed it found themselves repudiated by the remnants of the populist movement at a time when the Russian proletariat was still in its infancy, too small and ineffectual to sustain any systematic campaign of political agitation against the state. Many of the pamphlets smuggled into Russia after Deich's arrest and extradition in 1884 never reached the workers, and those that did seemed unable to galvanize these workers into action. To make matters worse, Western socialists viewed the Group with some suspicion because it seemed preoccupied with theoretical work and insufficiently concerned with the practical objective of overthrowing autocracy; Engels, in particular, remained infatuated by the chimera of an imminent revolution, and endorsed Plekhanov's *Nashi raznoglasiia*—at the time of its publication in 1885 the most cohesive statement of Russian Marxism—with a good deal less enthusiasm than he did the terrorism of the few Narodovol'tsy still at large.* For several years it seemed an open question

---

* Engels, letter to Zasulich, April 23, 1885, in *Perepiska K. Marksa i F. Engel'sa s russkimi politicheskimi deiateliami* (Moscow, 1947), pp. 249–52. Characteristically, Zasulich criticized the opening pages of Plekhanov's work for their "sharpness," believing that they needlessly antagonized the Narodovol'tsy and other populists with whom she felt that the Group might, under certain circumstances, still want to collaborate. N. Kuliabko-Koretskii, "Emigranty i naivnyi mirotvorets," in Deich, ed., *Gruppa 'Osvobozhdenie Truda,'* vol. 2, pp. 174.

whether the Group would survive. Dependent upon wealthy sympathizers to finance their publications, forced by their police records to live a miserable existence hundreds of miles from their country, and woefully short on managerial ability, the members of the Group must have thought that their prospects for creating a Russian workers' party guided by socialist principles were not very good.

Yet the very conditions that made the prospects of the Group appear so hopeless also made possible its eventual success. As if in recognition of their own strengths and weaknesses, Plekhanov and his colleagues determined from the beginning that their objective, at least in the immediate future, would be educational rather than political. As the first Marxists in Russia, the members of the Group would develop a Marxist literature that revolutionaries of future generations could utilize when the opportunities for revolutionary action would be better than they were in 1883. Through the Group's Library of Contemporary Socialism, translations of Marx and Engels as well as the original works of Plekhanov, Axelrod, and Zasulich would be made available to workers and intellectuals and anyone else inside Russia who expressed interest in reading them. There, these works would lie dormant like a dangerous bacillus, slowly penetrating the consciousness of revolutionary intellectuals, so that when the moment of insurrection finally arrived, these people would enter the struggle armed with a knowledge of Marxist ideology and of ways of transmitting this ideology to the workers. Because its purpose was primarily educational, the Group could calculate its prospects in 1883 comforted by the conviction that the fruits of its endeavor would appear only after an interval of incubation and development.[1]

Thus, the problems that plagued the Group, though real enough, did not necessarily mean that the organization would not be successful in the future. Indeed, the inability of the revolutionary movement to mount a sustained challenge to autocracy in the decade following the assassination of Alexander II allowed the Group to pursue its objective of producing and disseminating Marxist literature. The Group, more realistic than Engels and the Narodovol'tsy in its appraisal of the political situation, decided upon the less glamorous but more profitable objective of propagating Marxist ideology not merely because Plekhanov and his colleagues were more comfortable as propagandists than as political agitators, but also because the absence of a genuine proletariat—much less a revolutionary one—meant that an educational approach was the only one that promised eventual success.

Thus, with the revolutionary movement in disarray, the Group could proceed with its task unchallenged by Marxist rivals either in Russia or abroad. As Richard Pipes has remarked, Social Democracy and the Russian labor movement evolved in the 1880's largely independently of one another, the ties between them usually too ephemeral for either animosity or camaraderie to develop.[2] Moreover, the relative unpopularity of Marxism among what remained of the populist movement ensured that the Group would encounter little intramural opposition to the Russian Marxism it expounded until rapid industrialization in the 1890's created a new generation of Marxists willing to contest the Group for the allegiance of the Russian proletariat. In a very real sense, the powerlessness of revolutionaries in the 1880's was, for the Group at least, a blessing in disguise. The decade during which they were either scorned or ignored gave Plekhanov, Axelrod, and Zasulich the isolation necessary for producing the Marxist literature that they hoped would constitute a legacy to future generations of Marxists, a source of inspiration and legitimacy as well as a fund of practical and theoretical wisdom.

All this, of course, lay far in the future. Through the efforts of its agents inside Russia, the Group managed in the 1880's to establish contact with a few scattered revolutionary circles, such as the Blagoev group in St. Petersburg, but the police arrested most of their members before any progress could be made in the dissemination of the Group's propaganda.[3] In fact, the isolation of the Group was so complete in the late 1880's that Plekhanov and the others did not learn of the strike in the Morozov textile works (a strike significant in both its size and its political overtones) until some time after it had been suppressed.[4] Although neither Plekhanov nor Axelrod found émigré life as stifling as it was for Zasulich, there must have been moments when they wondered whether they would ever have any impact upon the course of events in their homeland.

Quite apart from their political isolation and impotence, Plekhanov and his two colleagues lived under difficult circumstances. To supplement his meager income from translations, Axelrod produced and sold *kéfir*, a fermented milk (native to the Caucasus), but the time and effort he expended in this enterprise severely limited the time he could devote to matters of politics. Plekhanov did what he could to sell his written work to sympathetic publishers, but seems to have lived largely off whatever he could earn tutoring children of well-to-do Russian émigrés. Zasulich did copywork in addition to her translations, but, like the others, could afford nothing more than the bare necessities of life; visitors to her disordered, sometimes filthy residence not far from Plekhanov's often noted that she tramped about in worn-out boots with holes in them.[5] Finally, in the late 1880's, she accepted what she euphemistically referred to as "loans" from her friend, Sergei Kravchinskii, who sent her money well aware that she would probably never be able to pay it back to him.[6]

Zasulich's health had not been good for years. Always neglectful of her physical condition, she was weakened further in the early 1870's by the travail of imprisonment and exile. In 1889, while helping to care for Plekhanov after he was stricken with tuberculosis, Zasulich contracted the disease herself. She suffered for the rest of her life from episodes of coughing, weakness, and fever that were probably aggravated and prolonged by her stubborn refusal to take even the most elementary measures to alleviate them.[7] After Rosaliia Plekhanova received her medical diploma in 1895, she provided Zasulich with various drugs to ease the discomfort that tuberculosis produced and even persuaded Zasulich to take these drugs when the symptoms of the disease became unendurable. At times, too, Zasulich would submit to the pleas of Plekhanov and Engels that she seek medical assistance.* But the tuberculosis itself was never com-

---

* Samuel H. Baron, *Plekhanov: The Father of Russian Marxism* (Stanford, 1963), p. 134; Letter, Zasulich to Plekhanov, April 5, 1895, *Gruppa*, vol. 4, pp. 292–93. In the spring of 1898 Zasulich finally heeded the pleas of Plekhanov and Axelrod and spent several weeks in Florence, Italy, in an unsuccessful effort to improve her health. Zasulich apparently agreed to the trip (which was financed by a wealthy sympathizer of the Group) only after Plekhanov offered to travel with her and find lodgings for her, which he did before returning to Switzerland. *Gruppa*, vol. 4, pp. 198–204.

pletely eradicated, and probably was the long-term cause of Zasulich's death in 1919.

In Geneva, Zasulich led a self-imposed solitary existence, living alone in rooms on the outskirts of Geneva, far from the cafés where émigrés of various nationalities and political persuasions tended to congregate. This detachment allowed her to avoid most of the endless feuds and intrigues that such a politically incestuous atmosphere tended to produce.[8] Uncertain both of the fine points of her convictions and of her intellectual capabilities, she wrote in isolation, agonizing over nearly every word, and would emerge from the room where she worked only for infrequent conversations with the Plekhanovs or to greet revolutionaries who considered it obligatory to pay their respects to the would-be assassin of Trepov. In 1889, when the Swiss government forced Plekhanov to leave the country because Russian terrorists in Zurich had caused an explosion, Zasulich faithfully followed him to the French village of Mornex, just across the border, where she lived quietly for the next five years. In 1894, after anarchist demonstrations in Paris prompted the French government to expel foreign nationals suspected of revolutionary activity, Zasulich and Plekhanov moved to London. Plekhanov was subsequently permitted to return to his family in Geneva, but the resources of the British Museum so delighted Zasulich that she remained in England until the spring of 1897.[9]

Precisely because of her political and personal isolation, Zasulich took even more seriously than did Plekhanov and Axelrod the claim of the Group to belong to the larger movement of international socialism. Unlike Narodnaia Volia and other organizations of Russian populism whose ideology emphasized the uniqueness of Russian culture and institutions, the Group considered conditions in Russia similar enough to those in the West for Russian revolutionaries to seek a common agenda with their counterparts in England, France, Germany, Italy, and Scandinavia. In its Draft Programs of 1884 and 1887 the Group maintained that it acted not only in the interest of the Russian proletariat but as part of a movement which transcended the boundaries separating the workers of one country from those of others.[10] For Zasulich, however, these ties that she and her colleagues felt with revolutionaries and with the working class in other countries were of psychological as well as political benefit.

Perhaps for this reason, the first essay of any magnitude Zasulich produced was an "Outline History" of the First International.[11] Timing its publication to coincide with the convocation of the Second International in 1889, Zasulich emphasized in her account of the First the psychological comfort that individuals derive from collective endeavor. Strikes in Western Europe were successful after the creation of the International in 1864 largely because the International had lent to them its prestige, its resources, and, above all, its claim to represent the interests of workers everywhere. In this way, the International gave striking workers the confidence, assertiveness, and esprit de corps that result only when one enlists in collective entities such as trade unions, student circles, and political parties:

Although the Norman weaver and Belgian coal miner joined the International without reading its statutes, the mere act of joining forced him at once to understand and to experience staggering things: the individual worker who, from his very childhood, perhaps, had not received help from anyone else, was only vaguely conscious of his solidarity with millions of fellow workers throughout the world. He could not help feeling that with the workers of a faraway distant city, the very name of which he had previously never known, workers who in the most difficult moments of his strike had sent him a few pennies of their own, he had a greater kinship than he did with all those in his own country who exploited him. The International enabled the working class to feel . . . that collective power which is the result of a unified organization.[12]

The importance of the International, then, was that it fostered allegiances, traditions, and alliances which alleviated feelings of isolation and powerlessness. In contrast to classical liberalism, which considered the individual and his autonomy the object of all political endeavor, Zasulich maintained that one could find happiness and protection only in the camaraderie of collective action: unless he joined his fate to others in an organization whose bonds transcended the limits of his experience, man would be powerless to effect beneficial changes in his life. Seemingly oblivious of the danger to personal freedom it contained, Zasulich espoused this ethos of collective action so passionately and consistently quite possibly because it seemed the best alternative in an age when the individual remained essentially helpless in his struggle for survival. Both to the workers in Russia and to Zasulich alone in exile in Western Europe, the only possibility of self-improvement seemed to lie in association with mass movements of one sort or another.

Three years later, in a review of Sergei Kravchinskii's novel, *The Career of a Nihilist*, Zasulich returned to this theme.[13] After describing the novel and pointing out what she considered its inadequacies, she evoked Turgenev's Rudin as a fictitious character who possessed the complexity that she thought was lacking in Kravchinskii's characters. Rudin seemed to her especially appealing because he personified a commitment to improving the public welfare at a time when most men of his class were preoccupied with concerns of a purely egoistic nature: "His task—the task of that time—consisted solely of developing in people a striving for the general and the great, to make people realize for the first time that there could be in the world concerns and issues other than the personal, that everything great is perfected through people, not through tsars and generals."[14] But Rudin was too far ahead of his time: because the opportunities for practical action were virtually nonexistent, he never developed the humility and self-effacement essential in a successful revolutionary. Indeed, the best corrective for Rudin's egoism and vanity would have been for him to join a revolutionary organization which demanded of its members a genuine commitment to the general welfare:

in [a revolutionary] organization all the weak and seamy aspects of Rudin's character would recede and only the more splendid ones would remain. . . . Conscious of his own superiority in certain aspects of revolutionary action, he would be forced to recognize his inadequacies in many others. . . . The investment of all resources of an organization to the general good, and the intimate camaraderie which makes possible the kinds of sacrifices even the closest friends cannot make for one another, eliminates from this world even the faintest trace of a personal struggle for individual survival.[15]

For Zasulich, then, a socialist party was something more than an association of like-minded individuals engaged in the pursuit of common goals. A socialist party, as her analysis of Turgenev's Rudin reveals so clearly, had the power to effect a moral transformation in those willing to subordinate their personal concerns and petty vanities to the greater good of revolutionary action. Not only a means by which to achieve political objectives, a revolutionary party was also an instrument of spiritual purification, the vehicle by which those in power after a socialist revolution would acquire the humility, the self-effacement, and the concern for the general good which she thought were essential for a virtuous socialist utopia.

Few others in the revolutionary movement, it seems, viewed the party in quite the same fashion as Zasulich. To Plekhanov and Axelrod, the party was the political expression of the proletariat and a means by which the workers would gain a consciousness of their role within society.[16] To Lenin, it was an elite of hardened revolutionaries acting in what it thought were the best interests of the proletariat.[17] Yet one finds again and again in the articles Zasulich produced in the 1890's the idiosyncratic notion that a revolutionary party elevates the moral caliber of virtually everyone who participates in it, transforming intelligent but self-centered men like Rudin into men possessing such compassion for what she calls "the general and the great" that they become, in effect, living proof of the superiority of socialism. In Zasulich's conception of a socialist party one sees also her vision of a socialist society, the self-sacrifice and dedication of party members being a harbinger of what will exist on a larger scale when these virtues have pervaded the proletariat as a whole.

Indeed, the moral purification that results when one commits oneself to a collective enterprise like a revolutionary party was Zasulich's most vivid illustration that a socialist society was preferable to a capitalist one. No doubt, Marxists everywhere agreed that workers' parties of one kind or another were essential in the struggle against capitalism, but none believed more passionately than Zasulich in the capacity of these parties to effect a moral transformation among its members *before* significant progress had been made in improving the objective conditions of society. By the camaraderie, élan, and ethic of self-sacrifice it engendered, a revolutionary party "socialized" its membership the way the proletariat, by virtue of its solidarity, would socialize all means of production once political power had passed into its hands. For Zasulich a revolutionary party was actually a socialist society in microcosm, its virtues evident to everyone.

Thus, in the spiritual transformation it produced among its

members, the party was an integral aspect of any socialist movement. Indeed, one of the reasons Zasulich tried so assiduously to preserve the unity of Russian populism and Russian socialism was that she saw the parties and organizations they fostered as the temporary repository of revolutionary virtue. In her view, party squabbles called into question the entire revolutionary enterprise, and if the organizations she belonged to could not achieve this spiritual transformation, they could hardly help the lower classes to do the same.

It was an idée fixe in Zasulich's thought that socialist parties ennoble all those who participate in them; living in Switzerland hundreds of miles from her homeland, Zasulich wanted so much to attach herself to movements transcending the limits of her shabby existence that she made no distinction in this respect between socialist parties in Western Europe and the socialist party she and her colleagues hoped to create in Russia. For Zasulich the ennobling experience of the party was a universal virtue, applicable in backward countries such as Russia no less than in the more economically advanced countries of Western Europe. In fact, Russia in the 1880's still so obviously lacked the voluntary institutions which in other countries served to shield the individual against the state that one could argue from Zasulich's assumptions that the party in Russia might be the only institution through which an individual could acquire this commitment to the general welfare that she considered a prerequisite of social justice. Lacking trade unions, choral groups, hunting lodges, and sporting clubs—all of which one could find in Western Europe—Russian workers could be protected and ennobled simultaneously only in a revolutionary party.

But Zasulich, like her colleagues, had to acknowledge differences between Russia and Western Europe that not even her commitment to collective institutions such as the International could obscure. Neither Zasulich nor Plekhanov nor Axelrod (nor any other Russian Marxist living and writing before the Revolutions of 1917, for that matter) could ignore the fact that, by all barometers of economic growth, Russia had yet to experience a so-called bourgeois revolution ratifying the triumph of capitalism; to debate whether Russia in the 1880's was "feudal" or (as Engels argued) a variant of "Oriental despotism" could not disguise the unpleasant reality that Russia was just beginning the process of modernization and industrialization that Marx, in his more sober moments, had said would have to be complete before a socialist revolution could occur.[18] Simply stated, the problem for Russian Marxists was this: if (as the vast majority of Russian Marxists agreed) Russia had not yet experienced a bourgeois revolution, and if this revolution would in turn be followed by a socialist one (how soon was a matter of conjecture), what should be the attitude of the proletariat toward the bourgeoisie? How should the proletariat act toward this class which would emerge triumphant in the first revolution only to lose its supremacy as a result of the second?

The answer proposed by Plekhanov and Axelrod was ingenious but, in practical terms, unworkable: differing only on details, the two men agreed that the workers should support the bourgeoisie in its efforts to overthrow autocracy but at the same time indicate that their ultimate objective was the destruction of the bourgeoisie in a socialist (or proletarian) revolution.[19] Lenin only stated in more graphic terms what Axelrod and Plekhanov had written in the late 1880's when he told British communists many years later that, in this transitional period between the two revolutions, the proletariat would support the bourgeoisie the way a noose supports a hanged man.[20]

But such a scenario, to which the two men remained faithful, seemed to create more tactical dilemmas for Russian socialists than it solved. Most of all, the scenario failed to take into account the possibility that the bourgeoisie might perceive the fraudulent nature of the proletariat's assistance, or that such a double-edged policy would prove too subtle for a workers' party to carry out successfully; in essence the workers would be told to support and oppose the bourgeoisie simultaneously, supporting it in the fight against autocracy, but opposing it in preparation for their own ascent to power. In the end, these dilemmas, from which Lenin and Trotsky would fashion solutions of their own, would be rendered moot by the events of 1917, when the "bourgeois" and "socialist" revolutions occurred within barely seven months of one another, with the proletariat playing a greater role in the February (or "bourgeois") Revolution than it did in the October (or "socialist") one. Nevertheless, one might argue that the Mensheviks failed so abysmally in 1917 because the two-stage scenario of Plekhanov and Axelrod that most of the Mensheviks still adhered to suggested that a seizure of power before conditions were right would necessarily be doomed to disaster.

Zasulich, for her part, reiterated this two-stage scenario of revolution. Indeed, when she produced her version of it in her "Revoliutsionery iz burzhuaznoi sredy" ("Revolutionaries of Bourgeois Background"), published in *Sotsial-demokrat* in 1890, there was much about it that was consistent with Marxist principles: an emphasis on class struggle, a belief in the material origin of ideas, a notion of change as a dialectical process, and so on.[21] She also agreed with Plekhanov and Axelrod that a progressive peasant revolution was inconceivable in Russia or in any other country and that populism was therefore devoid of predictive or explanatory value. But Zasulich differed with her colleagues in shadings and nuances, and also when she asked herself who would assist the proletariat in the period before the bourgeois revolution and before the proletariat possessed the political consciousness to understand its interests. To attempt here to elucidate her answer would be a pointless exercise were it not for the fact that her efforts reveal how someone ill suited to theoretical analysis could so confuse and manipulate Marxist categories as to render them virtually meaningless.[22]

Like Plekhanov, Zasulich began with the assumption (in 1890 it could not yet be considered a conclusion) that capitalism was inevitable in Russia. Although she herself did not use the exact terminology, it is clear from her essay that the various components of the Marxist dialectic were already working in Russia to create an order based on private property that was dominated economically by "capitalists"—writing in 1890, she could not have known that these "capitalists," in most cases, would be French, Belgian, English, and German rather than Russian. Unlike Plekhanov, however, who thought that the necessity of laissez-faire would force these capitalists to break with autocracy, Zasulich argued that a common fear of the working class reinforced by memories of the revolutions of 1848 in Western Europe would drive autocracy and the capitalists together.[23] However much their interests might ultimately diverge, at present autocracy and capitalism were in a symbiotic relationship, with the capitalists looking to autocracy to protect them from the proletariat while the government needed capitalism to commence a process of industrialization without which Russia could not remain a Great Power equal in strength to those in Western Europe. The memory of capitalists in Western Europe threatened in 1848 by a working class whose demands for change exceeded their own was yet another reason for capitalists in Russia to prefer a conservative alliance with autocracy to a revolutionary alliance with the proletariat.[24]

Having said this, Zasulich found herself in a quandary. If, out of self-interest, these capitalists joined forces with autocracy, then who would be left to make the so-called bourgeois revolution, the necessity and inevitability of which Zasulich did not choose to question? And if these capitalists did not participate in this bourgeois revolution, then how could she characterize this revolution as "bourgeois" when her analysis thus far seemed to equate the bourgeoisie with this stratum of capitalists, thereby excluding from the bourgeoisie other groups that might conceivably be included in it? Given her assumptions and her definitions, Zasulich either had to deny the inevitability of the bourgeois revolution or had to deny that this revolution, when it occurred, would be bourgeois in character.

Rather than acknowledge this dilemma, Zasulich simply ignored it by redefining her terms. The bourgeois revolution, she said, need not be carried out in Russia by the group which in her view had carried out such revolutions in Western Europe. Substitutes could be found for this class of businessmen and entrepreneurs, and if these surrogates for the bourgeoisie were not themselves members of the bourgeoisie as Marx (or Zasulich) defined it, then she would simply stretch the definition of the bourgeoisie to include anyone whom she considered sufficiently hostile to autocracy to want to destroy it.

But where would such surrogates be found? One possibility was Russian *obshchestvo*, which translates literally as "society" but which really means the educated elite. After a cursory analysis, one might think that this obshchestvo might perform in Russia the same function carried out in the West by the bourgeoisie:

For a long time Russian society has been revolutionary in the sense in which it is said, for instance, that the Western bourgeoisie was revolutionary. It is revolutionary if one takes it in its entirety, including its revolutionary elements. The "revolutionariness" of a society is expressed most clearly in that part of its youth that became revolutionary. In that alone was expressed the former "revolutionariness" of the educated strata of the Western bourgeoisie.[25]

But several pages later, Zasulich looked more closely at these youths produced by society and concluded that the few of them who claimed revolutionary aspirations were still paralyzed by a commitment to populism, the futility of which she exposed in yet another essay she wrote in 1890 for *Sotsial-demokrat*.[26] What was worse, "society" really had no institutions through which it could pressure the government for concessions, no political apparatus which could serve as the focal point for any revolutionary transformation. The *zemstva* she quickly dismissed as politically powerless and economically moribund; in any event, they would be abolished without hesitation by the Tsar should their members ever attempt to transform them into a genuine parliament—as the French had done in 1789 in the Estates General. So even though "the good intentions of 'society' toward its revolutionary obligations remain an open question, it cannot be doubted that 'society' cannot fulfill these obligations."[27]

For these reasons, "society" could not serve in Zasulich's scenario as a substitute for the bourgeoisie as a whole. But what about the intelligentsia, that component of "society" with which it is often confused? Again, Zasulich was prepared to substitute a social stratum for an economic class, but on closer examination this second potential surrogate for the bourgeoisie appeared to her to be just as reluctant as the first to conduct a bourgeois revolution comparable to those in Western Europe in 1789, 1830, and 1848. Indeed, it was the memory of 1848 that precluded the intelligentsia from serving in the 1890's as a revolutionary force. Memories of Russian intellectuals were long enough, in Zasulich's view, for them to remember that the working class, in the fever-pitch of revolution, had posited demands so radical in 1848 that neither the intellectuals who previously supported them nor the far larger number of capitalists who would benefit from the overthrow of Western monarchies could still consider the working class their natural ally. As the intellectuals and the proletariat finally revealed to one another their ultimate objectives, only very few in either group could fail to recognize the ideological and political incompatibility of these objectives. These two groups, which for several months had joined together in overthrowing autocracies, were subsequently forced by political differences they could no longer ignore to become, as it were, the deadliest of enemies. In the turmoil that followed, the forces of reaction, previously defeated but not entirely destroyed, could capitalize on this disunity among those who had defeated them, and return to power.[28]

Correct or not, this was Zasulich's interpretation, in general terms, of the 1848 revolutions in Germany and France. Its importance, however, is not in its historical accuracy (or lack of it) but rather in Zasulich's conviction that this interpretation was shared in the 1890's by the majority of Russian intellectuals who looked to history as a guide to practical action in the future. And since we are dealing here with Zasulich's perceptions of history rather than with history itself, whatever lessons Russian intellectuals may have actually drawn from the revolutions of 1848 are irrelevant to Zasulich's belief that these revolutions caused them to shrink, in their own lives, from seeking an alliance with the lower classes in Russia. Instead, the Russian intelligentsia, fearful of repeating the mistake of bourgeois revolutionaries in the West, would direct its offspring toward liberal goals rather than revolutionary ones. But, according to Zasulich, liberals could not make the bourgeois revolution any more than could the capitalists, the intelligentsia, or "society," since Russian autocracy, bolstered by the support of these capitalists, could not be forced to grant a constitution and the remaining desiderata of liberalism except in the unlikely event of liberals penetrating the police.[29]

Thus, having eliminated for the role of the bourgeoisie such potential surrogates as "society," the intelligentsia, and the liberals (not to mention, of course, the stratum of capitalists who, by Zasulich's definitions, should have filled this role in the first place), Zasulich might well have suggested that the proletariat make the bourgeois revolution by itself. Better yet, she might have suggested that the proletariat simply "skip" the bourgeois revolution and attempt in a pre-industrial society to make a socialist one. Given what Marx had written in the last years of his life about the obshchina serving as the basis for a socialist revolution, the idea of skipping stages was not altogether new to her. Indeed, so close did Zasulich come to proposing this second alternative, which Lenin, with his greater self-confidence, would advocate openly in 1917, that several revolutionaries in the 1890's confused Zasulich's implications for her conclusions and argued that she had indeed propounded a "one-stage" rather than a "two-stage" scenario of revolution.[30]

But a careful reading of "Revolutionaries of Bourgeois Background," as well as of other writings, reveals that Zasulich's opinion of the working class was not so high, and her opinion of the intelligentsia was not so low, that she could countenance the proletariat acting alone. If one looked hard enough, one could, in 1890, find revolutionaries of bourgeois background sufficiently disillusioned by populism and sufficiently convinced of the correctness of scientific socialism to chart through waters muddied by Russia's political and economic immaturity a path to socialism which would include both bourgeois and proletarian revolutions, and a decent interval for maturation between them.

The answer, after pages of seemingly endless peregrinations, was very simple: the surrogate of the bourgeoisie in the bourgeois revolution was that segment of the intelligentsia that believed in scientific socialism, that is, the Emancipation of Labor Group. Aided by the working class, the Group—or more precisely the future generations of intellectuals in whom it would have inculcated Marxist ideology—would make the bourgeois revolution where neither the capitalists, nor "society," nor the liberals, nor the intelligentsia as a whole was able to do so.[31] If Lenin, in 1917, would use revolutionary intellectuals to make for the working class what he thought would be a socialist revolution, Zasulich, writing in 1890, envisioned these same intellectuals making for the middle classes what she thought would be a bourgeois revolution. And if Lenin, paraphrasing Clemenceau, considered the socialist revolution "too important to be left to the workers," Zasulich considered the bourgeois revolution "too important to be left to the capitalists"—or to anyone else except a small coterie of Marxist intellectuals. Virtually the only caveat one must make about Zasulich's conclusions is that in 1904, evidently dissatisfied with her previous substitutions, she redefined the bourgeoisie again, this time including, rather than excluding, "society," the liberals, and the intelligentsia, and dropping in the peasants, of all groups, for good measure. As if in recognition of her ideological heresy, Zasulich argued somewhat defensively that such substitutions and additions were permissible because the Russian language had no precise equivalent of the French *bourgeoisie* or the German *bürgerliche*.[32]

The result, of course, is ideological chaos: peasants within the bourgeoisie and the entrepreneural middle classes seemingly outside of it, with "society," the liberals, and the intelligentsia described and defined more in terms of the ideas Zasulich attributes to them than in terms of their relationship to the means of production. Further complicating matters is that Zasulich changes her definitions not merely from one essay to the next but even within the essays themselves; the most glaring example of this is the case of the capitalists who constitute the bourgeoisie in the beginning of the 1890 essay only to be excluded from the bourgeoisie at the end of it. But these substitutions and additions which make such a mess of Zasulich's Marxism also serve to clarify her tactical objectives. By finally including peasants, intellectuals, and liberals in her original constituency of workers guided by Marxist revolutionaries, Zasulich created, at least on paper, the united front against autocracy that was the principal goal of her political career. Only as a result of such an alliance did she believe that autocracy could be overthrown, and only as a result of such a collective enterprise did she think that the working class could acquire the commitment to the general welfare that she considered the principal virtue of socialist parties and societies. Because this united front was essential to the success of socialism, Zasulich, in effect, was willing to make nonsense of her ideology in her efforts to achieve it.

To be sure, Zasulich remained faithful to a central postulate of Marxism, namely that, in the end, "the emancipation of the workers must be a matter for the workers themselves"—a phrase which appears countless times in her writings.[33] About the necessity of bourgeois intellectuals serving in the beginning as the teachers of the nascent proletariat Zasulich was really never in doubt—even in 1848, she maintained, one could find revolutionaries of bourgeois background willing to fight alongside the proletariat even after the economic interests of these groups had begun to diverge. Notwithstanding this contradiction between their convictions and their economic interests,

when republicans in 1848 were revolutionaries, when, risking their freedom and their lives, they turned to the workers and lined up with them in the courts and on the barricades, they honestly thought of the workers as their comrades, and sincerely called them to a struggle that would benefit them both. At the same time, these bourgeois revolutionaries performed a service for the workers, stimulating in them an interest in things intellectual, forcing them to become aware of those ideas and those interests that the two classes held in common.[34]

According to Zasulich, both in Western Europe and in Russia one could find bourgeois intellectuals capable of acting against the interests of their class, and surely the members of the Group were among them. But no matter how diligently intellectuals such as herself exerted themselves on behalf of the workers, or how much workers initially depended on revolutionary intellectuals for political and ideological support, "it must be made clear to the Russian people that without the working masses a revolution is unthinkable; it is necessary that bourgeois revolutionaries be convinced once and for all that any revolutionary movement that does not direct its energies in the direction of acquiring mass support among the people is 'abnormal' and condemned to failure."[35]

In Zasulich's view, the roles of the intelligentsia and the proletariat would at some point undergo a radical transformation, with the two groups essentially reversing the existing relationship between them. Although, at the outset, the intelligentsia would lead and the proletariat would follow, by the time conditions were ripe for revolution, the proletariat would dominate the revolutionary movement. In spite of the fact that the proletariat initially lacked the consciousness of Marxist doctrine to lead a socialist or even a bourgeois revolution, the efforts of the intelligentsia would, with the passage of time, have given the proletariat sufficient knowledge of its role and obligations for the intelligentsia simply to fade into the background, no longer required to fulfill its pedagogical function. By a peculiar working of the Marxist dialectic, the intelligentsia would create the conditions that would render it irrelevant: having educated the workers it would withdraw, handing over to them the party apparatus it had nurtured for so long. Zasulich does not indicate precisely at what point this transfer of political power was to occur, but her critical comments on the October Revolution suggest that she died without having seen the moment arrive.[36]

Unlike Plekhanov and Lenin, Zasulich had no "Jacobin" strain in her thinking. She considered coups d'état to be a violation of Marxism; a centralized, elitist party was a regrettable, and only temporary, expedient made necessary by a repressive autocracy.[37] Where Plekhanov seemed to waver on this point at various times in his career, on one occasion (at the Second Congress of the RSDLP in 1903) espousing the virtues of elitism, only to revert a few months later to the notion of a revolution by the masses, Zasulich was consistent in her hostility to any scenario of revolution which did not proclaim a priori the ultimate preeminence of the proletariat. She can therefore be included, along with Axelrod, Akimov, and Riazanov, among those Russian Marxists who were most obdurate in their emphasis on a true workers' revolution.

Zasulich and Lenin were virtually poles apart on the issue of who would really make the revolution. On any spectrum measuring the elitism of various Russian Social Democrats, the two would have to be placed at opposite ends, each adhering to the piece of Plekhanov's ambiguous intellectual legacy most congenial to the particular point of view. When Lenin argued in *What Is to Be Done?* that the proletariat required the assistance of intellectuals in order to understand its revolutionary obligations, he was merely repeating what Zasulich, Plekhanov, and Axelrod had stated nearly twenty years before when they formulated the first Draft Program of the Emancipation of Labor. Indeed, a passage in notes Zasulich wrote in 1901 attesting to the workers' lack of revolutionary consciousness could just as easily have been written by Lenin: "As soon as the proletariat sees from its own experience in trade union activity that its personal affairs can be conducted not too badly, it will be inclined to forget about [socialism]."[38] Lenin's formulation implied, however, that the dominance of Marxist intellectuals would be *permanent*, that this lack of revolutionary consciousness was an affliction so profound and unchangeable that any political party Russian socialists might create would have to reflect this condition in its structure and organization. Unlike the revolutionary pedagogues in Zasulich's party, the intellectuals in Lenin's would never fade into oblivion, but retain control over every aspect of the revolutionary struggle. It was precisely this authoritarian emphasis in Lenin's argument that prompted Zasulich to denigrate Lenin as a Russian Louis XIV when she publicly objected to Leninism in the summer of 1904.[39]

In a sense, both Lenin and Zasulich were impelled by a larger vision of what they considered the most appropriate instrument of revolutionary struggle—for Lenin a conspiratorial elite, for Zasulich a broad-based alliance—to make changes in the Marxist scenario that both had really inherited from Plekhanov and Axelrod. As a result, they remained political enemies until Zasulich's death in 1919. But this subordination of ideology to tactics constitutes an area of agreement which, on account of their differences on other matters, neither Zasulich nor Lenin was willing to acknowledge. Driven by different notions of the party to diverge in different directions from their original ideology, they could not concede that their motives in doing so reflected a shared belief that Marxism required tactical emendation if it was to be utilized successfully in Russia.

The other articles Zasulich wrote before moving to England in 1894 can be summarized briefly. In 1890 she composed a preface to "The Speech of Varlen before the Court of the Executive Police," a tribute to a self-educated Parisian bookbinder who organized his fellow workers to agitate for various concessions from their employer and was tried in court for his activities.[40] In the same year, she completed a critique of revolutionary populism (or *narodnichestvo*), in which she argued that the policy of the government since 1861 of placing impediments before peasants seeking to leave the commune was one which the populists implicitly endorsed, if for different reasons, and that this endorsement, implicit or not, had the effect of worsening the lives of those whose interests the populists claimed to represent.[41] In addition, Zasulich bemoaned what she thought was the reactionary nature of the populists' hostility to industrialization and to

the urban bourgeoisie: "whereas [the workers] battle the bourgeoisie for the future, the populists fight to withhold from it the
remnants of the past."[42] Narodnichestvo, especially when combined with "philanthropic activities or pious agricultural exer-
cises," actually deluded the peasants about this process of industrialization which Zasulich acknowledged would necessarily
exact a certain toll in human suffering; by declaring their hostility to industrialization to be total, however, the populists made
impossible rational debate over how the worst excesses of industrialization might be avoided, even if the process itself, in her
view, was inevitable.[43] Finally, in this same critique, Zasulich condemned as misguided the noblesse oblige that she still claimed to
see in narodnichestvo—a theme she would take up again in 1897
when she attacked liberal altruism as "a type of conspicuous
consumption" comparable to the acquisition of "objects of luxury."[44] To this extent, Zasulich's own desire to "help the people"
has, by 1890, become more discriminating, reflecting the fairly
recent recognition that altruism, by itself, is no guarantee of
moral virtue, and that unless it is placed in the service of a
"scientific" ideology, it could even be destructive of the goals it
purports to advance.

Nevertheless, Zasulich's reaction to the first significant event
in Russia after she completed this critique was entirely consistent
with everything in her career that preceded it. In the winter of
1891–92 a great famine swept across European Russia; many
peasants died of starvation or cholera, and thousands were left
nearly destitute. Although the government responded to the
calamity in ways that belied its reputation for inefficiency and
callousness, the mere fact that a famine had occurred at all
seemed to rouse the intelligentsia from its complacency, forcing
it to recognize the futility of seeking only gradual improvements
in people's lives.[45] Because the peasants' reaction to their plight
was on the whole devoid of animosity toward the state, the chief
political beneficiaries of the famine were not the populists but
rather the Marxists (because their appraisal of the peasants' political inertia had proved accurate) and the zemstvo liberals (because they organized various agencies of relief).[46] Moreover,
both groups benefited greatly from the perception of many
members of the intelligentsia that neither the government nor

the populists had done very much to improve the condition of the peasants in the thirty years since the Emancipation.

For a period after the outbreak of the famine there were efforts, reminiscent of those in the 1870's, to "go to the people."[47] But, this time, such efforts proved abortive. Rather than try to emulate the poor, and in that way help to perpetuate their poverty, students and intellectuals looked with a new respect not only upon the liberals but also upon the promise contained in Marxism that industrialization would ultimately destroy the political system which had made such famines possible in the first place. Thanks to recruits such as A. N. Potresov, who performed for the Group with considerable success the job of "letter carrier" that Zasulich had performed for Nechaev in the late 1860's, the Marxist pamphlets of the Group could reach this potentially receptive audience immediately after the famine.[48] By the early 1890's, contacts had been established between the Group and sympathizers in Odessa, Vil'na, Moscow, Kiev, and scores of smaller towns in southern Russia.[49]

Characteristically, when Zasulich learned of the famine, her first impulse was to call for the creation of a coalition of revolutionaries to assist the peasants; in this impulse one sees not only her social altruism but also her conviction that revolutionaries of disparate philosophies should work together in the pursuit of common goals. Whereas Lenin, recently licensed as a lawyer, refused to help the peasants on the grounds that "the worse it is, the better" (*chem khuzhe tem luchshe*), Zasulich sent a letter to Axelrod in Zurich requesting that he immediately come to Mornex to discuss with her and Plekhanov the formation of a "League of Struggle against Famine."[50] Zasulich had in mind an organization open to émigrés of all persuasions, and invitations were sent to Lavrov and Kravchinskii, among others, calling upon Russians everywhere to put aside their differences and do what they could to assist the starving masses in their homeland. Only a few of those who received the invitations responded favorably. Axelrod was able to establish a "section" in Zurich consisting of Marxists and populists whose objective was roughly that of Krasnyi Krest in the early 1880's; but as had happened in 1882–83, subsequent negotiations between Plekhanov and the populists collapsed in the wake of petty jealousies and rivalries, and the project for a Popular Front to combat famine was soon put aside.[51] Once again, the initial impetus for a united front had come from Zasulich, who, in certain circumstances, was still willing to ignore differences with her opponents and work for what she considered the public welfare. For all her demolishing remarks on the populists in 1890, two years later she could still envision collaboration.*

Zasulich's penchant for revolutionary unity was also reflected in the attempt of the Group to increase its membership in the early 1890's. Because Polish workers in Russia were much more active politically than their Great Russian counterparts, the Group considered it essential to establish ties with Polish socialists engaged in revolutionary agitation.† Accordingly, in the fall of 1891 the Group invited Leo Jogiches, Rosa Luxemburg's lover and a leader of Marxist radicals in Vil'na, to apply for membership. Convinced that Jogiches would accept their offer with alacrity, the members of the Group were astonished by his attempt to place strict conditions upon his joining them: in exchange for his full participation, the Group would have to agree to alter its existing procedures on matters such as voting, the dissemination of literature, and the disbursement of funds.[52] Despite this ultimatum from a man whom Axelrod's biographer describes as "arrogant, overbearing, and unscrupulous," the Group considered Jogiches's assistance invaluable in establishing contact with the Polish proletariat, and continued to negotiate with him in a conciliatory fashion.[53] Zasulich expressed her own attitude and that of her colleagues when she wrote to Jogiches in 1891, after he had already presented his demands to the Group:

We are elated by your desire to join the Group and are certain it will make you more aware of our concerns and our position. You will understand better what is not feasible for us; you can with some certainty make demands on us, and there will be less chance we would be placed

---

* It is noteworthy that Deich, like Kravchinskii a decade earlier, criticized Zasulich's willingness in this instance to cooperate with former Narodovol'tsy, arguing that she was sacrificing her principles and beliefs for a reconciliation that he thought would be spurious. Letter, Deich to Zasulich, November 18, 1892, *Gruppa*, vol. 2, pp. 297–99.

† It has been estimated that roughly six of every seven strikes in Russia in the early 1880's occurred in ethnically Polish areas. John Keep, *The Rise of Social Democracy in Russia* (New York, 1963), p. 42.

in an untenable position as a result of any demand that could not be fulfilled. Between us there would be greater mutual trust and solidarity, and less likelihood of misunderstandings in the future. From such a close association of people, all equally dedicated to identical goals, I cannot imagine results that would not be advantageous . . .[54]

In the months that followed, however, Jogiches's arrogance finally lost him the Group's good will. A last attempt by Jogiches to extract concessions in exchange for joining the Group and turning over to it money he had recently inherited only hardened the conviction of the Group that, on balance, it would be better off without him. By the end of 1892 relations between the two antagonists reached their nadir. The Group withdrew its offer of membership, and Jogiches proceeded to organize a "Social Democratic Library" of his own, its contributors mostly those who would later help him establish the Social Democratic Party of the Kingdom of Poland.

This conflict with Jogiches, petty and disagreeable in its outcome, had a marked effect on the already chilly relations between Polish and Russian Social Democrats at a time when a unified movement might have had greater influence than a divided one. More and more it seemed that each effort of the Group to broaden its constituency only served to increase its isolation within the Social Democratic movement. Subsequent efforts to establish ties with other Marxist groups were no more successful than this one; and because such efforts generally resulted in mutual recriminations and hostility, in the long run they probably did more harm than good to the reputation of Plekhanov and his friends. Indeed, a good deal of the ill will that existed in the late 1890's when the first attempts were made to form a genuine Social Democratic Workers' Party was a reflection of the conflicts that were unintentionally exacerbated when the Group attempted to relieve its isolation.

It would be incorrect to assume that the sentiments expressed in the letter quoted above characterized Zasulich's feelings throughout the protracted negotiations with Jogiches. If treated badly enough, Zasulich could muster the nerve to express the anger that she felt. As in her dealings with Dragomanov a decade earlier, she heatedly denied Jogiches's charges that she, Plekhanov, and Axelrod were behaving in a manner somehow unbecoming to dedicated revolutionaries; to this extent she perceived Jogiches's duplicity more quickly than she had Nechaev's in the late 1860's.[55] However, her conduct throughout the entire episode is remarkable in the degree to which she was willing to accommodate Jogiches before his behavior became so outrageous that she could no longer keep her objections to herself. So desirous was she of Jogiches's participation in the Group that, for a time, she was ready to abandon her own activities because she thought they might in some way offend him: in a letter to Axelrod in August 1892 she wrote that she had contemplated, but then decided against translating a biography of Engels because she feared that Jogiches would raise "innumerable objections."[56] Granted that a certain flexibility was required if the Group was to reap the benefits of Jogiches's participation, Zasulich seems to have gone further than either Plekhanov or Axelrod in attempting to assuage his sensibilities. In this instance she was ready to concede far more than what she and her colleagues would have received from Jogiches in return.

Unnerved by such conflicts, Zasulich welcomed the opportunity in 1894 to live in England, far from the increasingly acrimonious wrangling among the émigré community of Geneva. Having carried on for many years a cordial correspondence with Frederick Engels, whom she had met in 1893 at the Zurich Congress of the Second International, she could look forward to lengthy discussions in London with the man second only to Marx in the esteem of European socialists. In England, she could also work closely with Sergei Kravchinskii, who, despite his espousal of terrorism, remained a close friend and confidant throughout the 1880's. Finally, living in England offered her the chance to observe directly economic conditions in the most industrialized society in the world, and thus to apply to her ideology the most rigorous test of its empirical validity.

Ironically, during the three years that she lived in England, Zasulich managed to embroil herself in the same internecine quarrels that she had found so unsettling in Geneva—this time in connection with an émigré organization Kravchinskii had established to disseminate information about revolutionary movements inside Russia. Moreover, her observations of the English proletariat, and also a careful reading of the third volume of

Capital (published posthumously in 1894), produced an intellectual crisis so traumatic that thoughts of suicide once again passed through her mind.[57] In England Zasulich confronted the revisionist realities that Eduard Bernstein would detail in print at the end of the decade, and though his conclusions were not nearly so shocking to Zasulich as they would be to Russian socialists less knowledgeable about events in Western Europe, her belief in Marxism was tested as it had never been before. Almost the only solace she could take in her English interlude was that the British Museum and its archives proved to be an ideal location for the literary work she completed in this period.[58]

Although Bernstein was also living in London at this time, he and Zasulich met only fleetingly at a gathering at Engels's home in 1895, not long before Engels died. Zasulich mentioned the meeting in a letter to Plekhanov but said only that the German socialist had "bored" her.[59] Living in London, however, made it impossible for Zasulich not to recognize the same changes that Bernstein had discerned in Western capitalism since Marx and Engels had first claimed to penetrate its mysteries in the late 1840's. Like Bernstein, Zasulich was too keen an observer of social and political phenomena not to realize that much of what had recently transpired in Western Europe could easily make one deny the predictive value of Marxism. Whereas Marx had predicted the inexorable impoverishment of the proletariat, recent statistics on real wages suggested that, although the distance between classes may have been increasing, the proletariat nevertheless was becoming more prosperous, and increasingly reluctant to do anything politically that might jeopardize its newfound prosperity. Whereas Marx had claimed that the insoluble contradictions of capitalism would produce economic crises of increasing magnitude and frequency, careful study of economic conditions in Western Europe over the past half-century seemed to indicate that such crises were becoming fewer and discernibly less severe. And whereas Marx had argued that, as capitalism inexorably declined, the class structure of society would be simplified, with the lower middle class contracting to the point of insignificance, most of the available evidence suggested that this class was growing stronger rather than weaker, its rate of profit no less than that of capitalists engaged in large-scale production.

Everything considered, a dispassionate observer in Western Europe in the 1890's could conclude with considerable justification that the resiliency and adaptability of industrial capitalism was much greater than either Marx or Engels had imagined; if this was so, then perhaps socialism was not to be the inevitable consequence of capitalism.

However, socialists in Europe need not have been terribly worried by these apparent failures of Marxist prognostication, for just as capitalism seemed to be growing stronger and more resilient, so too, paradoxically, was international socialism. The 1890's was a decade of tremendous progress for socialists in countries that allowed them to engage in electoral politics: although England had no Labour Party until 1900 (which did not become socialist until 1918), enormous gains were registered by socialist parties in Germany, France, the Low Countries, Scandinavia, and Eastern Europe; only in Italy and Spain, where anarchist sentiment remained strong, did socialist parties fail to make significant progress toward achieving parliamentary majorities.[60] Indeed, the fruits of electoral success were so abundant—and in retrospect so ephemeral—that, by the turn of the century, Bernstein was speaking approvingly of "the inevitability of gradualism" and even hinting that the transition from capitalism to socialism need not be marked by revolutionary violence.[61]

It should be remembered that Marx and Engels themselves had occasionally hypothesized a peaceful transition to socialism: just as the exploits of Narodnaia Volia forced Marx to abandon his long-standing Russophobia and join with Engels in entertaining the possibility of Russia's reaching socialism by way of the peasant commune, so, too, did the vitality of capitalism in Great Britain and America impel them toward the end of their lives to speculate that events in these countries might not conform to the program of violent revolution implicit in their earlier writings.[62] As his letter to Zasulich suggests, Marx was quite willing to bend his ideology when events somewhere in the world seemed to portend an imminent transition to socialism, and Bernstein was quite correct (as well as complimentary) when he wrote that Marx and Engels were "the greatest Revisionists in the history of socialism."[63]

But to a Russian Marxist living in Western Europe or learning about its political tendencies in the mid-1890's, the economic realities he perceived there and also the attempts of Western socialists to come to terms with these realities could very easily have produced an intellectual crisis more severe than any experienced by Marxists or socialists in the West. Class struggle, violent revolution, the impoverishment of the masses, the self-destruction of industrial capitalism—all these concepts and phrases were articles of faith for Russian socialists such as Plekhanov and Axelrod who, unlike their counterparts in the West, faced the additional problem of adapting Marxist doctrine to a society still too backward for socialism to be established there during their lifetimes. Paradoxically, the various tactical adaptations and emendations to which Plekhanov and Axelrod had to subject their ideology made them more determined than ever to defend its essential validity as Marx and Engels had originally conceived it. In addition, Russian Marxists such as Plekhanov and Axelrod were so much further removed—literally and figuratively—than were West European socialists from the mainstream of political dialogue in their homelands that their discussions of ideology were commensurately more abstract and theoretical, and therefore less likely to allow for the inclusion of conflicting opinions based on empirical observation and evidence. The very passion with which Russian émigrés—and indeed the Russian intelligentsia as a whole—committed themselves to totalistic and abstract ideologies was perhaps a compensation for the utter absence in Russia of a political life in which their ideas could be tested and evaluated empirically. For these reasons it should not be difficult to understand why Russian Marxists should have reacted so emotionally and with such an outpouring of rhetorical vituperation when Eduard Bernstein systematically challenged virtually every facet of Marxist theory in articles published in *Die Neue Zeit* in the late 1890's.

Zasulich herself found little in Bernstein's articles that surprised her. For this reason she could tolerate, or at least acknowledge, the German socialist's heresy with an equanimity impossible for Plekhanov and Axelrod, neither of whom had paid much attention to the letters they had received from Zasulich replete with observations of economic conditions in England, and who were therefore unprepared for the revisionist onslaught when it broke upon them at the turn of the century. While it lasted, however, her anguish was no less than that of her colleagues, and, as the product of direct observation, was possibly even more difficult to endure.

Almost immediately after her arrival in England, Zasulich recognized the passivity of the English proletariat. In a letter to Deich written in the summer of 1895, she commented: "The English engaged in retail—neighbors, shopkeepers, and so on— I like very much; they are much more likeable than either the Swiss or the French. But taking a good look at England as a whole, one could despair if one forgot about the other countries and thought only of England."[64] In another letter to Deich the following winter, she noted that although she knew before she went to England how little influence the radical intellectuals had there, she was surprised by the prevalence of the "opportunist" mentality in the English working class: "The English are the real opportunists in the workers' world: they adhere to no principles, but seek only material gain. Up to now the Germans have received absolutely nothing material . . . and yet no one doubts that they represent an infinitely more powerful force in the life of their country than the English in theirs."[65] Engels only confirmed what she herself had clearly recognized when he told her that even universal suffrage would not impel the English worker to vote his class interests unless, as she wrote Plekhanov, "he could calculate upon receiving a direct monetary advantage from it": since "the English proletariat lacks the mentality to seize power, and life in England is not moving at all in a direction which would engender this particular mentality," the prospect of revolution there was virtually nil.[66] In 1896 she wrote to Axelrod that she "never felt so morose about the movement as I do now."[67]

Although Zasulich spoke no English, and, like most Russian émigrés, generally remained aloof from English politics, she could converse in French with Engels and with Eleanor and Edward Aveling, the daughter and son-in-law of Marx. Eleanor Aveling, troubled by personal problems that led to her suicide in 1898, for a time made Zasulich her confidante, and she and Edward introduced their Russian friend to their circle of English radicals.[68] Although I have found no evidence that links

Zasulich directly with the central figures of English radicalism at the turn of the century, such as Keir Hardie, John Burns, George Bernard Shaw, and Sidney and Beatrice Webb, she spoke on occasion (in French) to conferences of the Trade Union Congress, and seems to have been well informed of the most recent developments in the English labor movement.[69] In addition, her work with other Russian émigrés disseminating information about industrial strikes in Russia exposed her to English life in its most variegated forms. There is therefore reason to believe that her observations of the English proletariat were rather more reliable than those of other political exiles living in England at the time and reflected a serious effort to understand its peculiar lack of revolutionary consciousness.

Zasulich's pessimistic conclusions of what she saw in England seemed to confirm what she was reading concurrently in the third volume of *Capital*. As she wrote to Plekhanov in 1894: "The book produced in my mind a mass of anxiety. If you were here you would shout at me. . . . If Pavel were here I would not be allowed to remain on earth. I, for one, am now ready to affirm that England by itself will not evolve even slightly in the direction of socialism."[70] The notes and explanatory paragraphs Engels appended to Marx's unfinished manuscript seemed to prove that "anarchy in production" was decreasing. Marx's previous statements notwithstanding, it seemed to Zasulich that both in the real world and in the pages of *Capital* one could discern a trend that bore scant resemblance to what the two earlier volumes of *Capital* had argued was the inexorable course of economic development: largely because of improved communications, capitalists could now coordinate their efforts to avoid the dangers of overproduction. Cognizant of how much their competition was producing, capitalists could halt the fatal cycle of overproduction – falling profits – lower wages that Marx had said would eventually lead to an economic cataclysm.[71] In addition, the rise of cartels reduced the element of cut-throat competition and lessened the possibility that entrepreneurs would attempt to "swindle" one another out of the profits that each one had legitimately accrued. With a certain bravado, presumably to explain away its inapplicability to England, Zasulich declared to Plekhanov that she "had never liked" Marx's theory of the self-decomposition of capitalism, but it is clear that the section of Volume Three which cast doubt on its validity disturbed her greatly.[72] Zasulich never revealed to anyone except Plekhanov and Axelrod the doubts about Marxist theory she entertained, but the anguish they produced was very real.

While these doubts persisted, Zasulich remained completely immobilized, unable to complete the biography of Rousseau she was writing; her letters to Plekhanov are filled with allusions to a variety of physical complaints which one can safely say were at least partly the result of this intellectual crisis. Finally, after a period of protracted deliberation, Zasulich somehow managed to resolve her doubts and indecision. In a letter to Plekhanov written in February 1898 she says that "while Bernstein's essays would have excited me had they appeared three or four years ago, now for me this crisis has already passed."[73]

Her response involved yet another attenuation of her ideology. Unlike Plekhanov, whose critique of Revisionism will be described in the following chapter, Zasulich chose not to quibble with Bernstein's statistics, however vulnerable to attack she seemed to consider them: "On economic grounds one can, up to a certain point, brush Bernstein, Webb, and the others aside, and bite off one or another of their figures, but, in my opinion, this will not be genuinely and greatly serious."[74] Instead of disputing Bernstein's empirical data, Zasulich argued that they yielded conclusions different from those which the German socialist had induced. She conceded frankly that "economically, capitalism does not get worse, but is gradually freed of crisis and, generally, of the 'anarchy of production'"; indeed, her English experience had made this an "unshakable conviction." Still, she told Plekhanov, he should not think that she viewed the future entirely pessimistically or that she was prepared "to bid adieu to revolution and communism"; as she viewed the world in 1898, it was clear to her that "the psychic depends on the economic only within very wide limits. Capitalism inevitably destroys only the old (natural-economic) thoughts. The most various thoughts and feelings take shape in their place and exactly what takes shape also depends to a great extent upon politics."[75]

Thus, Bernstein's critique of Marxism was just as simplistic as the ideology it attacked. Regardless of how prosperous it made its proletariat, capitalism would be destroyed because it could not simultaneously create a way of thinking that would render this proletariat politically conservative, because capitalism left a void in the minds of the workers that the socialist intelligentsia could easily fill with revolutionary ideology. According to Zasulich, things more powerful than the purely economic ultimately determined political consciousness, and it is clear from everything she wrote in her lifetime that she accorded the intelligentsia inordinate influence in this regard. Reversing Marx's view of the relationship between "superstructure" and "base," Zasulich argued that changes in consciousness could produce changes in being: by a judicious application of its energies, the intelligentsia could turn the proletariat into a revolutionary vanguard forcing changes in the economic structure of society. For all its fabled powers of regeneration and adaptation, capitalism was powerless to preclude the development of ideologies which would ultimately destroy it. Bernstein's arguments, in Zasulich's view, were not so much invalid as they were irrelevant to the importance of ideas in creating revolutionary consciousness.

Implicit in Zasulich's emphasis on the role of the "psychic" was the notion that capitalism left its workers lacking in education and enlightenment: "capitalism inevitably destroys only the old thoughts and feelings," and presumably the intelligentsia supplies the thoughts and feelings to replace them. In the letter to Plekhanov of February 1898 she inadvertently revealed how crucial a role the intelligentsia would play in determining the consciousness of the Russian proletariat: "I ascribe enormous significance to those thoughts which occur to the masses at the moment (proceeding so quickly with us) of the destruction of the state of mind produced by the previous economic order. Our bloated intelligentsia consists of very zealous and fanatical individuals who can leave a loathsome residue in the souls of the workers. What sticks there is durable."[76] Just as in "Revolutionaries of Bourgeois Background," Zasulich in 1898 was forced by harsh realities which this time encompassed Western Europe as well as Russia to claim that the Marxist intelligentsia instilled in workers the political consciousness that otherwise would be a natural consequence of their economic condition. Writing in *Zaria* in 1902, she explained in greater detail the instructional nature of this relationship:

Whether it wants to or not, the intelligentsia will influence the proletariat in the evolution of its views. For the workers to answer their own questions without the whispers of the "bacillus" of the intelligentsia; for their Weltanschauung to be formed exclusively under the influence of their factory work and material existence, just as the Weltanschauung of the peasants was formed long ago under the influence of the land and adapted to an agrarian existence—this is just as impossible to achieve as it would be to insulate the factory proletariat from the *razno-chintsy* . . . who represent in their social position and education the natural ties which exist between the lowest strata of the urban poor and the world of the intelligentsia and of the book. . . . At the present juncture in history the intelligentsia cannot but shape the views of the proletariat.[77]

In sum, the greatest failure of industrial capitalism was its inability to do anything more than destroy "old thoughts and feelings"; beyond that, it was powerless. Whether it made the workers prosperous or not was in some sense irrelevant, an arid question better left to Bernstein and the Revisionists. According to Zasulich, the chief failing of capitalism was not its inefficiency, its self-destructive tendencies, nor even the cruelty with which it robbed the workers of a certain portion (that is, the surplus value) of their labor—all this, she admitted, had been legitimately questioned by Revisionist critics of Marxism. Rather, the chief failing of capitalism was cultural: it could not provide those whose labor it exploited with the education, traditions, habits, loyalties, and allegiances without which—as Zasulich never tired of repeating—no human being can lead a productive and happy life. Capitalism, as she saw it, left its proletariat in a state of cultural and intellectual isolation, and for that reason would meet the end it deserved. So long as Marxist intellectuals filled this void with propaganda of their own, with the intention to withdraw once this obligation was fulfilled, there was every reason to believe that the proletariat would proceed to create the socialist utopia.*

* To be sure, Zasulich's confidence in such an outcome would not be vindicated by events. If Marx underestimated the economic resiliency and adaptability of capitalism, Zasulich surely underestimated just as much the ability of workers to forge these traditions, loyalties, and allegiances without having to destroy the economic order in which they lived. At its most mature, capitalism generally permits its workers vehicles for collective endeavor, such as unions, which, in addition to serving as a force for political moderation, enable workers to generate the *solidarnost'* and camaraderie Zasulich extolled.

Because at first Zasulich was so troubled by what she saw and read in England, she took two years to complete her long-planned biography of Rousseau. When it was finished, she swore to Plekhanov that never again would she embark upon such a lengthy and time-consuming project.[78] Though turgid in its prose, clumsy in its structure, and in many places unclear in its meaning, this biography is nevertheless interesting as an indication of how readily Zasulich would seek historical precedent for the ideologies she espoused—a tendency understandable in revolutionaries, who, paradoxically, often find in history the inspiration and legitimacy for creating societies different in every way from all those that have preceded them in the past.* Writing to Plekhanov in 1895, she insisted that in Rousseau's ideas "the possibility of contemporary socialism is obvious."[79] Largely an attempt to rescue Rousseau from critics who, in Zasulich's view, habitually misrepresented nearly everything he wrote, her biography claims that Rousseau was a proto-socialist without knowing it; only his most obstinate opponents could fail to recognize that "for Rousseau production is the basic factor in the development of mankind."[80] Whereas *philosophes* such as Holbach, Helvetius, and even Mably espoused ideas conducive to the perpetuation of inequality and private property, "Rousseau was the only [eighteenth-century writer] who stood entirely on the side of the people, the only democrat in the serious meaning of this word. Not in the sense of wishing good to people—everyone from the King to the most extreme orator of the Palais Royal was in favor of this—but in the sense of a clear understanding of the opposition of the interests of the laboring classes with the interests of the upper levels of the population."[81]

Although Rousseau lived before the full flowering of capitalism, Zasulich attributed to him the prescience to realize that only people acting together in a common effort could eliminate the many evils it would eventually produce. In other words, Rousseau was actually a precursor of nineteenth-century socialism, a historical materialist of sorts among the monarchs and aristo-

* Zasulich also wrote a short biography of Voltaire, who appealed to her largely because his hostility to organized religion seemed to prefigure her own. The essay, published in Geneva in 1893 and entitled *Vol'ter, ego zhizn' i literaturnaia deiatel'nost'*, is reprinted in Zasulich, *Sbornik statei*, vol. 1, pp. 145–243.

cratic intellectuals of his day. This fairly ridiculous interpretation completely ignored Rousseau's belief that poverty was a virtue to be preserved rather than an evil to be eradicated; but it may well have been Zasulich's attempts in the essay to include Rousseau among the intellectual forerunners of Marx that prompted Lenin to praise her article lavishly when he procured a copy in 1899.[82] In any event, the biography of Rousseau was the longest of the various essays Zasulich completed, and it illustrates better than any other not only her limitations as a historian but also the way in which, all too often, the genuine insights of which she was capable were vitiated by a prose that was well-nigh impenetrable.

For Zasulich, however, work on this essay was perhaps her only outlet when her observations of the proletariat in England seemed destined to force a major reevaluation of her ideology. Whereas in the 1880's Zasulich could sublimate her intellectual doubts in the work she performed for Krasnyi Krest, her efforts of a similar nature a decade later seemed only to create more problems than they solved, and to indicate how unsuited she was for the political bickering so common within an émigré community. While working on her biography of Rousseau, Zasulich was invited repeatedly to assist a group of English intellectuals sympathetic to the Russian revolutionary movement who called themselves the Friends of Russian Freedom; consisting of Tories as well as Liberals and socialists, the group was united only by a revulsion for tsarist autocracy and a desire to help political prisoners in Russia through the dissemination of propaganda about their plight.[83] To acquire greater knowledge about conditions in Russia, these Friends of Russian Freedom often consulted Kravchinskii and Chaikovskii, both longtime residents of London and the leaders of an informal circle of populist émigrés known as the Fund of the Free Russian Press.[84] Zasulich had no reason to distrust or dislike the members of either organization, and she hoped that Kravchinskii's influence among both the Friends and the Fundists (as the members of these groups were sometimes called) would make possible her active participation in their joint philanthropic activities—for which her work in Krasnyi Krest had given her a special expertise. To assist the cause of political prisoners inside Russia had the same attraction in the mid-

1890's that it had in the early 1880's, and she had gone to England confident that her cordial relationship with Kravchinskii and his wife would preclude a repetition of the difficulties she had had with the Executive Committee of Narodnaia Volia.

Barely nine months after her arrival in London, however, Kravchinskii was fatally injured as he crossed the path of a speeding locomotive. Ignorant of their animus against Marxists, Zasulich was astonished and offended when the Fundists—especially Chaikovskii, Volkhovskii, Lazarev, and Goldenberg—objected to her proposal that the Group publish Kravchinskii's novels in a memorial edition: it hardly mattered to her that she was a Marxist and that Kravchinskii had been an anarchist and a terrorist.[85] It soon became apparent also that the Fundists were attempting to force the Friends to withdraw their invitation to Zasulich to partake in their joint activities. After months of almost continuous debate, Zasulich refused to have anything more to do with either group—as she told Plekhanov, their petty feuds were "too oppressive" for her to put up with.[86] The efforts of the Fundists to sabotage her collaboration with the Friends convinced her that, without Kravchinskii, the Fundists were "opportunists" and "clearly capable of anything"; she especially resented what she perceived as Chaikovskii's insidious defamation of her character.[87] Since Zasulich, for all her idiosyncracies, was perhaps the least likely of all the Russian Marxists to engender personal hatred and vituperation, the Fundists' diatribes against her must, one would think, have had something to do with Zasulich's shift in position: as a former populist turned Marxist, she epitomized to the Fundists the larger failures of their populism, and was therefore a threat to their claim to represent the Russian émigré community in its dealings with English radicals and socialists.

At any rate, the feud impelled Zasulich to seek other means of assisting revolutionaries in Russia. In the spring of 1896, when she learned of the massive strikes in the St. Petersburg cotton mills, she addressed an assembly of representatives of the Trade Union Congress (TUC), and was instrumental in the passage of a resolution pledging solidarity with the 30,000 striking workers in St. Petersburg.[88] Despite her trepidation about speaking before an audience which could understand her only through a translator, she succeeded in persuading the TUC to contribute a sizable sum to the General Fund for Striking Workers recently established inside Russia.[89] No formal ties between the TUC and the Russian labor movement were possible, since trade unions were still illegal in Russia and strict regulations governed the TUC's relations with its counterparts in foreign countries, but the donation and pledge of solidarity in 1896 were significant—and they were largely Zasulich's accomplishment, a testament to her tireless efforts to link together workers' organizations of different countries.

Zasulich realized that in England her notoriety as Trepov's would-be assassin probably did more harm than good to any organization that requested her assistance, so she reluctantly but firmly refused to address future gatherings of the TUC; whether her stage fright and natural self-effacement played a part in her decision must remain a matter of speculation.[90] Upon the conclusion of the strike in St. Petersburg, Zasulich remained aloof from English politics, content to work out a compromise with the Fundists whereby a Social Democrat more acceptable than she would expound the Marxist point of view to the Friends. In addition, it was agreed that direct correspondence be established and maintained between the Fundists and the Marxist-oriented Union of Struggle in St. Petersburg, thereby assuring the Friends of information more reliable and up-to-date than any with which the Group or Zasulich could provide them.[91]

Therefore when an emissary of the Union of Struggle arrived in London in March 1897, Zasulich felt that her presence there was no longer required. After the months of difficult negotiations, she was quite ready to separate herself as much as possible from the Fundists and return to the relative tranquility of Switzerland.[92] The dispute with the Fundists, however, was not without its larger repercussions, for it made Zasulich so skeptical of all forms of émigré debate that she had little inclination to fight the battles against Revisionism and Economism when these ideological heresies became known to the Group in the late 1890's. The dispute with the Fundists was yet another failure of the politics of revolutionary unity, and like the others that preceded it, it exacted its toll on her physical and psychological well-being.

Despite her brief moments of acclaim, Zasulich left England saddened and depressed by the quarrels she had seen there. To avoid similar conflicts in Geneva, she settled instead in Zurich near the Axelrods, who procured for her a residence more comfortable than any she could otherwise have afforded.

It was easy in the 1890's for Zasulich to be consumed by the little world of her exile and to lose sight of concurrent developments in Russia that might have lifted her spirits if she could somehow have foreseen their ramifications. Just when Zasulich in Mornex was attempting with Plekhanov and Axelrod to find ways of alleviating their political isolation, hundreds of miles away in St. Petersburg Tsar Alexander III appointed as Minister of Finance the man who more than any other would be responsible for making Russia's rate of industrial growth the highest in the world from 1892 to 1900. Sergei Witte, who was of Dutch stock from the Baltic provinces that had traditionally provided many of Russia's most efficient bureaucrats, was clearly more important a figure in the 1890's than either of his reluctant patrons, Alexander III and Nicholas II, who succeeded his father as Tsar in 1894. Driven by a messianic vision summoning Russia "to dominate not only the affairs of Asia but of Europe as well," Witte hoped that through a "multiplier effect" beginning with the construction of railroads Russia would at last achieve the economic strength without which she could not compete for political prestige and power on equal terms with Germany, England, France, Japan, and the United States.[93] Only when Witte recognized that other Russians saw this same vision as an excuse for military adventurism in Asia did he recoil from what he realized were its imperialist implications.

The multiplier effect on which Witte's system depended for its success was very simple: the building of railroads, especially the Trans-Siberian Railroad connecting European and Asiatic Russia, would stimulate the heavy industries in coal, iron ore, and steel that were essential in their construction. The expansion of these heavy industries in turn would stimulate light industries, and the new money which was the result of increased trade and access to new markets would increase even more the demand for industrial goods. In this way, the entire economy would eventually expand, and the sum total of Russia's wealth would increase dramatically.

Indeed, from 1892 to 1903, the years of Witte's tenure in the Ministry of Finance, sectors of Russia's economy grew at rates unsurpassed in her history until Stalin, using methods infinitely more brutal than Witte's, carried out the first of several Five Year Plans in the late 1920's and 1930's. The statistics themselves do not really do justice to Witte's accomplishments, but some deserve citation nevertheless: between 1892 and 1902, coal production doubled, the mileage of railroad track increased by 46 percent, steel production increased by 250 percent, and oil production in Baku expanded by 243 percent.[94] If, in 1870, Russia produced 3.7 percent of the world's industrial goods, by 1900 this figure had increased to 5 percent.[95] Without this industrial expansion, moreover, Russia would have been unable to recover from the dislocation caused by the 1905 Revolution and experience yet another industrial surge between 1906 and 1914 at rates nearly as rapid as those in the 1890's.

To be sure, Witte was forced by Russia's backwardness and by his own special sense of urgency to devise a series of "substitutions" which he hoped would compensate for Russia's social and institutional inadequacies. For the private initiative largely lacking in Russia that had sponsored industrialization in the West, Witte substituted the machinery and the resources of the government; for the domestic capital that Russia was lacking as well, Witte substituted foreign investment and loans; for Russia's lack of managerial expertise, Witte would build a small number of large factories rather than a large number of smaller ones so that the expertise that could be found would not be needlessly dissipated. Finally, to procure the money that was needed for foreign loans, Witte made the ruble convertible to gold and imposed a variety of direct and indirect taxes upon the peasantry, whose sensibilities, unlike those of other classes, he felt he could afford to offend.

The results of these "substitutions" were decidedly mixed. Foreign investment in Russia, so extensive that by 1914 the nation seemed to have become an economic dependency of Western Europe, greatly affected her foreign policy, and specifically her choice of France as a political ally. The substitution of the government for private enterprise as the principal impetus to industrialization tended to perpetuate the domination of state over society that Witte hoped his program would eventually alleviate through the creation of an entrepreneurial elite. The peasants, already burdened by the redemption payments that accompanied their emancipation, became increasingly restive under the additional hardship of Witte's taxes. Finally, the working class, which gradually lost its rural character as factory labor was increasingly its sole source of income, found it could organize and agitate more easily in large factories than in small ones; not surprisingly, the number of strikers in Russia increased from 17,000 in 1894 to 30,000 in 1896, reaching a peak of 97,000 in 1899.[96] This burgeoning proletariat, like its predecessor in England during the earliest days of the Industrial Revolution, lived in slums often conducive to serious injuries and illnesses, but whereas in England some of these slums were more tolerable than others, in Russia in the 1890's wages were so uniformly low that nearly all workers lived at the same level of misery.[97] Life for the urban poor in the 1890's was characterized by a wretched sameness in the home and at the factory unalleviated as yet by the improvements that generally come with the legalization of unions. But unions were not legalized in Russia until 1906.

In economic terms, Witte's achievements were undeniable, but they carried with them a political price that would be paid in 1905 when all those whom his policies had antagonized turned on the autocracy with a vengeance and a fury that nearly destroyed it. Still, in a very real sense, Witte was a victim not only of his enemies but also of his patron, the Tsar, and of the autocratic government that he served. In the 1890's Witte tried to modernize Russia's social and economic institutions while the Tsar tried to maintain the government's monopoly of political power, dismissing as a "senseless dream" a request (not a demand) from zemstvo officials that their assemblies be incorporated into the government. By creating new classes, new careers, and new avenues of individual advancement at the same time that it proclaimed its subjects unfit to participate in government, Russian autocracy in the 1890's took with one hand what it gave with the other, engendering considerable hostility as a result. This combination of economic modernization and political conservatism would not in itself, perhaps, have been so potentially incendiary had it not been for the fact that the same mixture of petty cruelty, arbitrariness, and inefficiency that in the 1860's had created an entire generation of student radicals would, thirty years later, help to radicalize another generation of students far more numerous, far more adventuresome, and far better armed with ideological ammunition than its predecessors.

Of these new ideologies, which included liberalism and a new variant of populism, Marxism was in some ways most attuned to the times. As many Russian peasants abandoned the countryside for the cities and acquired the habits and mentality of an urban labor force, large numbers of them found increasingly relevant an ideology which promised a better life without demanding that they "reverse directions" and return to the commune. The relative influence of Marxism in the genesis of Russian labor agitation remains a matter of dispute among historians, but recent evidence uncovered by Allan Wildman and others suggests that, in the 1890's, Marxism became a movement appealing to workers as well as to radical intellectuals, and its vision of proletarian dictatorship contributed greatly to the dynamism which marked such strikes as that in 1896 in the St. Petersburg textile mills.* At the very moment when it was being subjected to critical scrutiny by skeptical Revisionists in the West, Marxism experienced a resurgence in the East.

To the members of the Group, this resurgence was cause for genuine celebration. After many years of failure, their efforts were finally showing results. But with success came certain problems which they had not really anticipated and, for personal and political reasons, were unable to resolve. For the first time in its existence the Group had to contend with a new generation of Marxists, one which was impudent enough to challenge it for the leadership of Russian Social Democracy.

Among this new generation were men such as Lenin, Martov, Ivanshin, Struve, and Prokopovich. Unlike the generation of Plekhanov and Zasulich, theirs was a generation which matured when opportunities for revolutionary agitation were plentiful; with the industrialization of the 1890's there came into existence

---

* See, for example, Wildman's *The Making of a Workers' Revolution: Russian Social Democracy, 1891–1903* (Chicago, 1967), pp. 70–74. In response to this strike and other expressions of labor discontent, the government in 1897 introduced a law which limited the work day to eleven and one-half hours.

a proletariat in whose ranks could be found the manpower for a genuine workers' party. If the members of the Emancipation of Labor Group considered themselves primarily political theorists, their younger rivals were, for the most part, men of practical ability, convinced that the theoretical works produced by the Group could best be utilized in the strikes and demonstrations they themselves would organize; ultimately, as the ties between workers and intellectuals hardened, the two groups would coalesce in a national Social Democratic Party prepared to fight the autocracy on every front. In the view of this new generation, the time for contemplation had passed, and the moment for practical action had arrived.

Intellectually, Plekhanov and Axelrod agreed completely with this change in emphasis from theory to practice; in their hearts, however, they feared that this change would minimize their importance within the Social Democratic movement, and probably relegate them to the role of elder statesmen. Although their efforts in the 1880's had consistently been directed toward a geographical and generational transfer of authority, when it seemed imminent a decade later, the members of the Group seemed none too pleased with its implications for themselves. In the 1890's many younger Marxists made a pilgrimage to Switzerland to receive the blessings of their elders, and though these encounters were often cordial enough, differences of temperament and background as well as age made a mutual disillusionment nearly inevitable. Sometimes consciously, sometimes not, each generation perceived the other as a potential threat to its own authority, and the events immediately preceding the fateful schism in Russian socialism in 1903 between Bolsheviks and Mensheviks cannot be understood properly without reference to this underlying clash of generations.

Thus, when Zasulich returned to Switzerland in 1897, she left behind one altercation only to be confronted with another—one whose outcome could determine the ultimate fate of Russian socialism. Whereas previous disputes with Dragomanov, Tikhomirov, Jogiches, and the Fundists occurred when the internal dynamics of the revolutionary movement still had little impact upon developments in Russia, the conflicts Zasulich would attempt to mediate after 1897 involved issues that might ultimately touch millions of lives. To Zasulich it would be not merely ridiculous but a genuine tragedy for Russian socialists to be consumed by internal conflict when the opportunities for revolutionary action had never been greater, and she employed in the years between her return to Switzerland in 1897 and her return to Russia in 1905 all the prestige, diplomacy, and tact that she possessed to ensure that Russian socialists work together with the proletariat against the state. With Zasulich's return to Switzerland in 1897 we reach the most important and revealing chapter of her life.

FIVE

Zasulich and *Iskra*

T HERE ARE many reasons why Russian Social Democrats were unable in the years before 1917 to create a party with the mass support that most Social Democrats agreed was needed for them to have a share in the overthrow of autocracy. Allan Wildman and others are quite right to speak of a collapse of Social Democratic "hegemony" after 1901, and Wildman is also correct in suggesting that many of the fissures in the labor movement that led to this collapse were those that plague radical movements wherever an intelligentsia and a working class try to bridge the sociological and cultural differences between them.[1] Russian Social Democracy, it appears in retrospect, was weakened not merely by a clash between two generations of intellectuals, each attempting to impose upon the other what it considered the most efficacious means of instilling political consciousness among the proletariat, but also by its failure to sustain and strengthen the ties with the proletariat that had been tentatively established in the late 1890's.

Accounts of labor unrest in this period attest to this failure even in instances where a common hostility to autocracy or to factory owners enabled workers and Social Democratic intellectuals to work together in the pursuit of specific goals. The picture of agitators from the intelligentsia printing leaflets, making speeches, organizing discussion circles, and even joining the workers in armed resistance to the police is accurate enough, but one tends to forget about the numerous irritants that would shatter this alliance once the euphoria of collective action had passed. To be sure, in the mid-1890's groups of intellectuals publishing journals such as *Rabochee delo* (Workers' Cause), *Rabochaia gazeta* (Workers' Gazette), *Rabochee znamia* (Workers' Flag), and many others too numerous or ephemeral to mention ensconced their representatives in areas of Russia where industrial unrest seemed likely to occur: St. Petersburg, Moscow, Kiev, the Caucasus (its oil reserves near the Caspian Sea only now being tapped), and the older mining and metallurgical regions near the Urals which, until the late nineteenth century, had been Russia's principal source of iron ore and coal. In the beginning, these representatives tried to contact as many workers as they could find who had the literacy and political acumen to assist them in *kruzhkovshchina*, that is, in establishing small discussion groups where workers could learn in their leisure time that through their own efforts they could eventually destroy the political system which was the ultimate source of their poverty, exploitation, and degradation. Later, under the influence of intellectuals and workers impatient with the slow pace of propaganda, these representatives would eschew kruzhkovshchina for open encouragement of immediate action.[2]

As a result, Social Democracy achieved a measure of success. All over Russia Social Democratic agitators galvanized into action by the emergence of an urban working class succeeded in reaching a good many members of this class, and, using a variety of tactics both political and economic, began the slow work of making them a proletariat alive to revolutionary obligations. Indeed, Russian workers in the 1890's carried out more than adequately the functions that their Marxist teachers from the intelligentsia had intended for them. Labor unrest in the 1890's not only frightened the government but also extracted from it tangible concessions in matters pertaining to the workers' daily lives: wages in certain industries increased, the work day was to some extent reduced, and the worst abuses of child and female labor were abolished. In addition, an agreement reached in 1895 between the *theoretiki* of Plekhanov's generation and the *praktiki* of Lenin's and Martov's delineating what everyone hoped would be a permanent and equitable division of authority gave Russian Social Democrats reason to believe that they had solved the two problems that had plagued Russian dissent since the days of the Decembrists: intellectual dissent, previously isolated, would merge with the dissent of the masses and the intelligentsia would no longer be rendered powerless by its own internal conflicts and recriminations.

But one of the purposes of a biography of Zasulich is to suggest how ephemeral and tentative were the solutions to these two distinct, yet related, problems. For reasons that no amount of rhetoric about a socialist revolution could eradicate, workers and intellectuals could not work together. In the process of writing leaflets, printing manifestos, or explaining the historical origins of economic exploitation, a division of labor invariably developed between the two; even more, there was almost invariably a mutual resentment, and incomprehension, of background and cultural heritage. The agitators from the intelligentsia usually began by reserving all the important decisions for themselves, making it clear to the workers that even those of them who spent their leisure time studying Marxist principles lacked the tactical skill to lead a Social Democratic circle. The next step was for the workers to start demanding from their erstwhile "teachers" the right to run the circle on their own, arguing, not without reason, that the emancipation of the working class should be a matter for the working class itself, and that the conspiratorial tactics employed by the intelligentsia actually separated workers converted to Social Democracy from the larger numbers of workers in the factories whose interests they were committed to protect.

Many of these working class recruits, finding themselves increasingly isolated from their fellow workers while at the same time denied positions of leadership in Social Democratic circles, repudiated their initial commitments and looked for more satisfying alternatives. Among the most successful of these alternatives, if only for a brief period around the turn of the century, was the "police socialism" of Sergei Zubatov, a police official who shrewdly capitalized on the divisions in Russian Social Democracy and created unions secretly run by the police that would seek concessions concerning wages, hours, and working conditions. The idea was that these concessions would reduce political unrest and cement the workers' loyalty to the state. In the case of Zubatov's unions, however, the opposition of Sergei Witte, the Minister of Finance, was too much. Since Witte wanted to protect rather than intimidate Russia's tiny class of industrial entrepreneurs, he quickly secured the abolition of these unions in 1903.[3]

But even the eventual failure of *Zubatovshchina* could not eliminate the sociological and psychological chasm that divided the intelligentsia and the workers—and was made worse by certain practices of Social Democratic agitators. The workers, understandably resentful of the presumption implicit in kruzhkovshchina that the intellectuals understood their interests far better than they did themselves, became resentful also of the often high-handed way in which these intellectuals would exhort workers to take actions possibly endangering their jobs and then, in most cases, move on to another factory or town, leaving the workers to suffer any punishments that the government might choose to hand down. To be sure, the life of a Social Democratic agitator in the 1890's was not an easy one. But for the worker who felt the whip of a policeman on horseback, it was small consolation to understand intellectually that the agitators who had exhorted him to strike would probably be arrested later somewhere else. The representatives of *Iskra*, after its creation in 1900, were probably even more itinerant than those of the organizations that preceded it in the late 1890's, and this tendency to let the workers suffer the consequences of actions often initiated by the intelligentsia helps to explain the growing isolation of *Iskra*'s editors from developments in the Russian labor movement between 1900 and 1903.[4]

At the root of this hostility between workers and revolutionary intellectuals was what Pavel Axelrod—whose sensitivity in such matters was usually keener than that of his colleagues—called a division between a "bourgeois radicalism" of the intelligentsia and the needs and desires of the working class.[5] Hostility and distrust reflecting differences in education, upbringing, wealth, social class, and even appearance could not be passed off as a temporary aberration to disappear after workers and intellectuals had read Marx together and decided that socialism was the best of all worlds. If, in Zasulich's terminology, it seemed to many workers that by 1900 the time was right for the intelligentsia and the working class to reverse the roles of teacher and student, this reversal, when it finally came, was fraught with so much tension and animosity that Zasulich herself was forced to extend by several years the period of incubation during which she thought the workers would have to remain subservient to the intelligentsia.[6] In part for this reason, Zasulich would not realize when Lenin's *What Is to Be Done?* was published in 1902 that whereas she had only deferred the period of the workers' subservience, Lenin was prepared to make this subservience permanent.

Without belaboring the importance of 1900 as a turning point in the history of Russian socialism, it bears mention that, by 1900, Marxism was no longer the dominant radical ideology in Russia. As a result of Witte's economic modernization and Nicholas's political conservatism, other classes and strata besides the urban proletariat were alienated, and the dissent that erupted around the turn of the century came from a greater variety of sources than ever before in Russian history. Students antagonized by interference in their curricula, peasants exploited by excessive and discriminatory taxes, religious and ethnic minorities needlessly alienated by a policy of Russification, liberals emboldened by converts from Marxism such as Struve and Tugan-Baranovskii and by the vision of parliamentary constitutionalism that was already a reality in other parts of Europe—all these groups became not merely opponents of the government but rivals for the place in the political spectrum in Russia that since the 1860's had been dominated first by populists and then by Marxists. In this struggle for the loyalty of the proletariat, the Social Democrats found themselves in competition with liberal and neo-populist parties as well as socialist organizations such as the Jewish Bund that sought a special autonomy for the ethnic and religious minorities they represented.

Faced with this sudden emergence of groups challenging their monopoly of dissent, the Russian Social Democrats elaborated three possible courses of action: (1) to accept these other parties and movements as collaborators in the effort to overthrow autocracy, which would mean substituting a kind of Popular Front of Dissent for the bourgeoisie that, according to Marx, was to make the bourgeois revolution; (2) to continue their efforts to forge a Social Democratic Workers' Party consisting of workers and revolutionary intellectuals which would act mostly on its own in securing the fruits of any bourgeois revolution; or (3) to create a revolutionary party with an extraordinary centralization of authority which would act in the interest of the proletariat—perhaps without its active participation and support—in moving directly from a bourgeois to a socialist revolution. In 1900, at least, Lenin, Plekhanov, Axelrod, and Zasulich all held firm on the second course—this being, indeed, part of the tactical orthodoxy that the Emancipation of Labor Group had hoped to pass on to its political and ideological descendents. But as the other opposition movements grew, elements in Russian Social Democracy tended to veer in opposite directions. Zasulich was leaning toward the first course, because she recognized both the difficulties in elevating the political consciousness of the proletariat and the advantages to be gained from collaboration with parties and movements representing different sectors of the population. Lenin, on the other hand, would soon draw from this same view of proletarian consciousness (or lack of it) the opposite conclusion that the only course of action was to create a clandestine elite of revolutionary intellectuals. Axelrod seemed willing for a time to follow Zasulich in advocating a Popular Front, and Plekhanov seemed willing on occasion to follow Lenin in advocating a conspiratorial elite; but both Plekhanov and Axelrod would eventually revert to their original position.[7]

The important point about these possible courses of action designed to counteract or to utilize the growing strength of other opposition movements is that they were all a reflection of failure. Despite their success in the 1890's in establishing the basis for a national Social Democratic Party, Russian Social Democrats could not make this party a reality. The conflicts among Marxist intellectuals were too great, and the psychological and sociological differences between workers and intellectuals were too profound, for Russian Social Democrats to compete on equal terms with the liberals, the students, the national minorities, and the Socialist Revolutionaries not merely for the loyalty of the working class but for the allegiance of society as a whole. After 1900 the revolutionary tide in Russia seemed to rush on beyond the Social Democrats without so much as a passing nod in recognition of services they had previously rendered, and this tide would finally crest in 1905 in a revolution without the Social Democrats playing a significant role in its initial stages.[8]

Indeed, as labor unrest, student demonstrations, and a resurgence of revolutionary terrorism in 1902 and 1903 caused the
Minister of the Interior to dream wistfully of a "short, victorious
war" that would engulf domestic dissent in a surge of patriotism, Russian Social Democrats seemed caught on a treadmill of
failure, recrimination, and conflict from which they could not
escape. Even the proclamation in 1903 of a national Social
Democratic Party was followed a few weeks later by a schism
which left Russian Social Democrats bitterly seeking scapegoats
for their failure. This schism left Marxist revolutionaries for the
five years 1900–1905—and later for the six years 1906–12—
weak and politically alone, the victims not just of objective forces
over which they had no real control but, far worse, of their own
inability to contain the recriminations which were, perhaps, an
inevitable consequence of their political failures. Indeed, these
recriminations were particularly acute because the failures that
produced them followed immediately (and inexplicably) after
initial success, and because the political police force in Russia
was not efficient enough to make it necessary for the Social
Democrats to resolve their disagreements for the sake of survival. Pavel Axelrod, writing in 1903, captured this sense of
hope dashed by forces Russian socialists were only just beginning to comprehend:

In the course of [the 1890's] our movement acquired deep roots in the
proletariat, revolutionized the mood and even the consciousness of
considerable strata of the workers, and aroused them to revolutionary
activism. The political significance of the period of economic agitation,
a period circumscribed by the narrow limits of trade-union or parochial
interests, erupted to the surface in the revolutionary events of the first
year of the new century. Workers by the thousands threw themselves
into battle against the retinue of the autocracy, but Social Democracy
was caught completely unprepared to lead the masses in such tempes-
tuous times.[9]

Not surprisingly, the conflicts and recriminations induced by the
failures to which Axelrod refers would leave a distinctive mark
on Russian socialism, mostly by creating an atmosphere of suspicion and hostility (exacerbated by provocateurs from the police)
in which one's supporters were always potentially one's opponents and in which a certain paranoia was virtually a prerequisite of political survival.[10]

*

To trace Zasulich's activities between 1897 and 1905 is to follow these conflicts and recriminations from the perspective of one who genuinely abhorred them and did everything possible to minimize their impact. For Zasulich, revolutionary unity was both a tactical necessity and an ethical imperative: only in unity could Russian socialists assist the working class in overthrowing autocracy, and only in unity could Russian socialists indicate to the workers the virtue of collective endeavor which gave socialist societies their moral superiority. And because Zasulich herself was entirely lacking in personal ambition and arrogance, her prestige as an acquitted would-be assassin still assured her a degree of trust and affection reserved for few others in the revolutionary movement.

Zasulich was indeed the only possible mediator among the factions that would coalesce and dissolve with bewildering rapidity as Russian socialists confronted one divisive issue after another. The debate about Economism in the late 1890's, the establishment of *Iskra* (The Spark) in 1900, the composition of a party program in 1902, and the convening of a party congress in 1903 were all occasions requiring Zasulich to play the role of conciliator, cheerfully subordinating her personal convictions to bring about what she thought were satisfactory compromises; by her efforts she hoped Russian socialists would be able not merely to gain the support of the workers but, in addition, to reach a modus vivendi with other opposition movements (most notably the liberals) whose support she increasingly deemed essential to any bourgeois revolution. At the very point when Russian socialists seemed ready to turn inward, consumed by internal feuds and disagreements, Zasulich sought to direct their attention outward, trying to show, despite the counterarguments of Plekhanov and Lenin, that those who espoused radical ideologies different from theirs were not renegades and traitors but only misguided people with whom one could collaborate on the basis of mutual trust and respect.

This self-imposed task was a thankless one, and a difficult one personally as well as politically for Zasulich. Her health, never good, grew worse. Her psychological stability, always precarious, seemed to decline also. And though she managed to complete in this period lengthy essays on Pisarev and Dobroliubov, as well as a critique of Neo-Kantian Idealism demonstrating what she thought were the utilitarian roots of Marxist ethics, her output of scholarly articles and essays was far less than that of her colleagues in the Group and *Iskra*. All these problems together might have been sufficient to force Zasulich's withdrawal from revolutionary politics. But she was prepared to accept these problems, even to allow them to worsen, because she was driven—often, it must be said, to the point of exhaustion—by the overriding goal of revolutionary unity. As Zasulich, now in her fifties, approached a stage in life when the accumulated defeats of the past often reduce one's willingness to risk their repetition in the future, she persevered in this endeavor with unflagging determination, convinced that it remained her best, and possibly her only, reason for living.

The first altercation Zasulich had to mediate when she returned from London in 1897 concerned an organization known as the Union of Russian Social Democrats Abroad. Established in 1895, this Union at first was little more than an ancillary organ of the Emancipation of Labor Group, its membership determined solely by Plekhanov and Axelrod; its purpose, so far as one can determine, was simply to give the Group a haven for new recruits while maintaining the autonomy of the older organization.[11] In an effort to broaden their influence, Plekhanov and Axelrod also published two journals, *Rabotnik* (The Worker) and *Listok rabotnika* (Worker's Sheet), which they hoped would disseminate the views of the Group while bearing as well the imprimatur of the Union, thus suggesting a harmonious division of power between the two groups (and, by implication, between the two generations). This fiction was too blatant to perpetuate, however, and in 1897 the Group had to agree that previous participation in any Marxist circle inside Russia automatically entitled one to membership in the Union of Russian Social Democrats Abroad.[12] As police arrests decimated the ranks of clandestine Marxist groups in Russia following the strikes of 1895–96, those fortunate enough to escape abroad naturally gravitated to the Group in Switzerland, and eagerly joined its affiliate, the Union; those who, like Lenin, had to go to Siberia merely delayed their encounter with Plekhanov and his colleagues until their terms of exile had been fulfilled.

Thus, an organization originally intended as a vehicle for

Plekhanov and Axelrod was rapidly inundated with a flood of new émigrés, many of them openly dissatisfied with what seemed to them to be the bourgeois hauteur of their elders. By 1897 the Union was no longer a tool of the Group but its rival, containing mostly younger men such as Ginzburg, Ivanshin, Takhtarev, and Krichevskii, all of whom were in varying degrees unwilling to put up with the domination of Plekhanov and Axelrod. In 1898 this potential for open conflict was exacerbated by the arrival in Switzerland of E. D. Kuskova and S. N. Prokopovich, two young Marxists who would shortly add to the tensions already present an element of ideological discord that had only been implicit in previous disputes between Plekhanov and his rivals.[13]

These new recruits included men and women of considerable practical ability. Unaccustomed to the quiet solitude of life in exile, fresh from recent struggles against autocracy, they repeatedly implored the Group to publish pamphlets more relevant to current issues inside Russia. In the parlance of Russian Marxism, they begged the Group to shift its emphasis from propaganda to agitation: rather than train intellectuals for future struggles, the Group should involve the workers in current ones. Iulii Martov describes this attitude in memoirs written many years later: "We decided that the focus of our activity should be transferred to the sphere of agitation and that all propaganda and organizational work should be subordinated to this fundamental task. This implied agitation on the basis of the daily needs of the laboring masses which brought them into conflict with their employers."[14] The danger of this approach for a Marxist, however, was that an emphasis upon the immediate needs of the proletariat might cause Marxist goals and principles to be forgotten. Strikes and demonstrations inspired by demands for higher wages, shorter hours, and better working conditions might divert attention from the necessity of political revolution; if successful, such strikes might even deradicalize the Russian proletariat as the autocracy made concessions removing the ostensible causes of the workers' discontent.

Because they knew far less than Martov about recent strikes in the Vil'na-Minsk sections of Polish Russia, where workers combined such "economist" agitation with demands for changes in the political structure of society, Plekhanov and Axelrod could not feel very sanguine about any Social Democratic program that promised to satisfy the workers' most immediate needs.[15] Such a program seemed to them to smack of unconscionable opportunism and, in any event, could only delay the political radicalization of the proletariat. One only had to read the Group's program of 1885 to see that its authors openly acknowledged what Lenin later claimed in *What Is to Be Done?*—namely, that without the intervention of Marxist revolutionaries, workers could not advance beyond "trade-union consciousness" and perceive the advantages of socialism. Indeed, the very existence of the Group had been predicated on the assumption that, for the workers to perceive their long-term interests, theoretical works produced by Marxist revolutionaries were required. But Plekhanov and Axelrod were more disappointed than encouraged by this sudden upsurge of labor unrest in the late 1890's, for it suggested the hitherto unthinkable conclusion that even Marxist tracts might not be enough to convince the proletariat of its revolutionary obligations.

Something else that made "economist" agitation suspect from the vantage point of Russian socialists was the correspondence many of them maintained with leading socialists in Germany, England, and France. As the bacillus of Revisionism spread through Western Europe in the late 1890's, culminating in 1899 with the entry of a socialist into a bourgeois government in France, Plekhanov and Axelrod feared that this bacillus might infect the Russian proletariat as well, transforming it from a revolutionary vanguard into a participant in parliamentary elections offering a relatively painless—and wholly illusory—route to political power. Although Revisionism and Economism were two separate ideas, the former a phenomenon of highly industrialized societies, the latter a response to less developed ones, Plekhanov and Axelrod, in their trepidation, seemed to lump them together. With the publication of Bernstein's articles in *Die Neue Zeit* in 1898, both men felt themselves to be entering an ideological state of seige, as their carefully thought-out plan of slowly educating the workers to socialist consciousness was increasingly threatened by tactics which, if taken to their logical conclusions, seemed sure to lead to the deradicalization of the

Russian proletariat. Plekhanov wrote to Axelrod in April 1899: "The struggle against 'Bernsteinism' is the basic task of our movement. To the influence of our quasi-Marxists, we must oppose our influence as Marxist revolutionaries. . . . If you want to participate in the coming struggle, well and good. If not, I alone will follow the path which my duty as a revolutionary requires me to follow."[16]

Thus, neither Plekhanov nor Axelrod was especially amused when, in 1899, E. D. Kuskova, now a leader of the younger members of the Union, composed a "Credo" which denied entirely the utility of political struggle against the state. In the words of her manifesto: "The basic law that can be derived from the study of the labor movement is that it follows the path of least resistance. . . . Whereas in the West the weak forces of the workers were strengthened and consolidated after being drawn into political activity, in our country, on the contrary, these forces stand before a wall of political oppression."[17] Somewhat incongruously, Kuskova argued in this same Credo that Russian Marxists should collaborate openly with zemstvo liberals and participate in good faith in any parliament that might be created in the future. Lavish in its praise of Bernstein's "evolutionary socialism," this manifesto managed to combine an emphasis on economist agitation with a sympathy for parliamentary government.

This Credo was of course anathema to Plekhanov, whose own outline had a workers' party preparing for violent revolution at the very center of Social Democratic agitation, and it produced fits of apoplexy within the Group. In the spring of 1900 Plekhanov launched a vitriolic campaign against both Economism and Revisionism. Some of his remarks from the introduction to his polemic (entitled *Vademecum*) amply illustrate the anger with which the "Father of Russian Marxism" directed his verbal arrows against his "Sons": "The 'young comrades' regard themselves as representatives of a new direction in the Russian Social-Democratic movement but at the same time in this would-be trend there is neither socialism nor democracy." And again: "We have remained true to the sacred traditions of our revolutionary movement. We are proud of this, and shall always remain proud, however much this infuriates closed-minded pedants, political castrates, sophisticates of Marxism." Later on he asks: "And all these are comrades! And all these are Social Democrats! Is this not anarchy? Is this not chaos? Is this not infamy?"[18] Encouraged somewhat to find in Lenin someone of the younger generation equally repelled by Kuskova's apostasy, Plekhanov directed his energies in the next few months to the creation of a Social Democratic newspaper, the celebrated *Iskra*, whose readers he and Lenin hoped would eventually constitute the nucleus of a workers' party immune to these two ideological deviations. This was where matters stood until 1902, when Lenin and Plekhanov resumed their offensive against Economism and Revisionism.

Zasulich's reaction to this embroilment was in a way rather surprising, for it bore no sign of her usual tendency toward mediation. She was clearly on the side of Plekhanov, and indeed, with few exceptions, had never felt any great affection for the new generation of Russian Marxists. As early as 1893, when plans for a union of Social Democrats were first discussed, her opinion, as expressed in a letter to Axelrod, was that such a group would lack "true-believing" Social Democrats within its ranks.[19] Four years later she wrote Plekhanov that Prokopovich "values opinions only in so far as they help or harm his own activities"; and again, in 1898, she described Prokopovich as a "duplicitous rascal."[20] In a letter to Deich in 1899 she bemoaned the high incidence of "rogues and cheats" in the Union's membership; in a letter to Plekhanov she described as "dunces" those associated in St. Petersburg with *Rabochaia mysl'* (Workers' Thought), a newspaper of economist inclinations edited solely by younger Marxists.[21] Takhtarev was "a dunce and a dolt," and Ivanshin was enough to make her hair "stand on end."[22] Though all these remarks were leveled in private letters to Plekhanov, Axelrod, and Deich, her feelings, and those of her colleagues, were not kept to themselves, and Kuskova retaliated in kind in 1899 by referring to the members of the Group as "fossilized émigrés."[23]

Zasulich's unusual outspokenness on the subject of the younger generation of Marxists showed how much she, like Plekhanov and Axelrod, in a sense "cherished" her revolutionary past. The younger generation seemed to them to know little and care even less about the enormous sacrifices they had made in the previous decade creating a corpus of Marxist literature whose benefits only now were becoming apparent. In Zasulich's case too there seems to have been more than a passing recognition that the younger generation had the joie de vivre and youthful impetuosity which she herself had once had in happier days among the Iuzhnye Buntari. A letter she wrote to Deich in 1899 after the death of his wife shows an understanding of his loss and loneliness—which reflect her own:

Not to live alone, but with someone near and dear to you is a need felt by everyone. Family cannot always satisfy this need, but the camaraderie among friends certainly can. The older one gets, however, the more difficult it becomes to achieve this camaraderie, the less chance one has to cement friendships. People who have no blood relations almost always live alone, and it is as hard to come to terms with this as it is to become accustomed to hunger.[24]

Without overemphasizing the obvious, one can suggest that Zasulich, who was never outgoing, would naturally have clung loyally to her old friends Plekhanov and Axelrod in this clash with the younger generation, while still faintly envying the kind of political camaraderie and zest that seem possible only in youth.

In spite of these feelings, which were exacerbated when many of these young Marxists visited her in Zurich, Zasulich loyally agreed in 1897 to help Axelrod edit *Rabotnik* and *Listok rabotnika*. She and Axelrod plunged into the task, but when they earnestly tried to improve the quality of the manuscripts, which were mostly clumsily written and clumsily argued, they only managed to increase the tension. By 1898 both she and Axelrod were eager "to escape having to edit illiterate and semiliterate publications."[25] She wrote to Plekhanov in the spring of that year: "If only we could believe that our hard labor is of value to the Russian movement! But I am convinced it is not. What we have done so badly, [the younger Marxists] can do also."[26] The nearly fourteen months that Zasulich spent rewriting the essays submitted to the two journals convinced her that it would be best for everyone involved if she relinquished her position as co-editor.

Zasulich's decision was complicated by Plekhanov's wish that the Group should break irrevocably with the Union and relinquish not merely the editorial positions it controlled but also its membership in the organization. Besides being suspicious of the Union for what he considered its economist inclinations, Plekhanov was personally suspicious of Prokopovich and increasingly hostile to him. Prokopovich, far more than anyone of his generation, aspired to the role of Marxist theorist, and after he arrived in Switzerland in 1898 a clash between him and Plekhanov was only a matter of time. The clash came when Prokopovich had the temerity to criticize the Group's Draft Program of 1885, a document prepared almost entirely by Plekhanov.[27] Although Prokopovich concluded his critique with a plea for unity and mutual tolerance, the older man's response was to label him "an archswindler and a rogue," and to demand his expulsion from the Union.[28]

Zasulich, though she concurred in Plekhanov's low opinion of Prokopovich, perceived more clearly than her colleague the problems that such a drastic action might create and wrote at once to Plekhanov urging him to examine the situation "in historical context," and recognize that differences of opinion did not always imply that one's opponent was "bad." In many instances, she suggested, it was "simply a difference in years, understanding, and mood."[29] For all her contempt for the young generation, whose frequent calls for "economist" agitation she had dismissed in 1897 as "idiotic," Zasulich understood the balance of power within Russian Social Democracy.[30] In a second letter to Plekhanov, dated about two weeks later in May 1898, she dwelt at length on the balance of power that she realized was tipping against them:

For you reality is screened (and sometimes to madness) by a conception of what ought to be, but which is not. . . . You are wrong to think that there are only two fools against us, who need to be blasted away. Against us is virtually the entire younger generation in alliance with those elements of the students who are already acting or are getting ready to act seriously. They are full of energy; they feel that Russia is behind them. S. N. [Prokopovich] is not a serious problem. It is very probable that one could finish off his theoretical fantasies with one or two brochures. . . . But this general rise in the spirit against us is only outwardly connected with him. . . . A formal victory over our opponents in the Union is possible in one way or another, but it would be our greatest defeat.

She then discussed this conflict in a larger perspective:

We cannot carry out the function of the Union: to create a workers' literature. You say we cannot repudiate the cause for which we have worked for fifteen years. Yet in the last three years we have been doing entirely different work from that which we did in the preceding twelve. We could continue this work and I propose that we do so. But we cannot publish literature for the workers that would satisfy the demands of the Russians. And it appears to everyone that we are hampering those who can. . . . They will not achieve their ideal either, but they possess such an ideal and we do not. They have a thirst for activity of that kind but not under our direction. . . . We should simply declare that the results of our editing have not been brilliant, and that we will give our critics the opportunity to try their hand.[31]

A few months later, when Plekhanov, outraged by some real or imagined slight of his authority, demanded that the Group somehow "seize" the printing press of the Union, Zasulich retorted that that would be "an act of impotent malevolence"; the sad truth was that a split with the Union would only serve to illustrate the disparity between "our own unproductivity and the activity of the other group . . . one and one-half invalids (Pavel and I) against all the Social Democrats abroad."[32]

Zasulich's recommendation was matter-of-fact: that "we give the fresh faces complete autonomy." Rather than cause more dissension by all of them resigning from the Union, as Axelrod proposed, with a grand public chastisement of the members, she proposed that she and Axelrod simply divest themselves of their editorial responsibilities while still retaining their individual memberships; to do otherwise, she argued, would eliminate completely whatever influence the Group still possessed within the émigré community, and only isolate the group from Marxist circles still in existence inside Russia.[33] Acting on her own proposal, and with the assistance of Axelrod and Grishin, one of the few younger Marxists committed wholeheartedly to preserving good relations with the Group, Zasulich managed to convince Prokopovich not to publish his pamphlet attacking the Group's original program.[34] It is not known whether the quid pro quo for Prokopovich's concession was her resignation from her editorial positions, but she was true to her word in November 1898 when a congress of Union members convened in Zurich. At this congress Zasulich formally relinquished all responsibility for the publication of *Rabotnik* and *Listok rabotnika,* and also endorsed a proposed program for the Union which combined appeals for economist agitation with the affirmation that "the overthrow of autocracy" remained "the historical obligation" of Russian Social Democracy.[35]

Avoiding the extreme positions of both Plekhanov and Proko-povich, the program worked out with Zasulich's approval (Plekhanov and Axelrod were suspiciously absent when a vote was finally taken to endorse it) represented a triumph of sorts for the forces of compromise. Although Plekhanov's *Vademecum* in 1900 would eventually shatter whatever goodwill remained between the Group and the Union, the modus vivendi achieved in 1898 lasted long enough for Zasulich to devote the next few months to completing her essay on Pisarev, which she finally published in the spring of 1900.* Relinquishing her editorial positions helped to resolve some of the petty quarrels that had diverted her from tasks she considered potentially more reward-ing, and she could return secretly to St. Petersburg in the winter of 1899–1900 confident that her efforts to establish ties with Marxist circles there would not be undermined by internecine conflict back in Switzerland.[36]

This trip to Russia, after an exile of nearly twenty years, marked the end of one phase of Zasulich's mediation; from 1900 to 1903 she would be involved almost exclusively in reducing tensions between Plekhanov and Lenin (whom she now met for the first time). But before leaving this earlier phase behind, one must take note of Zasulich's feelings about the utility of econo-mist agitation—as distinct from her personal dislike of the youn-ger Marxists who espoused it. To be sure, Zasulich felt very strongly that agitation based entirely upon immediate demands would not ameliorate the workers' lack of political freedom; as she told Plekhanov in February 1898, she objected to Proko-

---

* In this period between 1898 and 1900 the Union transformed *Listok rabot-nika* into an explicitly economist journal entitled *Rabochee delo* (Workers' Cause). When Plekhanov attacked the Union for this, Zasulich wrote him a letter, begin-ning "My Dear Lord Beast," in which she asked him why he "embittered and abused good comrades." Letter, Zasulich to Plekhanov (undated; 1899), Deich, ed., *Gruppa 'Osvobozhdenie Truda,'* vol. 6, p. 240.

povich's notion that "under present conditions the workers can, by strikes alone, achieve the prosperity and political rights which the Russian bourgeoisie has already achieved."[37] In a similar vein she complained to Plekhanov a few months later that the articles she read in the economist-minded *Rabochaia mysl'* "could just as well have been written in the Ministry of the Interior."[38] If, by economism, one means the notion that agitation based on imme-diate needs could result in the granting of political rights, then surely at no time was Zasulich its proponent.

Like so many other terms in the revolutionary lexicon, how-ever, economism could be defined in many ways. As an epithet its meanings were numerous, its boundaries elastic. Zasulich's criticisms of economism are intriguing because, depending upon how one chooses to define it, she can very easily be de-scribed as its advocate. If, by economism, one means the convic-tion that agitation based on immediate needs could increase the political consciousness of the proletariat, possibly even to the point where workers would want to enlist in a socialist party, then Zasulich was indeed an economist. In 1897, at precisely the moment when she was condemning as "idiotic" the economism of *Rabochaia mysl'*, she wrote a brief paean to the Morozov strike of 1885 in which she applauded demands clearly "economist" in nature.[39] When workers in the Morozov textile works near Mos-cow staged a walkout in January 1885, they issued a proclama-tion demanding a shorter work day, prompt payment of wages, and the elimination of fines for trivial infractions of the labor codes. Praising this demonstration as an example of agitation at its best, Zasulich argued in her tribute that, with the assistance of groups such as the St. Petersburg Union of Struggle, compara-ble strikes in the future—like the Morozov strike in 1885—were bound to elevate the political consciousness of the workers who would take part in them. In this tribute she commended the Union of Struggle, composed largely of students and intellectu-als, for having "printed according to the dictates of the workers all the grievances of the workers against the factory owners, all the details of the employers' malpractices, all their malicious tricks and deceptions. . . . All this information was printed in leaflets distributed among the workers, urging them to defend themselves against these malpractices." As a result of such activities on behalf of the workers, "by the winter of 1896 the labor question already confronted the government in all its force, and by the summer of 1896, the entire world was speaking about the Russian workers' movement."[40]

The clear implication of Zasulich's article is that it was not only permissible, but even tactically advisable for socialists to assist workers in any agitation they should undertake on behalf of their immediate needs. In her opinion, economist agitation would not produce a favorable response from the autocracy; Prokopovich's economism was suspect precisely because he claimed that it would. Zasulich was more concerned with raising consciousness than with extracting concessions; it did not matter that strikes for higher wages and lower hours were unsuccessful, because the very act of involving workers in agitation for economic changes would make them cognizant of their lack of political freedom, and thus receptive to Marxist propaganda advocating the violent overthrow of autocracy. In retrospect, her position seems largely indistinguishable from that expressed in 1894 in a celebrated pamphlet entitled *Ob Agitatsii* (On Agitation):

The struggle incited by agitation [based on existing demands and needs] will teach the workers to defend their interests; it will raise their fortitude; it will give them a confidence in their forces, a confidence in the indispensability of unity; and it will confront them in the end with the more important questions which require resolution. Prepared in this way for a more serious struggle, the working class will proceed to the solution of its basic problems.[41]

Economist agitation, in other words, was not an end in itself but rather a vehicle by which the workers would come to realize that behind their employers stood the political system—with its whips, its policemen, and its prisons—that was the ultimate source of their misery. Possibly because by 1897 Zasulich had already formulated an answer of sorts to Bernstein's Revisionism, she could endorse without fear of inconsistency a position clearly "economist" in nature—and retain sufficient confidence in the orthodoxy of her views to ignore their apparent similarity to those of people such as Prokopovich whom she disliked. Provided one makes clear the fine, but very real, distinction between Zasulich's and Prokopovich's Economism, one can understand how she could simultaneously advocate economist agitation while condemning it when espoused in slightly different form by her opponents.

Zasulich's trip to Russia at the turn of the century, though limited to only three months' duration by the omnipresent threat of arrest, was a successful and happy one. Much of the depression she had suffered in London and in Switzerland miraculously vanished as she saw many of the people and places which had become ever fainter memories: in April 1900, when the police realized that she was traveling on a false passport supplied by the Rumanian revolutionary Christian Rakovskii, she wept at the prospect of going into exile once again. But during the period she spent in Russia she was also able to meet and evaluate other revolutionaries, including Lenin and Martov, whom Plekhanov and Axelrod hoped to recruit as editors of a journal to be published abroad by the Group.[42] This journal was intended to serve as the nucleus for a socialist party that would replace the one that disintegrated when the nine men who had founded it in Minsk in 1898 were immediately arrested.* Because she had been in England when Lenin made his first trip to Geneva in 1895, Zasulich was only now, in 1900, able to exchange ideas face to face with the man whom she would denounce four years later as the Russian equivalent of Louis XIV.

In the light of subsequent developments, it is perhaps surprising that Zasulich's first impressions of Lenin were generally favorable—and even more surprising, perhaps, that the affection Zasulich felt for Lenin was reciprocated. On her journey back to Zurich by way of Sweden and Germany she wrote to Plekhanov that Lenin was "not only orthodox, but what is more, a Plekhanovite"; a few months later she remarked to Plekhanov

---

* The manifesto that Struve wrote for this abortive party in some respects echoed Zasulich's argument of 1890 that the Russian bourgeoisie was incapable of leading the struggle for political freedom in Russia. But whereas Struve ascribed this phenomenon to the Russian bourgeoisie's numerical and political insignificance, Zasulich, in her "Revoliutsionery iz burzhuaznoi sredy," attributed it to what she saw as the desire of the bourgeoisie to elicit the political and economic protection of the government against workers inclined to question the basis of its power and privileges. Struve's manifesto is reprinted in Richard Pipes, *Struve: Liberal on the Left, 1870–1905* (Cambridge, Mass., 1970), pp. 193–96.

that "with his rough originality, Lenin pleases me."[43] Lenin, for his part, had read some of Zasulich's writings, most recently her attacks on the populists and her biography of Rousseau, and found nothing in them to make him doubt her dedication to Marxist principles.[44] In 1900 he described as "excellent" her analysis of Pisarev's philosophy; to Krupskaia, his wife, he affirmed that "Zasulich is true to the core," and reiterated his belief that "she is a woman of uncommon sincerity unswervingly loyal to the cause."[45] Finally, it bears repeating that in 1900 Zasulich and Lenin shared the perception that the working class in Russia still lacked sufficient political consciousness to determine its interests, and as a consequence would have to look to Marxist intellectuals for guidance. Only over the next several years would the two come to recognize the nuances that differentiated their positions.

However, despite these apparent similarities in their views, Zasulich returned to Switzerland in the summer of 1900 skeptical of Lenin's almost maniacal insistence (shared by Plekhanov and Axelrod without the same fanaticism) that only Social Democrats untainted by the heresies of Economism and Revisionism should publish this newspaper which would secure the allegiance of all Marxists groups in Russia. Such restrictions, she feared, would embroil her and her colleagues in the same petty arguments that had been resolved only with great difficulty at the congress of the Union in 1898.[46] Moreover, speaking from her dreadful experience editing émigré publications, Zasulich expressed a great reluctance to take on the thankless role of editor once again, even though she was to share the task on *Iskra* with Plekhanov, Axelrod, Martov, Lenin, and Potresov.

Nevertheless, Zasulich was extremely pleased that Lenin and Martov were prepared to collaborate with the Group, and she took special precautions to preserve this new-found harmony among the six prospective editors of *Iskra*. From her correspondence one senses that she had little inkling of the close relationship between Lenin and Martov, and therefore felt it necessary to warn them that they should not allow any issue to divide them, especially if they should also find themselves at odds with Plekhanov. But when Lenin arrived in Geneva in August, it became abundantly clear that the individuals most likely to disagree were not Lenin and Martov but Plekhanov and Lenin. Almost immediately after his arrival Lenin was shocked to learn that Plekhanov had no intention of heeding his suggestion that the pages of *Iskra* should be open to contributions expressing non-Marxist views—so that the editors could then publicly point out their fallacies. Ironically, the man who after 1903 would personify the tactic of "splitting," posed in 1900 as a champion of open access to the press—and threatened to resign from *Iskra* even before the first issue was under way because he objected to Plekhanov's "Leninist" insistence that former Marxists such as Struve and Tugan-Baranovskii should be denied the opportunity to contribute to it.[47] Several years later the two men would reverse their positions, but in 1900 Lenin was so perturbed by what he found to be the older man's pomposity and condescension that he uncharacteristically vented his disillusionment in print:

My infatuation with Plekhanov disappeared as if by magic. . . . Never, never in my life have I regarded any other man with such sincere respect and veneration. I have never stood before any man with such humility as I stood before him, and never before have I been so brutally spurned. . . . When a man whom we desire to cooperate with intimately resorts to chess moves dealing with comrades, there can be no doubt of the fact that he is a bad man, yes, a bad man, inspired by petty motives of personal vanity and conceit—an insincere man. Good-bye journal! We will throw everything away and return to Russia.[48]

As things stood in August 1900, the plan to publish a permanent Marxist newspaper appeared to have been stymied by a specific disagreement between Plekhanov and Lenin greatly exacerbated by purely personal antagonism.

That this disagreement was settled amicably was in large measure the result of efforts by Zasulich and Axelrod to mollify these two proud and often difficult men. Zasulich herself probably tended toward Lenin's position, since the year before she had remarked to Deich (in one of the last letters she wrote to him before he escaped to America) that the heresies of former Marxists such as Struve and Tugan-Baranovskii "infuriate Georgii but not me."[49] In the interest of unity, Zasulich kept her feelings to herself and concentrated on securing a truce between Plekhanov and Lenin, but the consequences of failure evidently weighed very heavily on her mind, for we have the testimony of Potresov and Lenin that they both feared she would commit suicide if the break between Lenin and Plekhanov proved irremediable.[50]

In the course of highly charged negotiations, Plekhanov complicated matters greatly by announcing that, no matter how the other editors might decide the question of accepting contributions from former Marxists, he himself would refuse to serve in any editorial capacity. Since, without Plekhanov, the entire enterprise was probably bound to fail, Lenin and Potresov pleaded with their older colleague not to repudiate his commitment—which may have been the kind of deference Plekhanov was trying to draw out. Properly mollified, Plekhanov now extracted his part of the bargain: he inquired how Lenin and Potresov proposed to resolve disagreements if the six prospective editors should find themselves evenly divided with no way of resolving a 3–3 tie. Again, the negotiations seemed on the brink of collapse, but Zasulich made a felicitous suggestion: that, in view of his seniority and long years of service to the revolutionary cause, Plekhanov be given an additional and potentially tie-breaking vote.* Pleased with Zasulich's proposal, to which the other prospective editors added their approval, Plekhanov promptly agreed to Lenin's demand that, if Plekhanov were given an extra vote, *Iskra* should be published somewhere other than in Switzerland, so as to reduce Plekhanov's control over its daily operations. Owing in great measure to Zasulich's intervention, Lenin departed amicably enough a few weeks later, convinced that Plekhanov's potential power was no greater than his own.† Although the few weeks they spent together in August 1900 caused each man to view the other with a suspiciousness which, in 1903, would lead to the severance of personal relations, Plekhanov and Lenin remained on their best behavior for two years following the publication of the first number of *Iskra* in Munich in December 1900.

---

* Bertram Wolfe, *Three Who Made a Revolution* (New York, 1948), p. 150. Though Lenin was understandably suspicious, there is no evidence that Zasulich offered her suggestion at the prompting of Plekhanov.

† One historian has speculated that, had it not been for Zasulich's mediation, the entire *Iskra* enterprise might have collapsed. See Pipes, *Struve*, p. 258.

Under this arrangement, *Iskra* proved in some ways to be the most successful of the numerous journals published by Russian émigrés and exiles. In circulation it surpassed even Herzen's *Kolokol* (The Bell).[51] Even the unfortunate tendency of *Iskra*'s agitators to let the workers in Russia suffer the consequences of strikes and work stoppages that they had themselves inspired did not seriously weaken *Iskra*'s reputation for thoroughness, integrity, and honesty. The lucidity of its prose, the regularity of its twice-weekly publication, and the depth (if not always the breadth) of its ideological commitment assured *Iskra*'s readers of information which, though perhaps biased in its reportage, was at least there to read and often was entirely absent in journals published by the government. Not all the copies reached Russia—some issues were lost entirely or succumbed to mildew in the course of being smuggled in, frequently in double-bottomed suitcases, by way of Germany—but enough reached their intended destination for the editors to consider the entire enterprise a political, if not exactly a financial, success.[52]

Temporarily freed from her role as mediator, Zasulich was able to find time in 1901 and in the first few months of 1902 to contribute articles to *Iskra* and also to *Zaria* (The Dawn), the journal devoted mainly to Marxist theory published less frequently but at regular intervals by the *Iskra* staff. Probably the most interesting point of these articles is the return to public criticism of political terrorism. Prompted by the assassination of the Minister of Education, Bogolepov, Zasulich in an essay in *Iskra* in April 1901 reiterated her previously stated objections to terrorism; the only addition to her litany of arguments was that, in its reliance upon a small elite to transform society, terrorism reduced the remaining citizenry to political passivity, no more a participant in the process of revolution than they were in determining government policy in an autocracy.[53] Zasulich's main charge, following a description of Bogolepov's assassination, was this:

to transfer the struggle for emancipation to a handful of heroes, no matter how superhuman their prowess, not only does not harm the autocracy, but is itself a consequence of the feelings and ideas inherited from autocracy. The servants of autocracy are inclined to think that all the business of the country, its laws, and its institutions depend entirely

on the higher authorities—in principle on one man—and these servants can, on their own initiative, only shout "hurrah." But if the parti-
sans of freedom invest all their hopes in a handful of heroes, and
thereby leave behind only the very same "hurrah" in the depth of the
soul or in a conversation with friends—is this really not a legacy of
autocracy?[54]

Because its modus operandi was conducive to authoritarianism,
political terrorism in Russia was, Zasulich argued, no more than
a substitution of one form of tyranny for another. Though in
the late 1870's and early 1880's, terrorism was understandable,
if rarely ever justified, as a reflection of political despair, by 1900
mass discontent was so obvious that to concentrate one's energies on terrorism was, in Zasulich's opinion, not only morally
wrong but politically foolish.

An article Zasulich published in *Iskra* in 1901 castigated the
liberal press for ascribing humanistic motives to the government; she entitled her article "A Eulogy to *Moskovskie vedomosti*"
because, as a mouthpiece of political reaction, this journal at
least gave its readers a true picture of what autocracy was like.[55]
But Zasulich's public criticism of Russian liberals was not intended to alienate them from Russian socialism. Rather, it was
intended to make them realize that socialists and liberals could
not attain the political freedom they both desired without establishing some kind of alliance. If liberals and socialists could only
recognize the degree to which their goals coincided, Zasulich
argued, then there need not be any repetition of conflicts such as
that in 1900 between Plekhanov and Struve, when the question
of whether Struve and other liberals could properly contribute
articles to Marxist journals was allowed to obscure the many
points of agreement that she claimed to see between liberalism
and socialism. The fact that socialists, by her own admission,
would be obliged to turn against the liberals once the bourgeois
revolution had been consummated seems not to have diminished her belief that liberals and socialists could work together
on a basis of mutual trust.[56]

In the summer of 1901 Zasulich was also successful in getting
Lenin to tone down the strident rhetoric with which he had
attacked Struve for his ideological heresy and what Lenin
thought were his attempts to insinuate his liberalism into *Iskra,*

Zaria, and a third Marxist journal, not yet in print, to be devoted to topics even more theoretical than those reserved for *Zaria.*[57] Characteristically, Zasulich coupled her assertion that Struve, as a prominent revolutionary intellectual, should not be needlessly antagonized with an affirmation of his personal and political integrity—a defense so impassioned that Struve would write rather extravagantly in 1934 that Zasulich felt toward Lenin "an antipathy verging on physical revulsion."[58] Struve, in her view, was still in 1901 very much a member of this larger fraternity of men and women whose services to the cause of revolution, past and present, were such that attacks on their integrity could not be tolerated. Criticizing liberals as a group in 1901 did not prevent Zasulich, as a matter of principle and in the interest of revolutionary unity, from defending individual liberals such as Struve against the polemics of Social Democrats such as Lenin.

However, the most important essays that Zasulich published between 1900 and 1902 were her analysis of Pisarev's philosophy and social ethics and her article on "Women in the Revolutionary Movement," first published in *Gleichheit,* an official organ of the German Social Democratic Party.[59] The article on women, written in the form of an open letter to Klara Zetkin, is of particular interest because it is the only expression in print of Zasulich's feelings about the emancipation of women, an issue of considerable importance within the Russian intelligentsia.[60] In this essay she laments the paucity of female workers in Russia inclined to participate in movements attempting to achieve the emancipation of women but says that this in itself is hardly cause for despair, for in revolutionary circles women were generally accorded the equality that they could find in no other sphere of Russian life. Indeed, female revolutionaries suffered the same hardships, endured the same punishments, and made the same sacrifices that men did, experiencing the same moral and intellectual transformation that benefits everyone, male and female, who participates in revolutionary endeavor: "Women are taking upon themselves those same revolutionary obligations that men undertake, and like them they are acquiring the qualities without which it would be impossible to fulfill these obligations. And according to the widely held opinion, the 'weak' woman thus is becoming a strong one, as was clearly revealed in the struggle of the seventies."[61] In the hardships and demands that it imposes, revolutionary work serves to destroy the old shibboleths about women as inherently "weak," and also indicates that women are surely equal to men in their capacity for heroism and self-sacrifice:

Constant ties between women of the intelligentsia and the working masses would gradually eradicate among male and female workers the prevailing prejudice about the lesser worth of women. The prejudice which considers a woman by nature more foolish, weaker, and more cowardly than a man must disappear, as well as the view that a woman by nature is incapable of public activity and that, because of this, only domestic obligations, not public ones, must fall on her.[62]

Because she believed that revolutionary struggle is in itself conducive to moral virtue, Zasulich was confident in predicting that "the Russian workers' movement will be supported also by numerous women workers and by workers' wives, conscious that besides their family obligations, they also bear responsibility for the welfare of their class comrades and society, and that this responsibility impels them to struggle for freedom of press, assembly, and elections, for the workers' defense, and for the victory of the socialist order." So, she concludes: "Inevitably the time will draw near when even in Russia a large army of female proletarians together with the proletariat of the entire world will achieve 'the first of May' by their indomitable will."[63]

In some ways this article is more significant in what it fails to say than in what it contains. Though Zasulich was sensitive to the discrimination against women in prerevolutionary Russia, at no point in the article does she propose the creation of a movement or party devoted solely to the advancement of women's rights; nor does she argue, as did Alexandra Kollontai and other socialist feminists of her generation, that the problems of working class women were different enough from those of working class men to warrant institutions within socialist parties established specifically for the purpose of solving them.[64] Presumably such institutions would be politically divisive and destructive of the camaraderie between men and women that develops through collective endeavor.

For very clear reasons, Zasulich believed that in Russia women

should participate in socialist rather than purely feminist movements because in Russia—quite unlike the situation in Western
Europe and America—the rights denied to women were denied
also to men; female revolutionaries in Russia, in contrast to the
suffragists in England and America, were fighting for human
rights, not just for women's rights. Only by participating in a
common effort to rid Russia of an autocracy that oppressed
them both could men and women hope to establish a true socialist society in which all forms of discrimination—sexual as well as
economic and political—were nonexistent. Organizations such
as the Society for the Mutual Help of Working Women, which
Zasulich addressed shortly after her return to Russia in 1905,
were only "superfluous enterprises" which diverted attention
from the overriding struggle for socialism.[65]

Indeed, Zasulich was very much against feminism per se, believing it to be not merely pointless but positively harmful to
women in the context of Russian politics. In this respect, Zasulich's opinion differed little from that of female socialists such as
Kollontai, Krupskaia, and Inessa Armand. Although Zasulich
did not go as far as Rosa Luxemburg in contending that, for an
economic determinist, a "woman's question" was an ideological
non sequitur, she shared with Kollontai, Armand, and Krupskaia the conviction that a resolution of this question could only
be a concomitant of a revolution in economic relations. However
strongly she disagreed with these women on the role of women's
groups within revolutionary movements, she was in complete
agreement with their conviction that economic equality was a
prerequisite of sexual equality.[66]

Nonetheless, it is pretty clear that the emancipation of women
was hardly uppermost in Zasulich's mind. Unlike revolutionary
women such as Kollontai, who considered political revolution
merely the prelude to a transformation of social and sexual
mores, Zasulich, despite her bohemian ways, seemed content
with the fairly conventional pattern of sexual behavior that she
encountered among her fellow revolutionaries, and probably
believed that such patterns would continue uninterrupted by
any political or economic revolution. If, as Zasulich maintained,
socialist parties were really socialist societies in microcosm, then

there was little reason to believe that the sexual and social mores one found in these parties should be changed with the establishment of socialism.

Another reason, less abstract and intellectual, for Zasulich's relative unconcern about female emancipation may have been her reluctance to jeopardize personal relationships from which she derived considerable gratification. One doubts very much, for example, whether Kollontai or Armand would have suffered the benevolent domination that Zasulich usually was willing to endure from Plekhanov and, to a lesser extent, from Axelrod and Deich. But Zasulich, except on rare occasions, tolerated this condescension possibly because it implied a genuine understanding—more implicit than expressed perhaps—for her numerous physical and psychological ailments. Under the circumstances, she was probably unwilling—and very probably also psychologically disinclined—to ponder the very real possibility that the condescension bore more than a tinge of latent chauvinism among revolutionary men which ought not to have any part in a perfect socialist world.

The other important essay of the 1900–1902 period, the analysis of Pisarev's philosophy, though perhaps less interesting to us today, is more typical of the kind of writing that Zasulich liked to do, and it indicates her readiness to defend against unwarranted criticism writers whom she considered precursors of the socialism she espoused. Whereas most of what Plekhanov and Lenin wrote dealt with subjects of a contemporary nature, roughly half of what Zasulich produced consisted of biographical and historical studies, mostly about individuals such as Rousseau and Pisarev, and institutions such as the International, which she considered effective in creating a revolutionary tradition upon which revolutionaries could draw for legitimacy, inspiration, and ideological guidance. If these writings, by and large, do little to elucidate the ideologies she espoused, they have the virtue, by their very existence, of reminding one how much revolutionaries like Zasulich used history to justify, to rationalize, and to explain the various political and ideological choices that they made.

In the case of Pisarev, Zasulich's principal objective was to demonstrate that his philosophy was more than mere diatribes against art and aesthetics, and that literary critics did him a disservice when they said that he lacked compassion for the underprivileged in society. In Zasulich's opinion, most analyses of Pisarev's philosophy concentrated too much on the works he wrote before he went to prison in 1862, and too little on what he produced during the four years that he spent there. She saw two distinct phases in his intellectual development: an early one, which fully justified the charge that he was a mere "preacher of unbridledness," and a later one, when he repudiated the goals of his youth and emphasized instead the individual's obligations to society.[67] In this long, rambling, often repetitive essay of some eighty pages, Zasulich returns again and again to the radical transformation in Pisarev's social ethics, seeking to place him in the same tradition of radical thought which produced Belinskii, Chernyshevskii, and Dobroliubov.

Having established this fundamental division in Pisarev's intellectual evolution, Zasulich does her best to sort out the many misconceptions surrounding Pisarev's idea—"the alpha and omega" of his social ethics—that the aim of political activity should be the creation of "critically thinking individuals."[68] Zasulich argues that Pisarev did not mean by this a complete denial of political revolution, or a repudiation of efforts to assist the lower classes in their struggle for education and enlightenment. Rather, what Pisarev envisioned when he called for the proliferation of "critically thinking individuals" was an elite of socially conscious intellectuals doing everything in their power to bridge the gap between intellectual and manual labor, bringing to the lower classes the education and enlightenment that, because of the backward state of Russian education, they had no possibility of obtaining on their own. This, in Zasulich's opinion was what Pisarev had in mind in this passage in his 1864 essay, "The Realists":

In the beginning, other people worked for me, but now I must work for others. I still belong to that society which molded me. All the forces of my mind constitute the result of someone else's labor, and if I should squander these forces on various pleasant follies, then I shall turn out to be an insolvent debtor and fraudulently bankrupt . . . an enemy of that same society to which I am totally obligated for everything. . . . When you arrive at such serious conclusions, then an aimless enjoyment of life, science, and art turns out to be impossible. There remains only one enjoyment—that which comes from a clear recognition that you are bringing genuine benefits to people, that you are paying little by little the mass of your debt which has accumulated, and that, with firm steps, not swerving either to the right or to the left, you are going forward toward the general goal of your entire life.[69]

Pisarev denied the social utility of art, Zasulich argues, not because he lacked the aesthetic sensibility to appreciate a melodious song, an engrossing novel, or a lyrical poem. Pisarev was neither a nihilist nor a cultural boor; he simply felt that artistic endeavor, if misdirected, induces political passivity. In a country as culturally backward as Russia, artists and intellectuals should not squander their energies producing works which only they can understand; therefore if Pisarev insisted that a pair of boots was worth more than the entire corpus of Pushkin's writings, Zasulich probably demurred only in her belief that Pushkin (and other writers of comparable stature) could indeed be rendered comprehensible to the masses. According to Zasulich, Pisarev believed that the principal obligation of the educated elite was "to act for the laboring masses," and it followed that if Pisarev felt that the way to do this was to develop one's critical faculties to their fullest extent, this was not to be interpreted as showing a lack of political consciousness.[70] By turning inward, men were simply preparing themselves for the time when the knowledge and critical insights they had accumulated would be utilized in the struggle for the intellectual and political emancipation of the masses:

It seemed to Pisarev that when he wrote ["The Realists"], in the absence of a demand for knowledge from the masses themselves, and given the infinitesimal number of "thinking individuals" in Russia, these few individuals would do more for the enlightenment of the masses if, for a time, they were occupied, as it were, in "self-reproduction," with the creation of an army of intellectuals drawn from the educated and semi-educated classes. This would be preferable to concentrating one's forces at this time on a philanthropically inspired instruction of grammar in schools for the general public. But, once the people begin to demand knowledge, this instruction will proceed very rapidly. . . . To awaken social opinion and to create critically thinking leaders of popular labor means to indicate to the laboring majority the road to a broad and fruitful intellectual development.[71]

One quickly sees here that part of Pisarev's appeal was his conception of the intelligentsia—at least as Zasulich interpreted him—as having a primarily pedagogical role in society. Pisarev, Zasulich explained, was sufficiently imbued with the utilitarian notion of "wise selfishness" (which Zasulich always seemed to confuse with self-sacrifice) to consider acting on one's own behalf a means of increasing the happiness of others. Thus, far from being the mindless iconoclast depicted in the accounts of hostile critics, Pisarev was actually a social altruist and, like Rousseau, a proto-socialist in his desire to eliminate the existing inequalities in society. Not surprisingly, this placement of Pisarev within a revolutionary teleology that included Rousseau at one end and Russian Marxism at the other has won the plaudits of Soviet historians such as R. A. Kovnator, who praises Zasulich for having done more than any other Russian socialist "to further the restoration of Pisarev's genuine ideological-political cast of mind."[72]

It is not surprising that Soviet historians familiar with Zasulich's writings do not view as favorably her critique of philosophical idealism, which she wrote for *Zaria* while living in Munich in 1901–2. This essay, "Elements of Idealism in Socialism," attacked the philosophy and social ethics of Nikolai Berdiaev, a recent convert from Marxism to an idealism fashionable in intellectual circles which, in the words of Struve, attempted "to inject a valuable moral content into the social-political ideal of the proletariat."[73] Berdiaev ultimately embraced Russian Orthodoxy as most congenial to his idiosyncratic concept of "creative freedom," but there was a phase in his intellectual evolution when his idealism was still entirely secular.

Berdiaev had at one point adopted but later repudiated a materialism which he considered the principal flaw in Marxist theory: in its emphasis upon the material origin of all ideas, Marxism lacked ethical content, so that its proponents had to determine the moral value of an action solely by its momentary utility in the struggle to achieve a socialist revolution. In Berdiaev's view, Marxists such as Zasulich and Plekhanov were actually engaged in disseminating an ethic of hedonistic self-enrichment which he claimed was identical to the "*burzhuaznost'*" that socialists were ostensibly determined to eradicate. According to

Berdiaev, the fulfillment of man's creative potential, the establishment of man's supremacy over nature, the elimination of all
barriers between intellectual and manual labor, and all the other
goals of Marxism would be rendered unattainable by the vulgar
and philosophical materialism that Russian socialists espoused
while attempting to achieve these ends.[74]

Berdiaev proposed instead that socialists redirect their energies to what he termed "the perfection of the individual personality." Man, in Berdiaev's view, was an end in himself, and the
political system in Russia blunted, but could not entirely eradicate his moral and creative potential. It was therefore only logical that in view of the difficulty of reforming social and political
institutions, revolutionaries could best serve their altruistic impulses by espousing the virtues of inner moral transformation;
only after this spiritual regeneration was complete would it be
possible—and morally permissible—to attempt to transform society. In Marx's scheme, changes in human nature could only be
the result of changes in man's environment; in Berdiaev's, this
sequence was reversed: man's environment could be altered legitimately only after he had rediscovered his spirituality.

What makes Zasulich's rebuttal so distinctive in comparison
with those of other Marxists is the utilitarian phraseology she
employed to embellish it. To Berdiaev's claim that Marxists have
no genuine system of ethics, Zasulich replied that whether they
do or not is irrelevant, because the only moral principle Marxists
require is what she refers to as *solidarnost'*, the notion that, if
necessary, one must sacrifice one's personal fortunes for the
greater good of society. Happily enough, serving society is almost always in one's personal interest, but in cases where one
can distinguish "individual" and "collective" happiness, there is
no doubt that the Marxist should prefer one to the other. In a
lengthy footnote Zasulich explicitly acknowledged what she
thought was this utilitarian morality in Marxism:

As far as I know, Marxism has no official system of morality. But it is
clear that Social Democrats and all those who struggle on behalf of the
proletariat have one all-embracing demand: solidarity. Not doing anything contrary to the general good is the minimum demand of solidarity;
doing everything one can for the general good, not sparing anything

personal for it, if necessary, even dying for it, is the maximum. . . . This is undoubtedly a utilitarian morality. What defines this demand is the general welfare, to which the fate of the individual's is inextricably joined.[75]

Zasulich found Berdiaev's social ethics—or more precisely his lack of them—so appalling not because she considered man's moral perfection ignoble or wrong; such a goal she even applauded when she perceived it—in the writings of Pisarev, for example—as the first step toward the transformation of society. But when espoused by Berdiaev, this ethic of self-perfection had become an end in itself, an easy substitute for the more important and far more difficult task of increasing the general sum of happiness in society. With considerable emotion she accepted Berdiaev's contention that Russia was intellectually backward, but maintained that the cause of this was something other than the vulgar materialism that Berdiaev had condemned:

It is true that now there is just as little concern for beauty as there is for truth, for social interest, for friendship, or for life in the purely human meaning of this word. The market struggle, which absorbs all spiritual forces, pushes aside and perverts all the higher human needs. It perverts even the means of their satisfaction, overcrowding the market with substitutes for truth and beauty and all things that by their very essence the market struggles and valuations do not nurture—and that can develop freely only above an economic level of existence which satisfies the lowest and most basic needs.[76]

Dismissing Berdiaev's idealism as an excuse for doing nothing to further the cause of social justice, Zasulich affirmed instead what she termed a "practical"—as opposed to a purely metaphysical— idealism which she said was possible "only when the individual merges his own personality with the general good, the common revolutionary cause."[77] Virtue itself, she wrote in her biography of Rousseau, consists of "the submission of personal interests to the interests of society."[78]

To be sure, what Zasulich defined in 1902 as utilitarianism was really nothing more than social altruism, an ethos that in its emphasis upon self-sacrifice directly contradicts the notion in utilitarianism that to advance one's personal interest is to advance the interests of society as well. Zasulich, in her enthusiasm, confused the two. But if one defines utilitarianism simply as an ethical imperative requiring people to work for the general welfare without concern for their personal interest, then Zasulich, in a manner of speaking, was a utilitarian. And what Zasulich's "utilitarianism" lacked in intellectual exactitude was more than offset by the attraction it had for individuals like Zasulich who felt guilty about their advantages in wealth and education and believed that such things should be more equitably distributed. Defined simply as a concern for the general welfare, utilitarianism became for Zasulich not only a means by which she could make her altruism intellectually respectable, but also a legitimate defense of her conversion to Marxism. Just as she had in 1890 when she tried to find an appropriate substitute for the "missing bourgeoisie," so, too, in 1902 did Zasulich distort a word beyond recognition in an effort to express intellectually convictions about the necessity of self-sacrifice that were really more emotional than intellectual in their genesis.

If nothing else, "Elements of Idealism in Socialism" demonstrates that Zasulich was a socialist because she found in socialism the best expression of what she defined as a utilitarian ideal. Whereas capitalism, in her opinion, openly encouraged self-enrichment, socialism would enable man to work for the general welfare without regarding his labor as a sacrifice of his personal interest; indeed, in Marx's system, the distinction between individual and collective happiness would disappear as economic forces creating conflict are eliminated. With his interests finally identical to his neighbors', man would live in a state of perpetual peace, secure in the knowledge that the elimination of private property and the profit motive made possible the fulfillment of all material and spiritual needs. With the awkward eloquence she displayed when writing about subjects she considered especially significant, Zasulich described the socialist utopia:

The socio-psychological and ethical significance of the replacement of the contemporary order by the socialist consists in the emancipation of people from anxieties concerning their personal or family welfare. It consists in the abolition of the degrading struggle among people for bread and for contentment, in the emancipation of the soul from the fear of tomorrow's hunger. It consists, consequently, in the destruction not only of the necessity but even of the very possibility of transforming the securing of personal satisfaction . . . into the supreme aim and highest value of life.[79]

Although manual labor would remain obligatory under socialism, the time spent performing such labor would be minimized sufficiently so that no one would lack the opportunity to realize his creative potential. Freed from the need to secure the material necessities of life, man could finally experience the satisfaction of intellectual accomplishment, cognizant that his efforts would benefit not only himself but society as well. To Zasulich the creation of a socialist society meant that after years of economic exploitation, when the perpetual struggle for survival made intellectual endeavor impossible, "man could at last make his own history."[80]

Having said this, Zasulich felt compelled to explain why some people more than others could develop the civic consciousness that she considered both a prerequisite and a concomitant of socialism; for a Marxist this meant explaining why only the proletariat should be qualified to make a socialist revolution. According to Zasulich, the proletariat was different from other classes, past and present, in that it had no reason to develop an ethic of self-aggrandizement. Because the fruits of the worker's labor were returned to him only after a significant portion had been extracted in the form of "surplus value," for the worker to contemplate personal enrichment was, in her words, "comparable to participating in a lottery without a ticket."[81] In contrast to the bourgeoisie and the peasants, who devoted their energies to protecting their interests, the worker quickly lost all incentive to advance his interests at the expense of his neighbors'; only the workers, in other words, could advance what Rousseau a century earlier had termed "the general will." And yet, though industrial labor tied the body of the workers to his employer, "his mind and emotions remained free . . . to concentrate on wider, more general concerns than all the complicated needs of independent producers."[82] Because his labor precluded the accumulation of wealth, the worker had the capacity to develop an ethos of collective solidarity and a consciousness of the general welfare without which no group of individuals could ever coalesce in a political party or movement committed to the transformation of society. Accordingly, as an ideology of revolution, "socialism can be a goal only of the party of the proletariat and can be realized only by the proletariat itself. This is not only because the socialist order is for the proletariat its only escape from its unbearable position . . . but also because it alone is prepared early in life psychologically for the conditions of a socialist order."[83] Although Zasulich always acknowledged that the assistance of intellectuals was required for the workers to understand the political necessity of socialism, she always coupled this belief with the assertion that only the workers could endow this socialist order with the moral virtue that justified its creation in the first place.

In practical terms this meant that Zasulich's preference for a workers' revolution rather than a coup d'état of socialist intellectuals was not based on any special reverence for majority rule: that the class which made the revolution would also constitute the majority was, in her mind, incidental to the fact that, of all the classes of society, the proletariat alone possessed the solidarity that was necessary to conduct a revolution and create a socialist order in the aftermath. To be sure, Zasulich's critique of the October Revolution would include a strongly worded admonition that democracy of some sort was required if socialism were not to degenerate immediately into tyranny.[84] Undoubtedly, the rule of a self-appointed elite in Petrograd troubled her greatly, and perhaps it was fortunate for her that she died before the Bolshevik party degenerated into Stalinism. But in 1902 Zasulich had no reason to be concerned about party democracy. One suspects that it was rather Marx's failure to predict the continued rise of real wages that impelled her to dwell on the psychological effects of industrial capitalism, to point out the positive role of workers' "alienation" in creating proletarian solidarity, and to deduce from all this the conclusion that only the proletariat could make a socialist revolution. In many ways the essay most revealing of Zasulich's political convictions, "Elements of Idealism in Socialism," possibly reflected a belief that new and different arguments were required for Marxism to withstand the attacks of those, such as Eduard Bernstein, who effectively refuted Marx's prediction of proletarian impoverishment. If, in her rebuttal, Zasulich so diluted Marxism with utilitarian phraseology that the product which emerged bore scant resemblance to the original theory, this was a risk she was willing to take. In her own way, she was just as flexible ideologically as Lenin, and she composed a polemic no less audacious than *What Is to Be Done?* in the degree to which it grafted onto Marxist ideology certain assumptions about the workers' capacity for solidarnost' that she thought would make Marxism even more compelling as an ideology of revolution, even more attractive as a vision of the future, and even more incisive as a guide to practical action.

During the many weeks she spent in Munich working on this essay, Zasulich established close personal relationships with both Martov and Potresov, who shared their quarters with her. She took great pains to engage her younger colleagues in extended conversations, and when *Iskra* was moved to London in April 1902, Zasulich and Martov felt themselves sufficiently compatible to continue their communal arrangement, this time with N. A. Alexeev, another co-worker in *Iskra*.* Because Martov, like Zasulich, was considerably less than fastidious in his personal habits, it is something of a medical miracle that the three of them managed to escape serious illness in a household where, for example, the sugar bowl more likely than not contained remnants of Martov's tobacco.[85] Leon Trotsky, who arrived in London in October 1902, remembers the "common room" of their apartment as perpetually "in a state of rank disorder," and only slightly less dirty than the kitchen, where Zasulich's method of cooking meat was to hold it directly over the fire and use a scissors to snip off the pieces that she wanted.[86] Because Zasulich retained even into her middle years the bohemian habits she had acquired in her adolescence, she seemed to her younger colleagues to embody the epic history of revolutionary struggle, and without exception Martov, Trotsky, and Potresov accorded her the respect and admiration due someone who has sacrificed

---

* Nadezhda Krupskaia, *Reminiscences of Lenin* (Moscow, 1959), p. 75; Lydia Dan, "Okolo redaktsii 'Iskry,'" *Protiv techeniia*, vol. 2 (1954), pp. 62–64. Some accounts include Deich (who had recently escaped from Siberia) in this arrangement, but none of them indicates whether he and Zasulich resumed their previous relationship. Indeed, Deich's memoirs tell us nothing about the nature of his marriage in Siberia in the late 1890's, the news of which drove Zasulich to despair.

so much in such single-minded dedication to a cause; she returned their warm-hearted respect with a maternal affection that she obviously could not feel for Plekhanov and Axelrod. Although, as Lydia Dan remarks in her memoirs, Zasulich took very little real part in the mechanics of *Iskra*'s publication and distribution, her presence alone had an inspirational value for the others on the staff.[87] Not surprisingly, Martov, Potresov, and Trotsky all considered it not merely impolitic but a breach of revolutionary etiquette for Lenin to suggest in 1903 that Zasulich was negligent in her duties as editor and that her position should be abolished.

It is certainly a testament to Zasulich's personal prestige and integrity that she should have retained the trust and veneration of her colleagues through the vicissitudes of her many attempts at mediation; even Lenin, when he broke with her in 1903, apparently did so with regret. Perhaps for this reason, Zasulich was able, on occasion, to score some significant victories. For example, in January 1902 Plekhanov presented to the editors of *Iskra* a preliminary draft of what he hoped would constitute the program of an all-encompassing Social Democratic Party. Predictably, Lenin rejected Plekhanov's draft as "too much like a textbook," and produced instead a program of his own.[88] In this program Lenin displayed on certain issues the ideological flexibility that would serve him well in 1917: whereas Plekhanov's draft had stated that in Russia "capitalism is more and more becoming the dominant form of production," Lenin's contained the breath-taking assertion that in Russia capitalism was *already* the dominant form of production—which implied that the preconditions for a socialist revolution were already developing.[89] As in 1900, when Plekhanov and Lenin, through their mutual hostility, nearly ruined the *Iskra* enterprise before it began, substantive disagreements combined with personal antagonism to create a situation so explosive that, but for Zasulich's intervention, *Iskra* might well have collapsed.

Zasulich herself harbored numerous objections to Lenin's program which she expressed privately in the form of notes she scribbled on a copy of the program that Lenin had given her. Because Zasulich considered Plekhanov's views on capitalist development more accurate than Lenin's, she took umbrage at the latter's suggestion that the proletariat could do without the assistance of the peasants; ironically, the very class which in 1917 Lenin would include within his revolutionary coalition he condemned in 1902 as hopelessly reactionary and obscurantist, destined for eternal passivity by what Marx had called "the idiocy of rural life." The most one could expect from the peasants was benevolent neutrality; by no means could they be considered genuine allies of the proletariat.[90]

Always ready to create or to broaden revolutionary coalitions, Zasulich expressed her profound misgivings about Lenin's view. In her hands Marxist categories were so malleable and elastic that she could respond to Lenin's program with the assertion that those who were not of the proletariat, even peasants, could join in a working class movement if they professed a belief in socialist ideas and promised to act in the spirit of camaraderie that the movement demanded. Solidarnost', though it was more easily attained by workers than by others, could nevertheless be achieved by peasants also. In this respect, Zasulich was contradicting or at least severely qualifying in her written comments on Lenin's program what she had recently written in "Elements of Idealism in Socialism." But, as on so many other occasions in Zasulich's career, ideological consistency took second place to tactical flexibility. The barriers surrounding Russian Social Democracy that Lenin would draw tighter and tighter until they finally excluded much of the proletariat itself Zasulich would loosen with such alacrity and abandon because she believed that in the absence of a genuine bourgeoisie—or at least of one fully cognizant of its revolutionary obligations—the participation of classes other than the proletariat was necessary for the bourgeois revolution to be successful. Thus, as she wrote to Lenin in rebuttal of his program, it was not nearly enough to seek the peasants' benevolent neutrality; only by permitting them to participate actively in Social Democratic and proletarian movements could Russian socialists serve both their own interests and those of the peasants.[91]

But rather than argue publicly with Lenin about the sections of his program to which she objected, Zasulich chose instead to propose the creation of a "commission" consisting of herself, Martov, and Fyodor Dan which would draft a program satisfac-

tory to both Lenin and Plekhanov.[92] Although this proposal
could not eliminate all the tension between the two men, it succeeded, at least for a time, in preventing a breach of personal
relations. The program produced by this "commission" was
based largely on a second draft submitted previously by
Plekhanov, but it also accepted Lenin's wording concerning the
extent of capitalist development in Russia.[93] This episode was in
some ways a preview of the permanent break that occurred a
year later as a result of another hair-splitting distinction involving Lenin and Martov, and it is a good illustration of the fragile
nature of the *Iskra* coalition, and the lengths to which Zasulich
would go to preserve it. Zasulich herself much preferred
Plekhanov's draft to Lenin's, but, on the all-important question
of capitalist penetration, she was willing to ignore her own opinion, and Plekhanov's, in the interest of unity.[94]

A few months later yet another dispute arose to threaten the
working arrangement achieved in August 1900. In April 1902
Lenin presented to the *Iskra* editors a commentary on the agrarian section of the party program agreed upon a few months
before. Lenin's notion was that the way for Social Democrats to
acquire the support, or at least the benevolent neutrality, of the
peasants was to promise them the return of the *otrezki*, the strips
of land taken from them and confiscated by the nobility after the
Emancipation forty years earlier.[95] The idea of returning this
land to the peasants after so long a time was quite impossible
because, as Pavel Axelrod had recognized, most of it had been
rented out, divided, or sold.[96] But Lenin persisted because he
recognized the political appeal of such a promise, and his proposal marks the first of many entreaties he would make to the
peasantry, culminating in the April Theses of 1917, promising
land, and the NEP of 1921, eliminating arbitrary expropriation
of grain.

Plekhanov's response to Lenin's proposal was predictable: it
was yet another attempt to usurp his preeminence in matters of
theory, and, on its merits, was wholly impractical. And it also
smacked of political opportunism, for it offered the peasants
private property that a socialist party was, by definition, committed to eliminate.[97] In words startlingly prescient of Soviet policy

after 1929, Lenin replied that the return of the otrezki would be, at most, only a temporary expedient, and that once a proletarian dictatorship had been consolidated, no means would be too extreme in the seizure of these lands by the state:

> The "kinder" we are to [the peasant] in the practical part of our program, the more "severe" our attitude must be toward these vacillating, double-faced elements in the "principle" part of the program. We cannot retreat one iota from our essential position. We will have to say to the peasant: "If you accept our point of view, all will be fine, but if you reject it, do not complain." With our dictatorship we will say of you: "There is no point in wasting words when force must be used."[98]

Zasulich's astonished reply to this was: "On millions! Just try! You will have to take the trouble to persuade them, and that is all there is to it."[99]

Plekhanov's next move in the dispute was to demand that the changes he proposed in Lenin's commentary be put to a vote of the editorial board, a novel procedure under the informal rules of *Iskra*'s operation. As in the past, tensions rose, but Zasulich, along with Axelrod and Martov, tried to soothe Plekhanov's ire and bring him round to a compromise with Lenin.[100] After two weeks of efforts, Plekhanov finally acknowledged that he had been hasty in his reactions and had never really doubted Lenin's fidelity to "the cause." Lenin replied that "a great stone was lifted from my shoulders when I received your letter, and we can put to an end all ideas of 'civil war.' "[101] Lenin subsequently agreed to Plekhanov's suggestions for further changes in the party program, and Plekhanov withdrew his objections to Lenin's commentary on the otrezki.[102]

For a year or so, relations between the two men were markedly improved. Plekhanov read approvingly Lenin's diatribes in *What Is to Be Done?* against the heresies of Economism and Revisionism, and by the summer of 1903, at the Second Congress of the RSDLP, they were in such agreement that they could stand together on a wide spectrum of issues against the combined forces of the four other editors. In some ways Zasulich's mediation had been too successful, for by restoring good relations between Plekhanov and Lenin she made possible an alliance that would ultimately force her resignation—as well as Axelrod's and

Potresov's—from the editorial board of *Iskra,* the only undertaking in this period of her life which seemed to sustain her psychologically.

While plans were being formulated for the Second Congress, Zasulich continued, during the summer and fall of 1902, to work to preserve the harmony that she had been instrumental in achieving. For example, in a letter she wrote to Martov in June 1902, she rebuked him gently for his hostility to Lenin, and reminded him that a cycle of "insult and counterinsult" would only increase the possibility of further conflict; in her mind "all comrades are the same."[103] In a similar vein she told Potresov a few weeks later that, metaphorically speaking, she was "keeping a record" of the occasions when he made "mocking remarks" about Plekhanov so that, when tempers had cooled, he could see for himself how foolish he had been.[104] Though she quite understood that clashes of personality were unavoidable in any revolutionary movement, the clashes did not have to result in longstanding animosity. She also warned him how untenable her own position would be in the event of a permanent split in *Iskra:*

What would there be for me to do if I alone can view this cursed business from all sides? It seems as if an avalanche is spreading from trifles in order to crush me because I alone know all the participants: I got to know Iu. O. [Martov] closely, and V. I. [Lenin] is such a simple and open creature that I am now fearful that I will soon have to lose everything. I feel (or so it seems to me) that I love everyone equally, absolutely equally, and I know beforehand that however the break might occur, I would not find a place for myself on either one side or the other. . . . It would be too bleak for me with [Axelrod and Plekhanov]. Having looked through the little window of *Iskra* at the present revolutionary movement, I would not now reconcile myself to work in the dark. But my position even among you would become impossible and false, and I would have to flee from you without looking back.[105]

Apparently this plea for harmony proved effective, and the sympathy this letter aroused in Potresov apparently moved him to repair his relations with Plekhanov and Axelrod.

One sees in the summer and fall of 1902 the formation of the alliances that would fight the decisive battles creating Bolshevism and Menshevism; as the ties between Lenin and Plekhanov strengthened, Axelrod, Martov, Potresov, and Zasulich began to close ranks against the intractability they perceived in Plekhanov and Lenin.* But while her colleagues, especially Lenin and Martov, were communicating to *Iskra*'s followers in Russia the mechanism by which delegates to this Congress would be selected, Zasulich managed to return to her writing—presumably part of the reason for her attending the Congress in an "advisory" capacity, without a vote on any procedural or substantive motion.[106]

Unlike the articles she wrote a few years before, those of 1902 and 1903 dealt exclusively with subjects of a contemporary nature. In July 1902 information recently received about the arbitrary punishment in 1898 of demonstrators protesting the illegal actions of a zemstvo official prompted Zasulich to reiterate in *Iskra* that nothing good could be expected from the government, and that, if moderates could not quite bring themselves to participate in revolutionary protest, they at least should help the revolutionary movement just as civilians assist an army in wartime.[107] An article in *Iskra* in January 1903 again flayed Russian liberalism for what she perceived as its tacit acceptance of the political status quo; to remain aloof from revolutionary struggle, Zasulich argued, was tantamount to repudiating it entirely, since a situation now existed in Russia where both moral and political neutrality were impossible.[108] Nonetheless, the general thrust of her message—in direct contrast to Lenin's—was that liberals should join forces with revolutionaries to battle against a common enemy together; if only liberals could perceive what was in their own interest, she implied, they would realize that it coincided, at least for the moment, with the interests of the revolutionary movement. Even in her *Iskra* years, the vision of socialists fighting alongside liberals, students, peasants, and workers for rights from which all these groups would benefit so excited Za-

---

* Yet another irritant in the relationship between Zasulich and Lenin was the presence of Trotsky, to whom Plekhanov took an immediate dislike, quite possibly in a kind of competitive resentment of Trotsky's apparent literary and intellectual skills. Zasulich regarded Trotsky with an almost maternal affection but apparently was by nature incapable of defending him against Plekhanov's insinuations and insults. This, in turn, infuriated Lenin, who complained to Krupskaia that Zasulich's reticence silenced the only person with the prestige to rebuke Plekhanov publicly. See Isaac Deutscher, *The Prophet Armed, Trotsky: 1879–1921* (New York, 1954), pp. 61–65.

sulich's imagination that it was usually only as an afterthought that she stated that the proletariat alone would be the ultimate beneficiary of this alliance.

Finally, Zasulich published a harrowing account of the Kishinev pogrom of April 1903 in which dozens of Jews were killed and hundreds more wounded.[109] This account is especially significant because it places Zasulich firmly with those who believed there was no advantage for the Left in such brutal outbursts of prejudice and violence; all too often anti-Semitism among the peasants had been applauded in the 1880's in leftist circles as evidence of "political consciousness" which could be tolerated, perhaps even encouraged. Zasulich had long felt otherwise, and in the 1880's had agreed to sign a manifesto started, but never completed, by Pavel Axelrod condemning this attitude as the worst perversion of revolutionary idealism.* Thus, when the Kishinev pogrom took place a quarter-century later, the conviction had already hardened in her mind that, regardless of its political repercussions, any manifestation of anti-Semitism could not pass unnoted in the pages of *Iskra*. Although her account was mainly descriptive, presumably because the facts of the matter required no editorial embellishment, she affirmed at the end that such atrocities would not divert the masses from revolutionary agitation, and only lower even more the prestige of the government with whose connivance the pogrom was carried out.

The Second Congress of the RSDLP has been described in such copious detail by historians that one need not recapitulate its lengthy proceedings except to recount briefly how the Congress gave rise to Bolsheviks and Mensheviks.[110] The purpose of the Congress convened in Brussels in July 1903 was to create an all-embracing Russian Social Democratic Party, and it included delegates from organizations as diverse in their origins and

---

* Abraham Ascher, *Pavel Axelrod and the Development of Menshevism* (Cambridge, Mass., 1972), pp. 72–73. The anti-Semitism of the Left was especially prominent in Narodnaia Volia, whose executive committee in 1881 openly encouraged its supporters to attack Jews, whom they called exploiters of the peasantry. See S. Valk, "G. G. Romanenko: iz istorii 'narodnoi voli,'" *Katorga i ssylka*, no. 48 (1928), pp. 36–59. Ascher notes that in the early 1880's all but one of the principal socialist journals in Russia spoke favorably of pogroms. See his "Pavel Axelrod: A Conflict between Jewish Loyalty and Revolutionary Dedication," *Russian Review*, vol. 24 (July 1965), p. 251.

viewpoints as the economist-minded *Rabochee delo,* the Jewish Bund, and the socialist groups of Poland and Latvia.* Lenin, however, had succeeded in "packing" the Congress with supporters of *Iskra,* and he thought he could count on roughly four-fifths of the forty-three delegates to support a complicated plan whereby a central organ, preferably located abroad, would exercise authority over the party through a central committee operating in clandestine fashion inside Russia. In an atmosphere tense with emotion as various factions of Russian socialists attempted to crack *Iskra'*s parliamentary majority, Lenin and Martov proposed slightly different versions of the article of the party statutes defining membership: whereas Martov's defined a party member as one who supported the party "by regular personal assistance under the direction of one of the Party organizations," Lenin's considered a party member one who supported the party "by personal participation in one of the Party organizations." Though most of the delegates seemed to regard the difference as hardly worth belaboring, Lenin explained that "my formula restricts the conception of party membership, while Martov's broadens it"; in other words, implicit in these definitions of party membership was the difference between a party run dictatorially by its governing elite, and one whose membership exerted some control over those who exercised authority on its behalf.[111] These two formulations were placed before the delegates for consideration, and Martov's carried by a vote of 28 to 23.†

At approximately the same point in the proceedings the Jewish Bund rose to demand that the Congress ratify its exclusive right to adjudicate on behalf of Jewish workers all matters germane to their welfare. When this motion was rejected decisively (41 to 5 with 5 abstentions), the Bundists abruptly left the Congress, followed shortly by two disgruntled economists representing *Rabochee delo.* Since the seven votes controlled by these two groups had supported Martov's resolution on party member-

---

* Although a "First Congress" had been convened for the same purpose in 1898, only nine individuals attended it, and most of them were arrested and imprisoned shortly after its adjournment. Leonard Schapiro, *The Communist Party of the Soviet Union* (New York, 1960), pp. 29–31.

† *Ibid.,* p. 48, The number of votes cast exceeded 43 because some delegates could vote twice.

ship, Lenin realized that he now had a working majority of two, and could propose a resolution reducing the Central Organ from six to three. It had generally been assumed that the six *Iskra* editors would be elected to the Central Organ pro forma, and cries of outrage and exasperation were heard throughout the room when delegates realized that Lenin's selection of himself, Plekhanov, and Martov to head this all-important party organ meant that Zasulich and Axelrod—two of the most respected figures in Russian socialism—would be stripped of all authority in the new party. Nonetheless, by a vote of 24 to 20, Lenin's resolution carried. His supporters subsequently were referred to as *Bolsheviks* ("those in the majority"), while those whom he defeated came to be known as *Mensheviks* ("those in the minority"). In the short span of three weeks (during which the delegates moved from Brussels to London after the Tsar had pressured the Belgian police to arrest them), Russian Social Democracy split irrevocably into factions which no amount of cajolery, diplomacy, or negotiation could ever succeed in dissolving. Through the vicissitudes of war, revolution, and repression, Bolsheviks and Mensheviks would remain distinct and recognizable entities, attracting people who saw through the personal jealousies that exacerbated their animosity sincere and irresolvable disagreement over the tactics, governance, and composition of a socialist party.

Despite her growing suspicions about Lenin's motives, Zasulich, like virtually everyone else at this Congress, seemed genuinely surprised and chagrined by the results. What shocked her most, it seems, was the extent to which Plekhanov and Lenin, by their actions and their justification of their actions, had betrayed fundamental canons of revolutionary solidarity. To be sure, Zasulich had little reason in 1903 to see in Lenin's formulation of party membership the authoritarianism that she and others would attack in 1904 and 1905. Zasulich and Lenin, after all, agreed on the necessity, *in the immediate future,* of limiting party membership to the small number of workers and intellectuals who possessed the toughness and political consciousness to participate in a clandestine organization. These words, written by Zasulich in December 1902, could just as easily have been written by Lenin precisely because neither he nor Zasulich had at that point indicated whether this clandestine party which they both advocated would be a temporary or a permanent instrument of revolutionary struggle:

> [The socialist party] will be an organization of "chosen, illegal revolutionaries," an organization which consists of people who have made revolution their chosen profession, who are dedicated solely to revolutionary activity, and who therefore can, at any and all times, alter their names as well as their conditions of existence in order to escape persecution, and who can always serve only their cause. Only under such conditions is intensified activity possible in Russia at this time. . . . Only under such conditions can revolutionaries acquire that conspiratorial acumen, that agility in revolutionary matters which even under different conditions could not be achieved unless one had a most outstanding ability.[112]

For a long period after the Congress Zasulich continued to attribute Lenin's unconscionable behavior to what she thought was "the mad rage" and "the fire for revenge" ostensibly induced by his initial defeat on the definition of party membership.[113] Only after the passage of many months and the publication of Lenin's *One Step Forward, Two Steps Backward* did she confront at last the genuine differences between her views and Lenin's which, for a variety of reasons, she had previously ignored.

Zasulich, as one might have expected, hardly cut a striking figure at this congress so pivotal in the history of Russian socialism and of Russia generally. One scans the protocols of the Congress in vain for any instance when she publicly defended her prerogatives against the encroachments of Lenin and Plekhanov; the few comments she offered dealt mostly with the structure and jurisdiction of the Party Council, a four-member body conceived by Lenin to ratify decisions already agreed upon by the troika in the Central Organ.[114] At no point did she publicly protest the loss of her editorial authority, nor did she make it clear that Lenin's explanation for this action—that a smaller editorial board would function more efficiently than the existing one—was offered only after the Congress rejected his suggestion that *Iskra* be *enlarged* to include a seventh member, Leon Trotsky, who Lenin erroneously thought could be easily manipulated.[115]

In keeping with her customary diffidence, Zasulich confined

her comments to private sessions of the *Iskra* editors that were held concurrently with the public sessions of the Congress. On one occasion she registered along with Martov and Axelrod her strong objection to Lenin's proposal that the Party Council elected jointly by the Central Organ and the Central Committee (which presumably would be dominated by Lenin and his supporters) be entrusted with the responsibility of selecting new members of the Central Organ and Central Committee if and when their membership, whether by illness or resignation, should be reduced; because all the editors agreed that the Congress itself should appoint a fifth member to this Council and because Lenin was certain that the Congress would elect Plekhanov to this position, Zasulich thought that Lenin's proposal would invest the Central Organ, or possibly Lenin himself, with powers that she thought should best remain in the hands of the party congresses themselves. To avoid this kind of "mutual selection" implicit in Lenin's scheme, membership on such agencies should, she said, remain a prerogative of delegates whose shifting composition from one party congress to the next would ensure congruence between the wishes of the party and the actions of its elected officials.[116]

But even in the privacy of *Iskra*'s separate deliberations, Zasulich chose not to oppose Lenin when, on another occasion, he presented his colleagues with a list of prospective members of the Central Committee that he hoped they would all find acceptable. Although Martov objected strenuously to Lenin's selections, Zasulich, along with Axelrod and Trotsky (whose presence Lenin tolerated because he thought that Trotsky would always act as his ally), decided in the interest of unity that, even though they agreed with Martov, the issue was not of sufficient gravity for them to state their feelings directly to Lenin.[117] And even when Lenin, sensing that power was finally shifting in his direction, took the extreme step of advocating Zasulich's removal from *Iskra,* Zasulich maintained a stoic silence in public when delegates offended by her ouster implored Lenin and his supporters to reverse their decision.[118]

Much about this congress is astonishing: Martov's decision to favor the expulsion of Bundists and Economists who had previously supported him, thereby transforming his electoral majority into a minority; Plekhanov's repudiation of Zasulich and Axelrod after twenty years of intimate collaboration; Lenin's attempts to manipulate party organs in ways which, in their audacity, went beyond even the rough and tumble revolutionary etiquette previously enforced with fair success. But perhaps most astounding of all, at least to one unacquainted with Zasulich's personality and political inclinations, was the trancelike way in which she accepted her public removal from the job that everyone agreed was the principal source of what little personal happiness she enjoyed. In the words of Lenin's wife, Nadezhda Krupskaia, "for Zasulich to leave *Iskra* would have meant cutting herself off from Russia again, sinking back into the slough of emigrant life abroad. . . . For it was not a question of ambition, but a matter of life and death."[119]

There are many possible explanations of Zasulich's behavior. It is conceivable that she remained mostly silent because she had tired of her editorial responsibilities. It is also possible that, because she lacked a vote, she considered it inappropriate for her to express herself at the congress. Another explanation, suggested by Trotsky, is that Zasulich, never very skillful in debate, recognized that she would serve her cause badly by attempting to argue it publicly.[120] Yet another explanation sometimes offered is that Zasulich could not speak more often on her own behalf simply because she was suffering from a severe attack of laryngitis.

But how, then, does one explain away seeming apathy when she was so deeply attached to *Iskra*? Others, like Axelrod, who also lacked privileges at the congress were not kept from talking when they deemed their comments relevant. Moreover, there is evidence that Zasulich, however detached she seemed in the public sessions, was genuinely angered by Plekhanov's betrayal; at one point during the congress Plekhanov half-jokingly complained to Lenin that he found it impossible to speak with her because "she takes me for Trepov."[121] And the notion that laryngitis was the principal cause of her reticence can be discarded by virtue of eyewitness accounts which attest to her hissing Plekhanov repeatedly as a means of expressing her disagreement with him.[122]

A far more plausible explanation of Zasulich's curious reticence at the Second Congress is that, in 1903, the substantive differences between her and Lenin were not nearly so great nor so readily apparent as they would be in 1904 and 1905, when the publication of *One Step Forward, Two Steps Backward* finally made it clear to Zasulich that the dominance of intellectuals over workers that she applauded as a temporary and tactical necessity would be a permanent feature of any Leninist party. One might also offer the suggestion that, between the establishment of *Iskra* in 1900 and the Second Congress in 1903, Zasulich had expended so much time and energy restraining what she saw as Plekhanov's authoritarian impulses that she failed to recognize these same impulses when they manifested themselves in Lenin to a much greater degree. Preoccupied with the "Jacobinism" of one man, she could not see its same expression in the words, temperament, and actions of another.

But both these explanations, though probably true, fail to take into account what may well have been Zasulich's overriding consideration not only at the Second Congress but throughout her political career. Zasulich may have kept silent about her objections to Lenin's formulation of party membership, his attempts to manipulate the party apparatus, and his successful effort to eliminate her position as co-editor of *Iskra* because she thought that speaking out would do more harm than good in further widening the fissures in Russian socialism that already existed. Her silence was certainly not due to political cowardice. On the contrary, it showed the kind of political courage so evident on other occasions in her life, when she subordinated her personal interests to what she thought was the general welfare of the party. In this case the party's welfare seemed to necessitate her own removal from party councils after nearly a lifetime's dedication to "the cause." Like the Decembrist Ryleev, whose moral virtue had consisted in his capacity to sacrifice his interests for the interests of others, Zasulich felt in 1903 that the unity of Russian socialism was so much more important than her personal happiness that she would acquiesce in her own humiliation if that were necessary to achieve her goal of revolutionary unity. However obtuse Zasulich may have been to consider Lenin's actions merely the reflection of "rage" or of a desire for revenge, one cannot deny a certain consistency, indeed a genuine nobility, in Zasulich's willingness, even eagerness, to imitate in middle age an example of political heroism that had first stirred her imagination in the 1860's when she was living with her relatives at Biakolovo.

Most of the time, Zasulich's unsuccessful quest for revolutionary unity left her unhappy and exceedingly annoyed with herself. Unlike some historical figures whose self-destructive impulses often cause historians to describe them as "martyrs," Zasulich seems not to have derived from her failures any compensatory feelings of martyrdom or of moral superiority.[123] Nor does she reveal in her actions any conscious or even subconscious desire "to lose." Revolutionary unity was always for Zasulich an attainable objective and one which she failed to achieve not for any lack of effort or persistence but because the situation in which Russian socialists found themselves throughout most of the period before the outbreak of World War I was simply not conducive to the reconciliation and harmony that she desired.

Unexpectedly, however, the Second Congress of 1903 had a happy and extremely gratifying dénouement. In October 1903 the newly established RSDLP convened in Geneva a meeting of the Foreign League of Revolutionary Social Democracy, which the party had officially designated as its representative abroad (thus replacing the Emancipation of Labor). Realizing that his supporters were in the minority, Lenin attempted at this meeting to alter the rules by which new members were admitted, and, failing that, to seek the immediate adjournment of the session. Plekhanov, though he had sided with Lenin in Brussels and London a few weeks before, in the interim had come to recognize Lenin's ruthlessness, and now recoiled at the prospect of yet another split in Russian socialism. It is, of course, also possible that Plekhanov experienced some guilt over what he had done to his erstwhile colleagues in *Iskra*, and resolved to restore them to their former positions. At any rate, after some elaborate maneuvers, Plekhanov managed to secure Lenin's resignation from *Iskra*. That accomplished, he subsequently invited Martov, Zasulich, Axelrod, and Potresov to join him in *Iskra*'s publication, and by the winter of 1904 the newspaper had become a forum for anti-Leninist polemics.[124] In the weeks and months that followed, Martov, Plekhanov, Axelrod, and Rosa Luxemburg all denounced Lenin in its pages, each of them in different ways warning *Iskra*'s readers of the incipient authoritarianism in Lenin's political behavior.

Zasulich's contribution to this campaign, an article in *Iskra* in July 1904, marks the only occasion when she criticized a fellow socialist in print; that she had initially regarded Lenin very highly indicates how radically her opinion of him had changed since the happy days in 1900 when they seemed so enamored of each other's abilities.[125] Unlike other critics of Lenin, however, Zasulich felt that the authoritarianism she saw in Lenin's politics was more the result than the underlying cause of his behavior at the Second Congress in 1903. Although she had realized almost immediately from the day she met him in 1900 that Lenin harbored authoritarian impulses, she failed to see, as Axelrod and Plekhanov did, that these impulses had been given political expression as early as 1902 in a view of the party and its relationship to the proletariat that was all the more dangerous precisely because of the logic and consistency with which Lenin defended it.[126] Whereas Plekhanov and Axelrod, writing in 1904, viewed Lenin's behavior since 1902 as a consequence of his politics, Zasulich attributed it almost entirely to his emotions, claiming that it was only after Lenin's defeat by Martov on the question of party membership that Lenin, in an effort to justify intellectually what she described as his "desire for revenge," first conceived a scenario of revolution that could be attacked for its dictatorial implications.[127]

Zasulich's argument, of course, ignores completely the far more subtle authoritarianism in *What Is to Be Done?* that Axelrod and Plekhanov, with their superior political acumen, could now discern. Nor is it particularly surprising, since Zasulich's own political judgments were always more instinctive than intellectual, that she should have found a human, personal explanation for what was in truth a ruthlessly intellectual course of action. Even so, Zasulich's break with Lenin must have been a wrenching experience for her. After avoiding since 1900 unpleasant truths about a man whom, despite his cantankerousness, she had always considered a valued colleague and friend, Zasulich was finally forced in 1904 to acknowledge these truths and to explain why the political authoritarianism they entailed had to be discredited as thoroughly and quickly as possible.

In her article, "Organizatsiia, partiia, dvizhenie" ("The Organization, the Party, the Movement"), Zasulich took great pains to distinguish a "party" from an "organization" and a "movement": whereas an organization is defined by the particular functions it performs and a movement is simply the "moods, views, and feelings" current in the society at large, a party is defined by the individuals who belong to it. An organization invariably necessitates a strict hierarchy of control with authority running unidimensionally from top to bottom; "a real-life party is born— even without any organization—when people who think and feel in the same way oppose themselves to people who think and feel differently." A rigid hierarchy of authority is unnecessary because disagreements are few and, for the most part, insignificant.[128]

Lenin had led Russian socialists astray, Zasulich argued, by confusing the two concepts and substituting a socialist organization for a socialist party. Whereas a socialist party, by Zasulich's definition, should include "that section of the population which Social Democracy had drawn to participate in its theoretical and practical struggle," Lenin had created instead an "organization" whose structure and function, as Zasulich defined them, limited its membership to those whose actions he could directly control.[129] Thus, Lenin excluded from the party most of those who, by virtue of their views, deserved to belong to it. The result, although she did not say so explicitly, would be a dictatorship of the elite over the masses.

To be sure, the socialist party that Zasulich advocated would have to maintain for the foreseeable future a division of labor between workers and revolutionary intellectuals, with the latter teaching the workers and inspiring them to develop the solidarnost' that Zasulich always felt was the singular virtue of socialist parties and socialist societies. In the process, these intellectuals would accumulate power, and Zasulich seems to have recognized that this was almost inevitable. But she never indicated in anything she wrote precisely what course of action the proletariat should follow if these intellectuals should somehow prove negligent in fulfilling either their pedagogical or their inspirational obligations, or if they should decide that their domination of the workers should be extended indefinitely. In some sense Zasulich's position is reducible to the argument that intellectuals who promise to relinquish power will eventually do so because only such intellectuals would promise to relinquish power in the first place. And it is hardly adequate for Zasulich to imply, as she did in *Iskra* in 1904, that this problem was really of no consequence because her definition of party membership insured that workers and intellectuals would be in agreement on virtually every matter of significance, with each group cognizant that this imbalance of power was only temporary and that the interaction between the two groups was an ennobling experience enabling them to work together in perfect harmony.

Paradoxically, the workers in Zasulich's party would consider themselves every bit the equal of the intellectuals who led them. Whatever the internal division of authority, the party as a whole would be communal property, belonging as much to the workers who lacked the political consciousness to control it as to the intellectuals whose political and ideological sophistication forced them into positions of leadership. It should be the goal of all those who profess socialist principles, she said,

for having all sections of the working class . . . think, feel and say, "our party, we are part of the party; I am a member of the Party," even if they do not pass the strict requirements [established by Lenin in Paragraph 1 on party membership]. . . . It is important that all these workers [who participate in strikes and demonstrations] consider the affairs of the Party as their own personal affair, and that they feel responsible for the business of the Party, not before the Central Committee, but in front of themselves.[130]

After a time, workers would develop what Zasulich now termed "party patriotism"—really a synonym for the *solidarnost'* in "Elements of Idealism in Socialism"—and would thereby rectify this imbalance of power without any prolonged or unnecessary conflict.

Zasulich, however, did not explain in 1904—nor at any other time in her career, for that matter—what socialists should do if Russia's workers decided on their own that socialism was not the solution to their problems and thus either failed to join socialist parties or withdrew from them. If one believes, as Zasulich did, that parties consist of people who share the same beliefs and that no amount of force can instill these beliefs in people who choose for one reason or another not to adhere to them, then the socialist party which Zasulich thought would acquire mass support would, in this case, simply contract into a revolutionary elite. Indeed, if it should happen that Zasulich actually exaggerated the attraction of socialism, then her conception of party membership, originally designed to enlarge the party, would, in actuality, diminish it. Reading Zasulich's article one cannot escape the unsettling conclusion that her definition of party membership could lead to a Leninist elite just as easily as Lenin's, provided only that workers simply disagree with Zasulich about the virtue of socialism.

That Zasulich was unable to see this can be attributed to her assumption that the virtue of socialism, if not immediately self-evident, would surely become apparent to workers once their teachers in the intelligentsia had explained it. In her optimism, Zasulich never questioned the two assumptions central to her view of the party that Marxist intellectuals would eventually relinquish power voluntarily and that the workers would eventually recognize the advantages of socialism. In this respect, her critique of Leninism, with its intricate distinctions among parties, organizations, and movements, is far less compelling and internally cohesive than those of Martov, Axelrod, Plekhanov, Luxemburg, and Trotsky, all of whom perceived with far greater clarity than Zasulich the problems that a party of workers and intellectuals might encounter. Far from recognizing that differences of opinion were, in fact, inevitable, and that democracy was the most ethical and effective method of resolving them, because of her belief in the magical properties of solidarnost', Zasulich envisioned a party of such ideological unanimity that rules regarding the resolution of disagreements were not really necessary. Although Zasulich, like many socialists, shared the liberals' optimistic belief in secular progress, she did not consider this progress the result of any free and open exchange of ideas.

Not surprisingly, Zasulich's relations with Lenin deteriorated rapidly after the publication of her article in July 1904. But whereas a few years earlier a breach in relations with another socialist might have distressed Zasulich as yet another breach of revolutionary unity, by 1904 she could find solace in the fact that forces other than Social Democracy were for the first time since the late 1870's engaged in sustained, if uncoordinated, struggle against the government. Student disturbances and demonstrations were, by 1904, practically a daily phenomenon. Simultaneously, Russian liberals agitated for constitutional government at "banquets" commemorating the fortieth anniversary of the creation of the zemstva. Despite the steady rise of real wages, workers were now so restive that even Zubatov's police-sponsored unions were no longer able to moderate or redirect their hostility; Zubatov himself had been dismissed in 1903. Squeezed by Witte's program of taxation, peasants were increasingly inclined to attack those whom they held responsible for their predicament, most often the nobility and the Jews. In the provinces, meanwhile, many of Russia's national minorities were demanding autonomy, if not yet outright independence, especially in Finland and in the oil-rich regions of the Caucasus, where Georgian and Armenian nationalism had distinguished pedigrees of many years' duration. And, as if all of this were not enough, the government was also plagued by a crescendo of terrorism directed by the "Combat Section" of the Socialist Revolutionary Party: in 1901 the Minister of Education, in 1902 the Minister of the Interior, and in 1904 another Minister of the Interior, the notorious Viacheslav Plehve, were all victims of SR assassins, some of them originally double agents of the police who, after a time, had confused or even consciously reordered their allegiances. Given the generally repressive measures with which the government responded to these assaults on its authority, sporadic offers of concessions (and even of ministerial positions) to responsible liberals such as Dmitrii Shipov and Miliukov only hardened the conviction of these men that the Tsar and his advisers simply could not be trusted.

Finally, the "short, victorious war" with Japan which Plehve had hoped would be a means of eradicating all domestic dissent turned out to be a political and military disaster. The only fortunate aspect of the whole fiasco was that the losses sustained by Russia's armed forces ultimately exhausted the limited resources of her opponent, forcing the Japanese in the summer of 1905 to accept terms negotiated by Theodore Roosevelt, the American President, far less favorable to Japan than the course of the war itself might have led one to expect. That the war came to an end when it did also worked to Russia's advantage, for it seems questionable whether the army would have remained loyal to the Tsar in the face of domestic disorder that intensified in the fall of 1905 if it had still been engaged in hostilities with Japan. If nothing else, the events of that fall, which included a general strike more extensive than any in Europe up to that time, seem to bear out the truism that a government can survive almost any amount of internal unrest provided that its police and armed forces do not disintegrate.

Even so, the damage to the government was serious, and by October 1905 it had become apparent to all but the most obtuse and reactionary (among them the Tsar) that autocracy, in its present form, would have to be modified. The shooting on January 9, 1905, of some of the 200,000 workers marching peacefully through the streets of St. Petersburg, bearing portraits of the Tsar along with petitions requesting better working conditions and a constituent assembly, seemed to catalyze a revolution so multifaceted that it is more accurate to describe the Revolution of 1905 as really several revolutions occurring at once. And what the various groups in these revolutions lacked in coordination and planning was more than compensated by the fever-pitch of their emotional and ideological commitment. In the weeks and months that followed "Bloody Sunday," the universities closed, workers deserted their factories, some army and navy regiments openly mutinied, and in July zemstvo leaders defied the Tsar by convening a conference to create the Constitutional Democratic (or "Kadet") Party, which proceeded immediately to demand the convocation of a legislative *duma*. No longer content with the consultative duma that their spiritual ancestors in the Tver nobility had demanded of Alexander II, these liberals, as well as other groups assaulting the autocracy, were not to be placated by half-hearted and halfway concessions. Just as in the late 1870's, the political atmosphere in Russia in 1905 reflected the growing conviction among the Tsar and his critics that government and society were natural enemies and that neither could survive without the destruction of the other.

When revolution finally erupted in January 1905, Zasulich was no less surprised than many other émigrés whose distance from Russia had obscured their vision and skewed their judgment. But once she understood the enormity of what was happening, she believed that the revolution was a personal opportunity as well as a political vindication; more than anything else, it raised the possibility that she might, in the foreseeable future, return home in triumph.* Faithful to her two-stage scenario of revolution, Zasulich considered the strikes and demonstrations of 1905 mere preliminaries to the bourgeois revolution she had long anticipated, and her correspondence with her colleagues throughout the summer and fall reflects an optimism previously absent in her articles and letters. For example, in a letter to Martov written in October, Zasulich declared that the General Strike recently proclaimed by railway workers in St. Petersburg would lead to the destruction of autocracy. How much a successful revolution meant to her is evident from her tone and phraseology:

Indeed, [this General Strike] is evidently "the last and decisive battle" for political freedom. This is what replaces the barricade; this is the form of popular revolution in the 20th century. It is as if all the towns all along Russia—and most of all in both capitals—were covered with barricades. The soldiers still have not crossed to the side of the people, but they stand and do not know (and it is not completely known if they are going to) how to take them, these barricades which are so intangible for them. So terribly much depends on the railway employees' delegates, so much that my heart literally palpitates. The principal strength is the railroad strike—with it all the rest will stand or fall. Somehow I believe very much in victory, possibly because it would be terrible to admit defeat.[131]

After nearly thirty years abroad it was finally possible to escape from the stifling confines of Western Europe; in the euphoria of the moment, Zasulich stated more strongly than ever before how insignificant were the feuds of warring socialists:

The Bolsheviks with their petty souls will celebrate a victory over the Mensheviks, but the devil with this! Now again and one hundred times more strongly than on January 9th one feels that the underground hen house with all its parties will finally end. Now (if victory is granted to us)

* Several times between 1901 and 1905 Zasulich had importuned her *Iskra* colleagues to authorize her surreptitious return to Russia, but fears for her safety made them reluctant to agree to such a risky operation. Editorial note, *Pis'ma P. B. Aksel'roda i Iu. O. Martova*, ed. F. Dan, B. Nikolaevskii, and L. Tsederbaum-Dan (The Hague, 1967), p. 141.

the working class will emerge in free Russia as an enormous, perhaps too enormous force. It is necessary to remold Social Democracy into something entirely different.[132]

The events of 1905 seemed to corroborate everything Zasulich had argued about the evolution of the Russian proletariat; the strikes, the demonstrations, and the forty tons of socialist propaganda disseminated in the twelve months after April 1904 seemed to demonstrate, in effect, that the program of the Emancipation of Labor Group had proved, in the long run, to be correct.[133] After a quarter-century of wandering aimlessly in the political wilderness, Zasulich and her colleagues could have the satisfaction of knowing that what was happening in Russia was at least partly the result of their work, and proof that the masses had finally acquired revolutionary consciousness. In her elation Zasulich drastically overestimated the influence of the revolutionary intelligentsia, but whatever else one might say about the Workers' Councils (or *Soviets*) that arose spontaneously in 1905, they seemed, at least, to bear out her conviction that the bourgeois revolution, when it finally erupted, would be a revolution involving strata of the population other than the industrial bourgeoisie. Given the consensus on the left that it was only a matter of time before the government would collapse, one can hardly criticize Zasulich for failing to see that by acceding to certain demands at the propitious moment the Tsar could destroy the unity of his opponents and subsequently recover much of the political authority he had lost.

When the revolution reached its apogee in October, Zasulich and Potresov were living in Paris (the other *Iskra* editors had settled in Vienna). Consumed by their desire to be on the scene, the two made plans to return to St. Petersburg illegally, and to demand a full-scale trial if they were caught by the police.[134] But events moved more rapidly than they had dreamed. By the time they arrived at the Russian border, the October Manifesto issued by the Tsar proclaiming civil liberties (including amnesty for political exiles) and a legislative duma had split off more moderate elements from those committed to continuing the struggle; only a last-ditch battle remained to be fought in the streets of Moscow. Zasulich thus had legal status for the first time since 1878, and, after a brief detainment in January 1906, could live as she chose in St. Petersburg.[135] But the failure of the revolution seemed to have drained from Zasulich the energy she had summoned for what she expected to be the climactic battle against the government; and so it was that her return to Russia marked the end of her active participation in revolutionary politics.

SIX

The Last Years

Z ASULICH'S decision to retire from politics was evidently a
deliberate one. By 1905 she was barely four years short of
sixty, an age when many who suffer from chronic illness and
depression disengage from active pursuit of long-term goals.
Zasulich always had much of the *"babushka"* about her even
in her youth, and her correspondence after 1905 suggests a
woman much older in spirit than in years. Unlike her old colleagues, Plekhanov and Axelrod, Zasulich simply withdrew from
revolutionary activities, content to derive a meager income from
translations and the publication of her *Sbornik statei* (Collected
Articles).

Almost immediately after her return to Russia she bought one
half of a desiatina of land in Tula province, where, in a summer
cottage, she wrote her memoirs in 1909.[1] Winters she spent in St.
Petersburg, assisting in projects such as the publication of *The
Literary Inheritance of Marx and Engels*, a collection of their letters,
essays, and memorabilia.[2] In addition, she began, but never completed or never published, translations (all from the French) of
works by Balzac, Emile Zola, and H. G. Wells. Zasulich's preference at this time for a pastoral environment as well as her long-
standing support of the proletariat may explain why Wells's *Time
Machine* so repelled her with its substitution of human labor by
machines that she abandoned her translation a quarter of the
way through.[3] Her income at this time consisted mainly of royal-
ties from a common fund shared with Axelrod and Plekhanov
(of which they generously gave her a disproportionate share),

but it was sufficient to allow her a certain choice in the works that she translated.[4] When, in 1909, the "Writers' Home" in St. Petersburg invited her to live there, she eagerly accepted its offer, and remained a permanent resident of this haven for retired intellectuals until a group of Bolsheviks acting without authorization succeeded in evicting her in 1918.* That the police ignored her in 1911 while conducting a roundup of prominent Mensheviks in St. Petersburg indicates how slight a threat her presence in Russia posed to the government.

Her political beliefs altered little in the years before the outbreak of the World War. Naturally, she was depressed by the failure of the 1905 Revolution, and composed an addendum to her "Revolutionaries of Bourgeois Background" acknowledging that she had been far too sanguine in her predictions about Russia's political and social evolution. In her view, the October Manifesto was a clever ruse by which the autocracy deluded the masses into believing that they had acquired civil liberties and a parliament even as vigilante groups openly encouraged by the government did their utmost to create an atmosphere conducive to the reassertion of autocracy.[5] Like many others on the left, Zasulich realized how effective Stolypin's agrarian reforms might be in creating a class of petit-bourgeois landholders loyal to the government; not surprisingly, the only event of this period that raised her hopes occurred not in Russia but in England—that strange and unpredictable country which, in the years immediately preceding World War I, suddenly seemed on the brink of civil war.[6] Shortly after the Lords' Crisis erupted in Parliament, Zasulich wrote excitedly to Axelrod: "I am convinced that this is the end of Old England. No one can predict what future system will emerge there, but the blows, although not consciously, are being inflicted upon capitalism itself."[7]

With such dismal prospects for revolution in Russia, Zasulich

---

* Letter, Zasulich to Potresov, September 24, 1909, B. I. Nikolaevskii and A. N. Potresov, eds., *Sotsial-demokraticheskoe dvizhenie v Rossii: materialy* (Moscow and Leningrad, 1928), p. 191. At this stage in her life Zasulich was not about to alter habits to which she had been accustomed for many decades, and her proverbial sloppiness and inclination for solitude remained unchanged except for a new-found fondness for cats, especially underfed and mangy ones, several of which she adopted as pets. A. Damanskaia, "O tom, chto ne zabyvaetsia," no. 4, part 2, Bakhmetoff Collection, Columbia University, New York.

took refuge in the politics she had espoused throughout her life. Virtually the only choice possible for Social Democrats, she argued, was a temporary alliance with liberals still participating in elections to the Duma. Although none of her writings at all suggests that she favored permanent collaboration with parties far less militant than her own, in a letter to Potresov in 1909 she commented that the Kadets were "the least of all the evils in our life," and confessed her incomprehension of the invective directed against them from the left.[8] Similarly, in a letter to Axelrod (1912) she commented that the opposition of the Left to an alliance with the liberals "made a powerful social movement impossible."[9] Unlike Lenin, who responded to recent failures by declaring his Bolshevik faction to be an independent political entity, Zasulich found in the powerlessness of Russian socialism additional incentive to try to broaden its base.

Evidently very much against her will, Zasulich was impelled in 1913 to defend what was referred to, usually in the pejorative, as "liquidationism": the view that the RSDLP should "liquidate" its underground apparatus (or as much of it as was politically prudent) and concentrate its energies on activities designed to revitalize the masses. Some liquidators, as Lenin dubbed them, advocated participation in elections to the Duma, others did not. But all agreed that, for the party to survive when its popularity had diminished so precipitately, it had to attract new members. Lenin, on the other hand, was more and more of the opinion that secrecy and strict centralization of authority were essential to the survival, and the success, of any revolutionary party, and therefore shared Plekhanov's opposition to the liquidationist position.

Other issues intervened to personalize the debate. Reverting now to his previous alliance with Lenin, Plekhanov revived bitter memories of the party schism in 1903 by offering in his polemics the novel argument that, in their resentment over Lenin's move to strip them of their editorial positions, Zasulich and Axelrod had been responsible for this fateful split in Russian socialism.[10] Axelrod preferred to ignore this absurd new tack, but a group of younger Mensheviks, among them Martov and Dan, published an Open Letter calling upon their two older colleagues to respond in print to Plekhanov's accusations, which were, the letter said, a form of character assassination intolerable in revolutionary circles. The authors of the Open Letter affirmed their responsibility to defend the revolutionary honor of their colleagues and reminded Plekhanov of his own role in creating a party schism. The tragic flaw in Plekhanov's character, the authors concluded, was that he combined "a mind worthy of Chernyshevskii with the soul of a Don Basilio."[11]

The letter had little effect upon Zasulich. However much Plekhanov's polemics may have offended her, she had worked with her old comrade so long that she knew every trait in his character, disagreeable and otherwise. Plekhanov's invective no longer surprised her, she wrote somewhat wearily to Pavel Axelrod: "with regard to the Party, Plekhanov is unprincipled in the extreme."[12] Presumably, that ended the matter for her—but not for Plekhanov. He responded to the letter in *Pravda* in April 1913, in an article in which he admitted that he had overstepped the bounds of revolutionary propriety: when he spoke harshly about "Menshevik liquidationists," he said, he had not meant to include Zasulich among them.[13]

The tone of this superficially apologetic article drew Zasulich into the fray. Many of the revolutionaries whom Plekhanov had impugned, notably Potresov, Ezhov, and Maevskii, had for many years been among her closest collaborators, and she sprang to their defense. Barely eight days after Plekhanov's article appeared in *Pravda*, Zasulich responded in the pages of *Luch* (The Ray), a journal published by the "August Bloc" of Russian Social Democrats who were trying to reunite the Bolsheviks and the Mensheviks.[14] If Plekhanov chose to attack Potresov and his friends, Zasulich declared, he should understand that in doing so he was attacking her as well, since she herself was no less a liquidationist than the others: were it not for the wretched state of her health, she would be actively involved in the struggle to rid the party of its clandestine apparatus. Though Plekhanov and Lenin regarded liquidationism as a term of opprobrium, Zasulich thought it was the first step Russian socialists should take toward achieving a party whose leadership would be truly proletarian in composition. Furthermore, she concluded, making her usual plea, nothing good could emanate from such intraparty polemics: their only consequence would be to show the workers that Russian socialists were ill prepared to assist them.

The debate about liquidationism continued. Plekhanov responded to Zasulich in *Pravda*, Zasulich replied to Plekhanov, this time in *Zhivaia zhizn'* (Living Life), and Lenin composed a critique of Zasulich's position ironically entitled "How Vera Zasulich Demolishes Liquidationism."[15] It was all a good illustration of the way in which the specter of failure, especially after 1905, seemed to drive the Social Democrats to feuds and squabbling. But it was not all superficial. The debate about liquidationism— Adam Ulam and other historians notwithstanding—showed that genuine differences divided Lenin and his critics.[16] Beneath the personal conflicts and polemics two basic tendencies in Russian Social Democracy were at work, one of them attempting to perpetuate an elitist, clandestine party, the other genuinely critical of such a direction as a harbinger of revolutionary dictatorship. To Lenin an elitist party was not only a necessity but a virtue. To Zasulich, as her articles on liquidationism in 1913 indicate, an elitist party was harmful to intraparty democracy, and she believed that the time had come when the party could finally shed its clandestine apparatus and assume the posture of an organization seeking popular support:

We have now a broad section of workers who would have every right to join any socialist party in the West. All our forces should be in this rapidly growing section of the workers, who lack only the opportunity of formally joining a party to found one, and no matter what we call this section we shall both think of it and speak of it as the party. A formally disorganized party of workers, strongly tied to the entire working class, is preferable to an organized, underground party distinct from it.[17]

It would be difficult to find a substantive issue over which two people could disagree more than Zasulich and Lenin did over the structure, function, and evolution of a socialist party. In retrospect it seems that their debate was a stalemate: if the liquidationists were wrong in believing that a mass party could function effectively in what Richard Pipes has described as "a monarchical police state," they were quick to perceive the authoritarian potential in Lenin's alternative.[18]

Before 1914 Zasulich wrote only one other article, a brief

exhortation to "the young generation" to emulate the men and women of the 1860's in their dedication to social service and political action.[19] However, two years after the outbreak of war in August 1914, she redirected what little energy she still had in this period of steadily deteriorating health to a defense of Russia's participation in the Triple Entente against Germany. It is clear that she regarded the issue of "war guilt" as important enough to warrant a belated attempt to resolve it. In addition, as if to emphasize her solidarity with the war effort, in 1917 she joined the Central Committee of Edinstvo (Unity), an organization established by Plekhanov three years earlier to serve as a focal point for all those on the left who favored Russia's participation in the war.[20] Despite the coolness of their relationship a few years earlier, Zasulich apparently welcomed the opportunity to collaborate again with Plekhanov when he returned to Russia in 1917, and the few months that they worked together in Edinstvo must have been like old times recaptured.

Zasulich espoused the so-called "defensist" (or pro-war) position for reasons very similar to Plekhanov's. She repudiated Lenin's argument that, since the ultimate cause of war was imperialism, all countries had an equal share in the responsibility for its outbreak; although her comments on the war itself were few and fragmentary, she made it clear that she considered German imperialism a greater threat to international socialism than the survival of Russian autocracy.[21] The ultimate cause of the war, in her opinion, could be traced to Bismarck, whose militaristic foreign policy had so convinced the German people of their superiority that even the German Left had been infected by its spirit (in a letter to Potresov in 1917, she angrily denounced German socialists as "imperialists").[22] And the only way to avoid wars in the future was through multilateral disarmament—a notion which she knew would appeal as much to liberals as to socialists; although only socialism could eliminate conflict entirely, disarmament would at least remove from men's hands the deadly weaponry with which they acted out their aggressive impulses.[23] Unlike other socialists such as Trotsky, who, in his *Literature and Revolution*, extolled technology as a means by which man could conquer and transform his environment, Zasulich revealed in her article on World War I an awareness that technology could be misused by men in ill-conceived adventures resulting in the destruction of both man and his external environment.

To be sure, Zasulich and the other socialists who supported the war had to explain in 1915 and 1916 why support for the war seemed to diminish among the segments of the population, most notably the proletariat, which they thought would benefit most from the defeat of German imperialism. The problem, as Zasulich explained it, was not a result of proletarian solidarity; that is, the workers had not rationally calculated the general interest or the interest of their class and determined that it consisted of repudiating the war. On the contrary, the workers were plagued by a lack of solidarity, which in turn could be traced to an absence of political consciousness. Properly educated, workers would always select a course of action which objectively served the general interest, and the fact that workers in 1915 and 1916 did not agree with Zasulich's definition of this general interest forced her to attribute their mistake to political and ideological immaturity.[24] Quite apart from the arrogance implicit in her assumption that she knew what was in the workers' best interest, her assertion of proletarian immaturity contrasts rather sharply with her assertion during the debate on liquidationism that the RSDLP was ready to become a true proletarian party.

After the February Revolution in 1917, Zasulich's "defensism" needed fewer apologies. Whereas in 1916 several prominent Mensheviks could criticize her support of the war as, in effect, a defense of autocracy, in 1917 she could argue that Russia must fight to preserve its bourgeois revolution, which nearly everyone on the left agreed was a prerequisite of socialism.[25] In a pamphlet entitled *Fidelity to the Allies*, she contended that only on the basis of a democratic order could Russian socialists hope to create the preconditions for a socialist revolution; for Russia to sign a separate peace with the Germans would be "shameful," an act of unmitigated foolishness and moral turpitude that would leave the Provisional Government at the mercy of German imperialism.[26] Writing in 1917, when the outcome of the war was still not certain, Zasulich saw Russia's only hope for survival in a continuation of friendly relations with Britain and France. Though their long-standing democratic traditions would presumably make them more sympathetic to the Provisional Government than they had been to the Romanovs, the alliance with the Western democracies served a purpose more noble than that of realpolitik, she asserted, and quite apart from the advantages it offered in the common struggle against Germany, it ought to be preserved simply because the Russian government before the war had agreed to it. Alliances were solemn agreements to be faithfully adhered to—the closest equivalent in foreign relations to the popular fronts that she tried to create within the revolutionary movement. Possibly because Zasulich's devotion to the war effort was so obviously devoid of ulterior motives, her pamphlet was printed by the government-sponsored Military Industrial Committee—the only article of hers to receive the official blessing of the state.

As a member of Edinstvo, Zasulich presumably favored its policy of collaboration with the Kadets; the most one can glean from her private letters is that she assisted in the publication of its proclamations.[27] Because its membership consisted mostly of isolated and politically powerless intellectuals, Plekhanov established a second, more heterogeneous organization (which he called the League of Personal Example), whose members actually toured the major cities of Russia in an effort to increase support for the war. It is a testament to the strength of Zasulich's convictions that, despite her age and worsening health, she not only joined the League of Personal Example but even journeyed to Moscow to address a crowd of 5,000 assembled in the Zimin Theater.[28] With Plekhanov, Deich, and the British diplomat-historian Bernard Pares, Zasulich did what she could to assist the League as its members shuttled about from Petrograd to Moscow and Kiev, even though a recurrence of the respiratory ailments that had plagued her periodically severely limited her public appearances. She managed somehow to appear also with Kropotkin and her long-time friend and fellow revolutionary Katerina Breshkovskaia at pro-war rallies organized independently of both Edinstvo and the League.[29]

All these efforts proved unavailing. By September 1917 the enthusiasm for the war that had revived in February had completely dissipated as a result of Kerenskii's catastrophic July Offensive. What remained of the once-proud army that had gone to war in 1914 was in disarray and without support, despite the desperate attempts of the Provisional Government, now in the hands of Kerenskii, to sustain it. In October, weakened by its foolhardy continuation of the war, forced to share its power with the workers' Soviets, saddled with a faltering economy, threatened from the right by disgruntled army officers, and from the left by Lenin's cadres of revolutionary agitators, the Provisional Government collapsed with barely a murmur of resistance.

More than once before the October Revolution Zasulich, whose faith that socialism could emanate only from a workers' revolution had never wavered, had expressed her irritation that the Bolsheviks were making rational debate impossible by impugning everyone who supported the Provisional Government as acting "objectively" on behalf of the bourgeoisie.[30] Writing in *Nasha zhizn'* (Our Life) in February 1918, not long after the Bolsheviks had forcibly disbanded the Constituent Assembly, she made clear her belief that the October Revolution was nothing less than a perversion of Marxism. The reason for this, she said, was that Lenin's coup d'état did not allow for a decent interval between the bourgeois and the socialist revolutions, an interval during which the proletariat would acquire the necessary education and political consciousness to create a true socialist order. In this, the last article she would complete before her death, Zasulich maintained that a premature revolution such as that of the Bolsheviks was actually worse than no revolution at all: "From the point of view of socialists who remain faithful to the legacy of socialism, who formerly nurtured Russian Social Democracy, there are at present no greater enemies of socialism than the men of Smolny [the Bolsheviks]. They will not transform capitalist means of production into socialist ones, but annihilate capital and destroy heavy industry. . . . The hands of Smolny will ruin everything they touch."[31] After a lifetime of struggle for the principles and ideas that she believed in, Zasulich could not look kindly upon a government that she thought was repudiating them. To the pain, disappointments, and personal misfortunes of the past was now added, in the last year of her life, the humiliation of watching helplessly as the Bolsheviks tarnished the socialist legacy for which she had sacrificed so much of her happiness.

Not even a celebration in April 1918 of the fortieth anniversary of her acquittal could dispel the misery of her last months. In the winter of 1918–19 Bolshevik soldiers evicted her from her lodgings in the Writers' Home, and although Lenin called their action a "disgrace," it is not known whether he managed to secure her safe return.[32] Convinced she would die if she were forced to live elsewhere, Zasulich became increasingly despondent in the spring of 1919.[33] During the winter she had contracted pneumonia and had been confined in a hospital for weeks. At the end of April she suffered a relapse, and on May 8, 1919 (N.S.), she died. Two days later, N. L. Meshcherniakov wrote anonymously in *Pravda* that "in the person of Vera Ivanovna one of the oldest and most venerable revolutionaries has departed from us"; although recently she had "diverged" from the revolutionary proletariat, Russian socialists nonetheless valued highly the services she had rendered to it in the past.[34] In *Izvestiia* Vladimir Bonch-Bruevich described her as "a legendary figure" whose life should serve as an example for others in the revolutionary movement.[35] In an unusual display of generosity, the Soviet government assumed the expense of her funeral, at which Potresov delivered the principal eulogy.[36] She was buried next to Plekhanov in a section of the Volkhov Cemetery reserved for writers and political thinkers of distinction.[37]

What can one learn from Zasulich's life about Russian radicalism in the roughly thirty-five years during which she was intimately a part of it? In her self-effacing fashion, Zasulich would probably disapprove of efforts to ascertain her significance, but so many revolutionaries of her generation have attested to it in their memoirs, reminiscences, and autobiographies that her biographer has an obligation to examine the matter with the full benefit of historical perspective.

Perhaps the most obvious assertion about Zasulich is that in some indescribable way she was simply too decent to be a truly effective revolutionary. Perceptive enough to recognize that revolution must, by its very nature, be a dirty business, at the same time Zasulich could never quite make the sacrifices that her profession demanded: unlike her colleagues, she maintained cordial relations even with those who disagreed with her, and spent a good part of her life seeking reconciliation with them in ways which suggest incomprehension of the extent to which revolutionary politics makes impossible the casual relationships formed by others less driven by a political idea. When, in 1900, she wrote to Deich that "I am not so free from human compassion that I cannot feel sympathy for my enemies," she revealed not only a sentiment that ratified her superiority as a human being, but also an absence of political toughness that made her unusually inept in the practice of revolutionary politics.[38] At once her great strength and principal weakness, Zasulich's implicit faith in the goodwill of others caused Lenin to conclude rather cynically that "with Vera Ivanovna too much is built on moral foundations and sentiment."[39] In the life of the revolutionary movement, where paranoia was really a normal rather than a pathological response to one's environment, the very qualities which made Zasulich so "lovable" (the adjective most commonly employed to describe her) also account for her numerous failures. She never aspired to political power in the manner of Lenin and others, but she would hardly have been successful if she had, for she lacked the inclination to make the acquisition of power the principal determinant of all political and personal relationships.

Nor, it must be said, was Zasulich a theorist. The best of her works have originality but little insight (though many of those who knew her or who have commented on her works have often confused the two qualities), and she often seemed incapable of subtle intellectual distinctions. Merely to mention some of her attempts at intellectual analysis underscores how readily the intellectual categories she used could obscure rather than elucidate her thought: one thinks especially of the confusion of utilitarianism and altruism, the attempts to graft utilitarian terminology onto Marxism, the search for substitutes for the bourgeoisie in the so-called bourgeois revolution, the profusion of terms and categories that were needed to prove that Lenin harbored dictatorial ambitions, and the belief that workers could somehow acquire a commitment to the general welfare sufficient to suppress any lingering suspicion that their personal interests might conceivably conflict with it. Virtually the only idea Zasulich presents which constitutes a significant contribution to the corpus of Marxist or socialist theory is her dialectical perception of the evolving relationship between the intelligentsia and the workers, her view that the two groups essentially reverse their relationship as one group slowly educates, inspires, and ennobles the other to the point where power can be transferred without any diminution of ideological or political continuity.

To be sure, Zasulich lived all of her adult life in a milieu in which ideas were evaluated for their moral content even as they were used to legitimize and justify political choices that often had little to do with moral or philosophical issues. Russian revolutionaries, as the heirs of Belinskii, Chernyshevskii, and Dobroliubov, as well as of Marx and Engels, felt obliged to cloak impulses more often visceral than cerebral, and judgments more often pragmatic than principled, in a vocabulary possessing a special potential for exacerbating conflict because of a constant infusion of moral and philosophical absolutes. To support candidates in elections to the Duma was, for Russian revolutionaries, not merely a tactical decision but a matter of morality as well, and any and all who disagreed with it could be accused of ideological and even moral deviation. Although the populists and Marxists with whom Zasulich associated often disagreed with the specific prescriptions of their spiritual ancestors in the Russian intelligentsia, they inherited from them the conviction that political decisions were not merely pragmatic judgments based on reason and observation, but ethical imperatives based on absolute and abstract moral principles. From this milieu of the intelligentsia came the commitment, the integrity, and the devotion to "moral wholeness" characteristic of revolutionaries such as Zasulich, but it also produced a penchant for equating disagreement and betrayal, and an intolerance, often tending toward fanaticism, characteristic of revolutionaries such as Lenin. Not surprisingly, the tensions and disputes inevitable in revolutionary movements and containable in most of them became especially intractable in the Russian.

Because she lacked the self-confidence to impose her conclusions on others, Zasulich largely avoided this intolerance and inability to compromise even as she attempted, in the spirit of the intelligentsia, to give expression to half-formed intuitive ideas which she hoped would produce a spiritual transformation in those who were exposed to them. Just as they were for the revolutionaries who inspired her in her youth, ideas and ideologies for Zasulich were really vehicles for the expression of one's most precious moral imperatives, reflecting in Zasulich's case commitments to the poor, the underprivileged, and the uneducated that were far more emotional and ethical than rational or utilitarian in their genesis. Zasulich could not have shot Trepov, nor could she have sacrificed her happiness, indeed her life, for a philosophical ideal, if her incentive had not been a moral imperative that came from her heart.

As a revolutionary, Zasulich manifested an abhorrence of conflict that pervaded virtually everything she did. Most significantly, it prevented her from recognizing that conflict might be a liberating force intellectually and politically, producing through the multiplicity of opinions it engendered a true "market place" of ideas out of which a lasting consensus might emerge. About the origins of this abhorrence one can only speculate. But its existence and importance in Zasulich's thinking are undeniable, and it served as the principal motive for what this study has persistently described as a yearning for revolutionary unity. To establish alliances against autocracy was the overriding and dominant impulse in her political career, and the mere enumeration of the numerous occasions when this impulse seemed to determine her behavior should be sufficient proof of its centrality in her thinking. Her work in Krasnyi Krest, her dealings with Dragomanov and Jogiches, her negotiations with Narodnaia Volia, her reaction to the famine of 1891–92, her relations with the Fundists in London, her role in the creation of *Iskra,* her mediation between Plekhanov and Lenin, her advocacy of collaboration with the Kadets after 1905, her friendships with ideological opponents such as Kravchinskii, Struve, Mikhailovskii, and Kropotkin—all these facets of her life reflected the all-consuming desire to unite disparate revolutionaries in an alliance that not only would be politically effective but also would demonstrate a commitment to collective endeavor that she considered the principal expression of revolutionary virtue. Occasionally her efforts proved successful, but more often than not they ended in failure. Russian revolutionaries, irrespective of their ideology, were simply ill equipped to strive for common objectives with a minimum of feuds and personal squabbling; indeed, in the absence of police repression of a severity that might have made these feuds and squabbling an unconscionable luxury, there was little additional incentive to try to curtail them. Conflict was endemic to Russian radicalism when Zasulich was most actively involved in it, and in retrospect it is reasonable to suppose that no single individual could have contained this conflict within manageable limits. From 1881 to 1917 the failures were too great, the opportunities for positive action too limited, and the potential for insurrection too small for revolutionaries to avoid recriminations about the past or a profusion of conflicting strategies for the future. Their restless energy effectively thwarted by the state, many revolutionaries proceeded to turn this energy against themselves with a vengeance born of frustration and despair, and very nearly destroyed themselves in the process.

A comparison with German Social Democracy is revealing. German Social Democrats also experienced discord, and quarreled nearly as much as the Bolsheviks and Mensheviks, or Narodnaia Volia and Chernyi Peredel. Among German socialists, Kautsky, Bernstein, and Luxemburg came to personify distinct and recognizable strains of thought which encompassed the various questions of tactics and ideology that arose between 1890 and 1914. Moreover, just as in Russia, the personal conflicts and ambitions of German socialists gave to their political debates a cutting edge as sharp as any within the RSDLP, and surely Rosa Luxemburg was no less adept than Lenin and Plekhanov in cutting an opponent to ribbons through polemical devices sometimes fair and sometimes foul. In spite of all this, however, the SPD retained its unity, and through its choral groups, its hunting lodges, and its sporting clubs German Social Democracy became not merely a political choice but a way of life, cementing its members' allegiance to the party in ways that were unimaginable in Russia. Thus, in the history of German socialism there is no equivalent to the schism of August 1903, and the SPD remained a single entity until disillusionment over Germany's pursuit of (or lack of success in) World War I precipitated the creation of an Independent Social Democratic Party, and sometime later the Sparticist League of Liebknecht and Luxemburg. Indeed, if Zasulich had been a German rather than a

Russian, her politics of revolutionary unity might have had more solid and lasting results.

The reason, one suspects, is that, unlike the Russians, German socialists made significant progress—however illusory it appears in retrospect—in the period from 1890 to 1914. As its representation in the Reichstag increased, and as its leaders increasingly affected a way of life (if not always a rhetoric) that exuded bourgeois respectability and moderation, assuming power became a real possibility. With the prospect of success to bind it together, the SPD survived debates that would have ripped the RSDLP to shreds. Even including the Revolution of 1905, the record of Russian socialists could not match that of German socialists before 1914, and where the debate about Revisionism shook the SPD but did not destroy it, an argument about a single paragraph of the party statutes in 1903 split Russian socialism irrevocably.[40]

Thus, however valiant her efforts, Zasulich could not preserve the unity of a party or a movement whose very lack of appreciable success except for fleeting moments in 1881 and 1905 virtually ensured its continued fractionalization. In this, the most pressing endeavor of her life, Zasulich failed. But this is not to say that her story tells us nothing about the era in which she lived or about the people who both admired and respected her and whose achievements, at least in politics and ideology, were in many cases more constructive and profound. Zasulich touched people more by the strength of her personal example than by the force or the coherence of her ideas. Even revolutionaries more intelligent, more astute politically, and more attuned to the nuances of ideology than she was found in her perseverence in the face of adversity a moral rectitude that made them want to redouble their efforts to create a just and equitable society in Russia. In a sense, many revolutionaries considered Zasulich, an individual, the most tangible and obvious embodiment of revolutionary virtue even as Zasulich herself persisted in seeing this virtue embodied in collectivities such as the Proletariat and the Party. In an ironic reversal of the mythology of socialism, individual fortitude in confronting forces beyond one's control inspired revolutionaries to strive for socialism far more than the vision expressed in *The Communist Manifesto* of socialism as a collective enterprise dynamized by a faith in man's ability to control and reorder his environment. In the language of Greek mythology, the Myth of Sisyphus rather than the Myth of Prometheus—man's stubborn defiance of nature rather than his control of it—seemed, at least in the case of Zasulich's admirers, to be the principal inspiration for them to continue their struggle.

Thus, Zasulich seemed to capture in her own life a fraction of the nobility of spirit that she hoped revolutionaries would inspire in the proletariat by virtue of their commitment to socialism. To this extent, Zasulich's conception of a socialist party, with its emphasis on the workers' capacity for solidarnost', properly nurtured by a coterie of intellectuals, reflected the same ethos of social altruism and philanthropy that had originally impelled her to revolutionary politics. Inasmuch as revolutionaries inculcated in the lower classes the political consciousness to create a new social order, they performed a function not too dissimilar from that which Zasulich had performed as an adolescent in the late 1860's, when she worked for a justice of the peace and taught illiterate workers to read and write. The only alteration this ethos underwent in nearly thirty-five years of revolutionary activity was that the principal object of Zasulich's altruism changed from the narod of Russian populism to the urban proletariat of Russian Marxism. Because she considered the workers to be the repository of virtue in a socialist society, they were worthy of the intellectuals' solicitude in the period before the socialist revolution when they still lacked the political consciousness to determine their own interests and those of society.

In sum, Zasulich regarded the relationship between workers and intellectuals as mutually reinforcing: the ennobling experience of the party would, with time, imbue both with the requisite solidarity and civic consciousness to make a social order superior in every way to those that had preceded it. The purpose of revolution, she always seemed to be saying, was not merely to foster social justice but also to increase the general sum of moral virtue. But the history of Russian radicalism, in both its populist and Marxist phases, seemed to favor individuals like Zheliabov and Lenin, whose instincts told them it would be politically suicidal and psychologically debilitating to endure in relative weakness the many years it might take to inculcate revolutionary ideas among the masses. If, in the links that her politics of gradualism would forge between workers and intellectuals, Zasulich could promise a society more virtuous and egalitarian than the one actually created later by her rivals, her skepticism about quick (and elitist) solutions made her politics distinctly unpalatable to those who were impatient for radical change within their lifetimes. However prescient was her contention that Russian socialism could not be born without an adequate period of gestation, it was perhaps too much to ask of revolutionaries that, in the name of creating solidarnost', they deliberately defer to some future epoch a socialist revolution whose fruits they might otherwise enjoy themselves. As it happened, the temptation in 1917 to fill a power vacuum was so irresistible that Lenin and the Bolsheviks were willing, despite their fears, to bring about a revolution and take the risk that its fruits might not be ripe. Although Lenin was the better politician, Zasulich was the better prophet.

Reference Matter

Notes

❦

Complete authors' names, titles, and publication data for the works cited in short form are given in the Bibliography, pp. 247–54.

Chapter One

1. The exact date of Zasulich's birth is not beyond question. B. P. Koz'min, the editor of Zasulich's memoirs, says that she was born on July 29, 1849. John Keep, Leonard Schapiro, and Avrahm Yarmolinsky offer, respectively, the dates 1850, 1851, and 1852. Most secondary sources agree on July 27, 1849, and this date is given in *Sovetskaia istoricheskaia entsiklopedia* (Moscow, 1964), vol. 5, p. 631.

2. Much of the information about Zasulich's background and family history comes from the memoirs of her sister Alexandra, who married the revolutionary Pyotr Uspenskii, which were published under the title, "Vospominaniia shestidesiatnitsy," in *Byloe*, no. 18 (1922), pp. 19–45. I draw on this in these initial paragraphs. A brief sketch of Zasulich's youth can be found in Deich's "Vera Ivanovna Zasulich," the Introduction to Zasulich, *Revoliutsionery iz burzhuaznoi sredy* (1921).

3. Uspenskaia, p. 19. See also Zasulich [76], p. 16.

4. Uspenskaia, p. 19.

5. Zasulich [76], p. 113; Uspenskaia, p. 19.

6. Uspenskaia, p. 21. Vera in her memoirs says not a word about her only brother.

7. Zasulich [76], p. 113.

8. *Ibid.*, p. 11.

9. *Ibid.*

10. *Ibid.*

11. *Ibid.*, p. 15.

12. *Ibid.*, p. 16.

13. *Ibid.*, p. 15.

14. For more on the status of women see Stites, pp. 3–25 and Dorothy Atkinson, "Society and Sexes in the Russian Past," in Atkinson, Dallin, and Lapidus, eds., pp. 3–38.

15. Uspenskaia, p. 21.
16. *Ibid.*, pp. 21–22.
17. Zasulich [76], p. 16.
18. *Ibid.*, pp. 114–15.
19. Quoted in Venturi, p. 343.
20. Kovnator, p. 5. The fact that Andrei Kolachevskii and his sisters also came from the Gzhatsk district of Smolensk may have been a bond that influenced Zasulich's thinking. See E. S. Vilenskaia, *Revoliutsionnoe podpol'e v Rossii (60-e gody XIX v.)* (Moscow, 1965), p. 245.
21. Zasulich [76], p. 15.
22. Peter Lavrov, *Historical Letters*, edited by James P. Scanlon (Berkeley, 1967), p. 24.
23. Zasulich [76], p. 58.
24. Uspenskaia, pp. 22–23.
25. *Ibid.*, p. 23.
26. Kucherov, *Courts, Lawyers, and Trials under the Last Three Tsars*, p. 88.
27. Quoted in *ibid.*, p. 89.
28. Kovnator, p. 4.
29. Zasulich [76], p. 16.
30. Uspenskaia, pp. 24–28.
31. Pomper gives a very detailed description of Ivanov's murder in his biography of Nechaev, pp. 99–132. See also Stephen T. Cochrane, *The Collaboration of Nečaev, Ogarev, and Bakunin in 1869* (Giessen, 1977), especially pp. 35–47, 228–31.
32. Zasulich [76], pp. 58–60. See also Pomper's biography of Nechaev.
33. Venturi, p. 384.
34. Zasulich [76], p. 60.
35. *Ibid.*
36. Uspenskaia, pp. 39–40.
37. Zasulich [76], p. 61.
38. Uspenskaia, p. 28.
39. Zasulich [76], p. 62.
40. Baron, p. 22n.
41. Zasulich [76], p. 60.
42. *Ibid.*, p. 25.
43. Ulam, p. 186.
44. Zasulich [76], pp. 27–28.
45. Pomper, p. 65; Nevskii, ed., vol. 2, p. 330.
46. Gallinin, pp. 50–52; Uspenskaia, p. 30.
47. Gallinin, p. 51; Uspenskaia, pp. 30–31. Ekaterina was not released from prison until 1870.
48. Nevskii, p. 330; Kelly, p. 28.
49. Zasulich [76], p. 131.
50. *Ibid.*, p. 56.
51. Pomper, pp. 201–2.

Chapter Two
1. Koni, p. 8.
2. Nevskii, ed., vol. 2, p. 330; Uspenskaia, p. 40.
3. Koni, pp. 123, 139; Kucherov, "The Case of Vera Zasulich," p. 88.
4. Koni, p. 123; Kunkl', "Meloch' proshlogo," p. 80. One year after his arrest in 1869, Nikiforov was exiled to Tver, where he was joined by Ekaterina after her release from prison in 1870.
5. Nevskii, p. 330; Koni, p. 123; Kucherov, "Vera Zasulich," p. 88.
6. Koni, pp. 8, 121–23. In his reminiscences of these events, Deich confuses certain details, claiming Zasulich arrived in Kharkov in 1875 and describing her as a medical assistant. Deich, "Pamiati ushedshikh: Vera Ivanovna Zasulich," p. 203.
7. Rochefort, *The Adventures of My Life*, vol. 2, p. 190.
8. Zasulich [76], p. 131; Deich, "Pamiati ushedshikh," p. 203.
9. Koni, pp. 137–38.
10. The letter may be found in Kunkl', "Meloch' proshlogo," pp. 80–81.
11. See Zasulich [34], reprinted in Zasulich [58], vol. 2, pp. 375–87.
12. *Ibid.*, pp. 384–86.
13. *Ibid.*, p. 386.
14. Deich, "Iuzhnye buntari," pp. 47–49. This article describes the membership and activities of the circle.
15. For analyses of these reappraisals see Venturi, pp. 469–506; Yarmolinsky, pp. 181–209; and Wortman, *passim*.
16. For accounts in English of this affair the reader is referred to Venturi, pp. 581–84, and Daniel Field, *Rebels in the Name of the Tsar* (Boston, 1976), pp. 113–207.
17. See Deich, *Za polveka*, vol. 2, pp. 310–11; Iakimova, pp. 183–84.
18. Venturi, pp. 581–83; Deich, *Za polveka*, vol. 2, pp. 59–90.
19. Deich, "Iuzhnye buntari," pp. 44–45.
20. *Ibid.*, p. 50.
21. Zasulich [49], in Zasulich [58], vol. 2, p. 423.
22. Frolenko, p. 245.
23. Deich, "Iuzhnye buntari," pp. 47–48, 71.
24. Frolenko, pp. 241–46.
25. L. G. Deich, *Chetyre pobega* (Moscow, 1926), pp. 1–20.
26. Zasulich [19], in [58], vol. 2, p. 124.
27. For information on their common-law marriage see Deich, *Za polveka*, vol. 2; L. G. Deich, "Pis'mo k chlenam gruppy 'Osvobozhdenie Truda,'" in Deich, ed., *Gruppa 'Osvobozhdenie Truda,'* vol. 5, pp. 91–94; Lev Deutsch (L. G. Deich), *16 Years in Siberia: Some Experiences of a Russian Revolutionist* (London, 1903), pp. 1–6.
28. Ulam, pp. 260–61.
29. Iakimova, pp. 178–79.
30. Deich, "Iuzhnye buntari," p. 70.
31. Iakimova, p. 178; Frolenko, p. 246.

32. Aptekman, p. 197.

33. Iakimova, pp. 183–84; see also a letter from A. I. Zundelevich to B. I. Nikolaevskii, February 14, 1923, cited in *Perepiska G. V. Plekhanova i P. B. Aksel'roda*, vol. 1, p. 212.

34. Koni, p. 140.

35. Kravchinskii, p. 107.

36. Deich, "Iuzhnye buntari," p. 54.

37. R. M. Plekhanova, "Stranitsa iz vospominanii o V. I. Zasulich," *Gruppa*, vol. 3, p. 86.

38. L. I. Aksel'rod, p. 37.

39. Plekhanova, p. 85.

40. Frolenko, pp. 246–47.

41. Trotsky, *Lenin*, p. 41.

42. Kravchinskii, pp. 108–9.

43. *Ibid.*, p. 109.

44. Deich, "Iuzhnye buntari," p. 56.

45. Kravchinskii, p. 113.

46. Koni, pp. 444–45.

47. *Ibid.*, pp. 67–68; Venturi, pp. 373, 588. Wolfgang Geierhos argues—in my view unconvincingly—that Trepov may have been an illegitimate son of Nicholas I and thus a half-brother of Alexander II. See Geierhos, pp. 44–45.

48. Accounts of this episode can be found in Koni, pp. 49, 109–20; Gertsenshtein, pp. 243–50; and Glagol, pp. 147–52.

49. Glagol, p. 150; Gallinin, pp. 47–48.

50. Koni, p. 54; Kantor, pp. 92–93.

51. Debagorii-Mokrievich, p. 252; Aptekman, p. 235.

52. In an interview with Edward Aveling in *The Clarion* (London), February 23, 1895, p. 64.

53. Koni, pp. 58–59.

54. Frolenko, p. 246; M. F. Frolenko, *Sobranie sochinenii* (Moscow, 1931), vol. 2, p. 44; M. R. Popov, "Iz moego revoliutsionnogo proshlogo," *Byloe*, no. 5 (1907), p. 297.

55. E. G. Karpov, "Zasulich nakanune pokusheniia," *Vestnik literatury*, no. 6 (1919), p. 3.

56. Koni, p. 448.

57. L. G. Deich, "Valerian Osinskii (K 50-letiiu ego kazni)," *Katorga i ssylka*, no. 5(54), (1929), pp. 22–24.

58. Zasulich [76], p. 65.

59. *Ibid.*, p. 67.

60. *Ibid.*, p. 69.

61. *Ibid.*, pp. 65–69; Gallinin, p. 3; Koni, pp. 98–106; Rochefort, "Vera Zasulich i narodovol'tsy," p. 86. Trepov ultimately recovered from his wounds and passed away peacefully in 1889.

62. Koni, pp. 66–67.

63. Quoted in N. K. Bukh, *Vospominaniia* (Moscow, 1928), p. 162.

64. Koni, pp. 72–74.

65. *Ibid.*, pp. 85–88.
66. *Ibid.*, p. 71.
67. *Ibid.*, pp. 66–67.
68. *Ibid.*, pp. 45–46, 58–62, 71–75. See also Narishkin-Kurakin, pp. 53–56.
69. Koni, pp. 83–84; Kantor, p. 91; *Pis'ma Pobedonostseva k Aleksandry III* (Moscow, 1925), vol. 1, p. 120.
70. Katerina Breshkovskaia, *Hidden Springs of the Russian Revolution* (Stanford, 1931), p. 160; N. G. Kuliabko-Koretskii, "Moi vstrechi s V. I. Zasulich," *Gruppa*, vol. 2, pp. 74–76.
71. Koni, p. 69; *The Times* (London), April 15, 1878, p. 3.
72. Bezobrazova, p. 601.
73. Reprinted in *Revoliutsionnoe narodnichestvo 70-x godov XIX veka*, vol. 2, pp. 49–50.
74. Koni, pp. 92–93.
75. *Ibid.*, p. 152.
76. Glagol, pp. 150–51.
77. K. V. Mochulsky, *Dostoevsky: His Life and Work* (Princeton, 1967), p. 580.
78. Koni, pp. 94–97.
79. *Ibid.*, p. 120.
80. *Ibid.*, pp. 124–27.
81. *Ibid.*, pp. 133–34.
82. *Ibid.*, p. 13; Glagol, pp. 151–52.
83. Koni, pp. 124–26.
84. *Ibid.*, p. 145.
85. *Ibid.*, pp. 145–46.
86. *Ibid.*, p. 148.
87. *Ibid.*, p. 149.
88. *Ibid.*, pp. 152–56.
89. *Ibid.*, pp. 156–57.
90. *Ibid.*, pp. 157–68.
91. *Ibid.*, pp. 171–72.
92. Quoted in Gradovskii, pp. 8–9.
93. Gallinin, p. 109; Koni, pp. 172–73, 179–80; "Iz S. Peterburga," *Obshchina*, April 1, 1878, p. 23.
94. Kovnator, p. 8.
95. A Soviet historian who believes that the police fully intended to arrest Zasulich is V. F. Antonov, in *Revoliutsionnoe narodnichestvo* (Moscow, 1965), p. 217.
96. Accounts of this episode can be found in *Severnyi vestnik*, no. 89 (April 1, 1878); *Obshchina*, April 1, 1878; Gertsenshtein, pp. 255–57; Ertel, pp. 251–52; Kunkl', "Vokrug dela Very Zasulich," p. 60.
97. Koni, p. 17.
98. Plekhanov, "K russkomu obshchestvu," p. 18.
99. Reprinted in Koni, pp. 407–8.
100. See Dragomanov, pp. 6–10.

101. D. A. Miliutin, *Dnevnik* (Moscow, 1947–50), vol. 1, p. 41.

102. Koni, p. 17.

103. Plekhanov, "K russkomu obshchestvu," p. 17.

104. Gradovskii, pp. 435–36.

105. Quoted in Koni, p. 19.

106. Gustave Valbert, "Le Procès de Vera Zassoulitch," *Revue des deux mondes*, May 1878, p. 216.

107. Dragomanov, p. 1.

108. Quoted in Koni, p. 19.

109. Peter Kropotkin, *Memoirs of a Revolutionist* (London, n.d.), vol. 2, p. 225.

110. Brailovskii, p. 11.

111. Bezobrazova, pp. 601–2.

112. Koni, p. 229.

113. *Ibid.*, pp. 18, 190–91.

114. *Pis'ma Pobedonostseva k Aleksandry III*, vol. 1, p. 117.

115. Ertel, p. 250.

116. Kelly, pp. 47–48.

117. Gallinin, pp. 114–16.

118. The reason given for annuling the verdict was that Koni had violated Articles 575 and 576 of the Code of Criminal Procedure. According to Article 576, the defense counsel could summon individuals to testify even if the President of the Court had previously ruled their probable testimony irrelevant or unnecessary provided only that the defense counsel do so at his own expense and within one week of the President's decision. Alexandrov did this in Zasulich's trial after Koni, on March 22–24, ruled that Trepov's guilt or innocence had no bearing on Zasulich's and that therefore testimony concerning the Bogoliubov flogging was irrelevant. The Senate, however, ruled—in defiance of logic—that, in upholding Article 576, Koni had actually violated it, and also Article 575, which prescribed that persons who had not given testimony in the preliminary investigation could testify at the trial only if the President of the Court deemed their testimony vital. Several of the individuals Alexandrov called as witnesses had not participated in the preliminary investigation of the Trepov shooting, but Koni permitted them to testify anyway because, as he explained later, he considered their testimony (which concerned the genesis of rumors about Bogoliubov's flogging) vital to an understanding of Zasulich's motivation. Kessel's appeal for cassation (or annulment), Koni's response, and the text of the Senate's decision are all reprinted in Koni, pp. 408–40.

119. Kucherov, "The Case of Vera Zasulich," p. 93.

120. Kudelli, p. 145.

121. *Ibid.*, p. 146; Alexander II quoted in A. E. Perets, *Dnevnik* (Moscow, 1927), pp. 49–50.

122. Geierhos, pp. 77–82.

123. Vera Figner, *Memoirs of a Revolutionist* (London, n.d.), p. 64.

124. Rostislav Steblin-Kamenskii, "Grigorii Anfimovich Popko," *Byloe*, no. 5 (1907), pp. 188–91.

125. L. G. Deich, *S. M. Kravchinskii* (Petrograd, 1919), p. 24.

126. N. A. Morozov, "Vozniknovenie 'Narodnoi Voli,'" *Byloe*, no. 12 (December 1916), pp. 19–20.

127. O. Liubatovich, "Dalekoe i nedavnee," *Byloe*, no. 5 (1906), p. 241.

128. Zasulich [19], in Zasulich [58], vol. 2, p. 141.

129. *Ibid.*, pp. 141–45, and Zasulich [17], pp. 119–24.

130. Zasulich [45], no. 12, p. 365.

Chapter Three

1. Zasulich [76], pp. 74–75.
2. *Ibid.*, pp. 71–74.
3. Rochefort, *The Adventures of My Life*, vol. 2, pp. 191–93.
4. Zasulich [76], p. 78.
5. *Ibid.*, p. 77.
6. *Ibid.*, p. 80.
7. *Ibid.*, p. 74.
8. See the two letters from Zasulich to Deich, April 3 and 4, 1879, reprinted in Nevskii, ed., vol. 2, pp. 347–48 and 348–49; also L. G. Deich, "Chernyi Peredel," in *ibid.*, p. 271.
9. Deich, "Vera Ivanovna Zasulich," p. 4; E. P. Ol'khovskii, "K istorii 'Chernogo Peredela' (1879–1881 gg.)," in B. P. Koz'min, ed., *Obshchestvennoe dvizhenie v poreformennoi Rossii: Sbornik statei* (Moscow, 1965), p. 127.
10. Deich, "Chernyi Peredel," p. 278.
11. *Ibid.*, p. 271; Baron, p. 43.
12. Aptekman, p. 190.
13. Deich, "Chernyi Peredel," pp. 269–71.
14. For more on this see Wortman, *The Crisis of Russian Populism*.
15. One such individual was Gleb Uspenskii (no relation to Pyotr Uspenskii, Zasulich's brother-in-law), whose emotional collapse is described in *ibid.*, pp. 61–100.
16. Quoted in Venturi, p. 649.
17. Accounts in English of the split can be found in *ibid.*, pp. 633–65, and in Yarmolinsky, pp. 217–23. Plekhanov's role in this split is described in considerable detail in Baron, pp. 30–47. Venturi (p. 656) says that Zasulich attended the final session of the Voronezh conference, which would mean that she returned to Russia no later than the last week of June. However, he offers no documentation to corroborate his assertion. In this case one is inclined to accept Deich's account in "Chernyi Peredel" of Zasulich's movements, in which he states explicitly that she returned to Russia only after the Voronezh conference had disbanded.

18. The quotation is from an "Open Letter" in *Obshchina*, nos. 8–9 (October 20, 1878), signed by Deich, Zasulich, Kravchinskii, and Stefanovich.

19. Volk points out that, in the spring of 1880, the Chernoperedel'tsy added to their program a point recognizing the "importance" of terrorism. One has to remember, however, that some members of the group, notably Plekhanov, agreed to this addition reluctantly, and that for most of the others it did not imply any lessening of their commitment to mass agitation. Volk, p. 236.

20. Aptekman, pp. 189–96.

21. Baron, pp. 54–55.

22. An analysis of Plekhanov's views in these matters can be found in A. Walicki, *The Controversy over Capitalism* (London, 1969), pp. 147–56.

23. G. V. Plekhanov, "Zakon ekonomicheskogo razvitiia obshchestva i zadacha sotsializma v Rossii," reprinted in Plekhanov, *Sochineniia*, vol. 1, pp. 69–70.

24. A. V. Lunacharskii, *Revolutionary Silhouettes* (London, 1967), pp. 59–60, 85–95; Leon Trotsky, *My Life*, pp. 155–65; Baron, p. 213; V. I. Lenin, "Kak chut' ne potukhla 'Iskra,'" reprinted in Lenin, *Sochineniia*, vol. 4, pp. 309–24. For Zasulich on Plekhanov's faults see, for example, her letter to Kravchinskii, October 8, 1888, in Deich, ed., *Gruppa 'Osvobozhdenie Truda,'* vol. 1, pp. 200–201.

25. Venturi, pp. 705–6.

26. Plekhanov, "Zakon ekonomicheskogo," p. 67. For an analysis of Axelrod's intellectual evolution, very different from Plekhanov's in its reliance upon empirical evidence and observation, the reader is referred to Abraham Ascher's excellent study, *Pavel Axelrod and the Development of Menshevism*, especially pp. 25–55.

27. Plekhanov, "Zakon ekonomicheskogo," p. 67.

28. V. I. Nevskii, "Gruppa 'Osvobozhdenie Truda' v period 1883–1894," in Nevskii, ed., vol. 2, p. 28.

29. Deich, editorial note, *Gruppa*, vol. 2, p. 218.

30. See V. P. Vorontsov, *Sud'by kapitalizma v Rossii* (St. Petersburg, 1882); also Theodore Dan, *The Origins of Bolshevism* (New York, 1964), pp. 141–46.

31. Deich, editorial note, *Gruppa*, vol. 2, p. 218.

32. Letter, Zasulich to Marx, February 16, 1881, *ibid.*, p. 222. It is not clear whether Zasulich was writing for others as well as herself. B. I. Nikolaevskii, P. A. Berlin, and V. S. Voitinskii, the editors of *Iz arkhiva P. B. Aksel'roda*, claim in an introductory note that Zasulich wrote to Marx on behalf of Chernyi Peredel. A Soviet historian, Iu. Z. Polevoi, argues the same in *Zarozhdenie Marksizma v Rossii*, p. 163. Deich says in an introduction to "Pis'ma Fr. Engel'sa k Vere Ivanovne Zasulich," *Gruppa*, vol. 1, p. 133, that the question of the commune was simply of "general interest." In the second volume of *Gruppa 'Osvobozhdenie Truda,'* however, Deich asserts that Zasulich sent her letter after an

argument over Vorontsov's ideas involving Kravchinskii, Stefanovich, Deich, two Polish socialists, and herself. Deich, "Introductory Note" to "Pis'ma Plekhanovym," *Gruppa*, vol. 2, pp. 217–18. Deich's second explanation of Zasulich's motives seems the most plausible one.

33. Letter, Zasulich to Marx, February 16, 1881, *Gruppa*, vol. 2, p. 222.

34. *Ibid.*, pp. 222–23.

35. The letter, originally written in French, was reprinted in Russian translation in *ibid.*, pp. 223–24. Italics mine.

36. Karl Marx, "Address of the Central Committee to the Communist League," reprinted in Robert W. Tucker, ed., *The Marx-Engels Reader* (New York, 1972), pp. 363–73.

37. K. Marks and F. Engel's, *Izbrannye pis'ma*, p. 314.

38. Letter, Karl Marx to F. A. Sorge, November 5, 1880, in *ibid.*, pp. 338–40.

39. Baron, p. 66; *Iz arkhiva P. B. Aksel'roda*, p. 14.

40. Letter, Deich to Plekhanov (undated; March 1881), *Gruppa*, vol. 2, p. 219.

41. L. G. Deich, "Kak G. V. Plekhanov stal marksistom," *Proletarskaia revoliutsiia*, no. 7 (1922), pp. 138–39; L. G. Deich, "Iz Karliskikh tetradei," *Gruppa*, vol. 4, pp. 135–36.

42. Zasulich [74], p. 35.

43. *Ibid.*, p. 36.

44. Quoted in Solomon M. Schwarz, "Populism and Early Russian Marxism on Ways of Economic Development in Russia," in Ernest J. Simmons, ed., *Continuity and Change in Russian and Soviet Thought* (Cambridge, Mass., 1955), p. 51.

45. Letter, Zasulich to Deich (undated; 1884), *Gruppa*, vol. 3, pp. 185–86; V. Rakhmetov, "K voprosu o menshevistikikh tendentsiakh v gruppe 'Osvobozhdenie Truda,'" *Proletarskaia revoliutsiia*, no. 9/80 (1928), pp. 35–37.

46. Zasulich [8], p. v.

47. *Ibid.*, p. iii.

48. *Ibid.*, p. iv.

49. *Ibid.*, p. v.

50. *Ibid.*, p. vii.

51. Kelly, p. 135.

52. Letter, Axelrod to Zasulich (undated; February 1888), *Literaturnoe nasledie G. V. Plekhanova*, vol. 1, pp. 234–36.

53. *Perepiska K. Marksa i F. Engel'sa s russkimi politicheskimi deiateliami*, p. 248.

54. Zasulich [14], in Zasulich [58], vol. 2, pp. 28–29.

55. One thinks especially of Plekhanov's *Nashi raznoglasiia*, reprinted in Plekhanov, *Sochineniia*, vol. 2, pp. 89–356.

56. Interview with Edward Aveling in *The Clarion* (London), February 23, 1895, p. 64.

57. Editorial note in Nevskii, ed., vol. 2, p. 408.

58. Deich, "K vozniknoveniiu gruppy 'Osvobozhdenie Truda,'" pp. 196–97.

59. "Dokumenty dlia istorii Obshchestva Krasnago Kresta partii Narodnoi Voli," *Byloe*, no. 3 (1906), p. 288.

60. *Ibid.*, p. 289.

61. Letter, Zasulich to the Executive Committee of Narodnaia Volia (undated; March 1882), Nevskii, ed., vol. 2, pp. 394–98. It is not known whether Garibaldi complied with her request.

62. "Dokumenty dlia istorii Obshchestva Krasnago Kresta," pp. 290–97.

63. Letter, Executive Committee of Narodnaia Volia to Zasulich, February 2, 1884, in Deich, "K vozniknoveniiu," pp. 213–14.

64. Letter, Kravchinskii to Zasulich (undated; winter 1881–82), *Gruppa*, vol. 1, p. 216.

65. Letter, Zasulich to the Executive Committee of Narodnaia Volia (undated; March 1882), Nevskii, vol. 2, p. 396.

66. Letter, Zasulich to Lavrov (undated; October 1883), Deich, "K vozniknoveniiu," pp. 200–203.

67. See, for example, the letter of V. I. Iokel'son to a fellow Narodovolets, reprinted in Nevskii, vol. 2, pp. 401–5.

68. Letter, Zasulich to Lavrov (undated; October 1883), Deich, "K vozniknoveniiu," pp. 202–3.

69. *Ibid.*, p. 202.

70. Letter, Plekhanov to Lavrov, October 31, 1881, *Dela i dni*, no. 2 (1921), pp. 86–87.

71. L. G. Deich, "O sblizhenii i razryve s narodovol'tsami," *Proletarskaia revoliutsiia*, no. 8 (1923), pp. 15–18.

72. Quoted in Volk, pp. 393–94.

73. *Ibid.*, p. 395.

74. Letter, Kravchinskii to Zasulich (undated; April 1882), *Gruppa*, vol. 1, p. 225.

75. *Ibid.*, p. 224.

76. *Ibid.*, p. 226.

77. Zasulich to Kravchinskii (undated; 1882), Tsentral'nyi Partiinyi Arkhiv, Instituta Marksizma-Leninizma, Moscow, parts of which are reprinted in Volk, p. 397.

78. The Narodovol'tsy allowed that the Chernoperedel'tsy could join as a group, but that this process would take several months. P. B. Aksel'rod, *Perezhitoe i peredumannoe*, Book I, pp. 433–34.

79. Baron, pp. 78–88; G. V. Plekhanov, "Pochemu i kak my razoshlis' s redaktsiei 'Vestnika Narodnoi Voli,'" *Iskra*, no. 54 (1903), pp. 2–4.

80. Plekhanov quoted in Baron, p. 88; Aksel'rod, *Perezhitoe*, Book I, p. 434.

81. G. V. Plekhanov, "Ob izdanii 'Biblioteki Sovremennogo Sotsializma,'" reprinted in Plekhanov, *Sochineniia*, vol. 2, p. 22.

82. An offer that Lavrov refused. Ascher, *Pavel Alexrod*, p. 88.

83. Mikhail Dragomanov, "Obaiatel'nost' energii," *Vol'noe slovo*, no. 34, pp. 1–3.

84. This letter was reprinted in the so-called *Kalendar 'Narodnoi Voli' na 1883 god* (Geneva, n.d.), pp. 173–75.

85. This correspondence can be found in Deich, *Gruppa*, vol. 5, pp. 72–79.

86. P. B. Aksel'rod, "Gruppa 'Osvobozhdenie Truda,'" *Letopis' marksizma*, no. 6 (1928), p. 97.

87. Ascher, *Pavel Axelrod*, p. 90; Letter, Zasulich to Deich, April 3, 1879, Nevskii, vol. 2, p. 348; Letter, Zasulich to Plekhanov, November 7, 1896, *Gruppa*, vol. 5, p. 179; Letter, Deich to Zasulich, June 22, 1891, *Gruppa*, vol. 2, p. 278; Letter, Zasulich to Deich, May 16, 1899, *Gruppa*, vol. 4, pp. 261–63. Because their letters to one another had to undergo the scrutiny of the censor, they only hint at a relationship more passionate than the generally restrained language of these letters might suggest.

88. M. Visconti, "Chleny gruppy 'Osvobozhdenie Truda,'" *Gruppa*, vol. 2, p. 155.

89. R. M. Plekhanova, "Nasha zhizn' do emigratsii," *ibid.*, vol. 6, pp. 95–96.

90. Zasulich's characterization of the 1880's can be found in an obituary she wrote of N. K. Mikhailovskii in *Iskra*, no. 60 (February 25, 1904), reprinted in Zasulich [58], vol. 2, p. 444.

91. One such analysis of Marxism emphasizing and explaining its appeal in underdeveloped and non-Western countries is Adam Ulam, *The Unfinished Revolution: An Essay on the Sources and Influence of Marxism and Communism* (New York, 1960). One example drawn from Marxist history of this insidious equation of moral virtue and success is Isaac Deutscher, *Stalin* (New York, 1949), especially pp. 340–44, 565–70. That this equation appears, albeit more subtly, in the works of E. H. Carr makes it clear that not only Marxists and Marxist historians are susceptible to it. See, for example, Carr, *What Is History?* (New York, 1961).

92. L. I. Aksel'rod, pp. 39–40.

Chapter Four

1. G. V. Plekhanov, "Ob izdanii 'biblioteki sovremennogo sotsializma,'" reprinted in Plekhanov, *Sochineniia*, vol. 2, pp. 21–23.

2. Richard Pipes, *Social Democracy and the St. Petersburg Labor Movement, 1885–1897* (Cambridge, Mass., 1963), pp. ix–x, 8–12.

3. Baron, p. 126.

4. *Ibid.*, p. 127.

5. Deich, ed., editorial note, *Gruppa 'Osvobozhdenie Truda,'* vol. 3, p. 238.

6. Letter, Zasulich to Kravchinskii (undated; 1889), *ibid.*, vol. 1, pp. 213–14.

7. Baron, p. 131; Deich, editorial note, *Gruppa*, vol. 3, pp. 227–28.
8. N. Kuliabko-Koretskii, "Moi vstrechi s V. I. Zasulich," *Gruppa*, vol. 3, pp. 68–72, 77–78; Ts. S. Gurevich-Martynovskaia, "Znakomstvo s G. V. Plekhanovym i V. I. Zasulich," *ibid.*, vol. 2, pp. 160–67.
9. Baron, pp. 131–33.
10. These programs have been reprinted in Plekhanov, *Sochineniia*, vol. 2, pp. 357–62, 400–404.
11. Zasulich [10], reprinted in Zasulich [58], vol. 1, pp. 245–318.
12. *Ibid.*, p. 317.
13. Zasulich [19], reprinted in Zasulich [58], vol. 2, pp. 111–47.
14. *Ibid.*, p. 119.
15. *Ibid.*, pp. 120–21.
16. For Axelrod's views on this point, the reader is referred to his "Ob"edinenie rossiiskoi sotsial-demokratii i eia zadachi," *Iskra*, nos. 55 (December 15, 1903) and 57 (January 15, 1904).
17. V. I. Lenin, *Chto delat?* reprinted in V. I. Lenin, *Sochineniia*, 5th ed. (Moscow, 1959), vol. 6, pp. 30–31, 124–27.
18. F. Engels, "On Social Conditions in Russia," written in 1875 in the course of his controversy with Pyotr Tkachev, reprinted in Lewis S. Feuer, ed., *Marx and Engels: Basic Writings on Politics and Philosophy* (Garden City, N.Y., 1959), pp. 470–74.
19. See G. V. Plekhanov, *Sotsializm i politicheskaia bor'ba* (Geneva, 1883). Axelrod's biographer maintains that Axelrod generally agreed with Plekhanov's outline. Ascher, *Pavel Axelrod*, p. 95. See also P. B. Aksel'rod, *Rabochee dvizhenie i sotsial'naia demokratiia* (Geneva, 1883), *passim*.
20. V. I. Lenin, *Left-Wing Communism: An Infantile Disorder*, reprinted in V. I. Lenin, *Selected Works* (Moscow, 1961), vol. 3, p. 434.
21. Zasulich [14], reprinted in Zasulich [58], vol. 2, pp. 1–54.
22. Kelly's detailed and cogent critique of this essay was very helpful in formulating my own analysis, but our accounts differ on several points of interpretation and emphasis. See Kelly, pp. 132–78.
23. Baron, pp. 107–8.
24. "Revoliutsionery iz burzhuaznoi sredy," pp. 3–9. See also Zasulich [29], "Bibliografiia" (1897), pp. 16–21, and her "Cherez 16 let," an addendum to "Revoliutsionery iz burzhuaznoi sredy," written in 1906 and first published in Zasulich [58], vol. 2, pp. 55–64.
25. "Revoliutsionery iz burzhuaznoi sredy," p. 44.
26. "Literaturnye zametki: nashi 'sovremennye' literaturnye protivorechiia," Zasulich [15], reprinted in Zasulich [58], vol. 2, pp. 65–108.
27. "Revoliutsionery iz burzhuaznoi sredy," pp. 47–48.
28. *Ibid.*, pp. 3–15, 23–24, 35.
29. *Ibid.*, p. 48.
30. M. S. Aleksandrov, "Gruppa Narodovol'tsev (1891–1894)," *Byloe*, no. 11 (1906), pp. 9–10.
31. "Revoliutsionery iz burzhuaznoi sredy," pp. 53–54.

32. "Revoliutsionnoe studenchestvo," Zasulich [50], reprinted in Za-sulich [58], vol. 2, pp. 427–38.

33. Zasulich [16], p. 2. On occasion Zasulich would substitute "the people" for "the workers" in her formulation, as in "Revoliutsionery iz burzhuaznoi sredy," p. 29.

34. "Revoliutsionery iz burzhuaznoi sredy," p. 15.

35. "Kar'era nigilista," Zasulich [58], vol. 2, p. 146.

36. Zasulich [70], "Sotsializm Smol'nogo" (1918), reprinted in Zaria, nos. 9–10 (1922), pp. 285–86.

37. For example, Zasulich [62], "Po povodu odnogo voprosa" (1913), pp. 2–3.

38. Quoted in "Lenin. Zamechaniia na proekt programmy," Leninskii sbornik, vol. 2, p. 67.

39. Zasulich [52], p. 6.

40. Zasulich [16].

41. Zasulich [15], reprinted in Zasulich [58], vol. 2, pp. 65–108.

42. Ibid., p. 101.

43. Ibid., p. 98.

44. Zasulich [28], in Zasulich [58], vol. 2, p. 184.

45. Richard G. Robbins, Famine in Russia, 1891–1892 (New York, 1975), especially pp. 168–73.

46. Haimson, pp. 49–50.

47. Martov, p. 86.

48. B. I. Nikolaevskii, "A. N. Potresov: opyt literaturno-politicheskoi biografii," in B. I. Nikolaevskii, ed., A. N. Potresov: posmertnyi sbornik proizvedenii (Paris, 1937), pp. 18–25.

49. G. Zhuikov, Gruppa 'Osvobozhdenie Truda' (Moscow, 1962), pp. 102–8.

50. Robert Conquest, V. I. Lenin (New York, 1972), p. 14; editorial note in Perepiska G. V. Plekhanova i P. B. Aksel'roda, vol. 1, p. 74. The letter itself has evidently been lost.

51. Iz arkhiva P. B. Aksel'roda, pp. 117–32. See also Ascher, Pavel Axelrod, p. 109.

52. The correspondence between Jogiches and the members of the Group is reprinted in Proletarskaia revoliutsiia, no. 82–83 (1928), pp. 255–85. See also Peter Nettl, Rosa Luxemburg (London, 1966), vol. 1, pp. 65–69.

53. See also Ascher, Pavel Axelrod, pp. 108–9.

54. Letter, Zasulich to Jogiches (undated; end 1891), Proletarskaia revoliutsiia, nos. 82–83, p. 265.

55. Letter, Zasulich to Axelrod, August 24, 1892, Arkhiv P. B. Aksel'roda, Nikolaevskii Collection, Hoover Institution, Stanford. Za-sulich sent a copy of this letter to Jogiches.

56. Letter, Zasulich to Axelrod (undated; August 1892), Arkhiv P. B. Aksel'roda, Nikolaevskii Collection, Hoover Institution.

57. Baron, p. 169; Letter, Zasulich to Plekhanov (undated; 1896), Gruppa, vol. 5, pp. 157–58.

58. Letter, Zasulich to Plekhanov (undated; 1894), *Gruppa*, vol. 4, pp. 280–81.

59. Letter, Zasulich to Plekhanov (undated; 1895), *ibid.*, p. 296.

60. Julius Braunthal, *A History of the International* (New York, 1969), vol. 1, pp. 195–242.

61. Gay, pp. 220–37.

62. See, for example, Marx's address in Amsterdam of September 8, 1872, reprinted in Saul K. Padover, ed., *The Karl Marx Library* (New York, 1971), vol. 1, pp. 63–65.

63. Quoted in Gay, p. 255.

64. Letter, Zasulich to Deich (undated; summer 1895), *Gruppa*, vol. 4, p. 249.

65. Letter, Zasulich to Deich (undated; winter 1895–96), *ibid.*, p. 251.

66. Letter, Zasulich to Plekhanov, January 1, 1895, *ibid.*, pp. 286–87.

67. Letter, Zasulich to Axelrod (undated; 1896), Arkhiv P. B. Aksel'roda, Nikolaevskii Collection, Hoover Institution.

68. See the letter of Eleanor Marx-Aveling to Zasulich. April 18, 1898, Arkhiv P. B. Aksel'roda, Nikolaevskii Collection, Hoover Institution. On one occasion Zasulich described the Avelings as one of her "small torments." Letter, Zasulich to Plekhanov (undated; 1896), *Gruppa*, vol. 5, p. 159.

69. See the 1896 letter from Zasulich to Plekhanov in *Gruppa*, vol. 5, pp. 163–64, and the letter from Zasulich to Axelrod (undated; end 1896), in Arkhiv P. B. Aksel'roda, Nikolaevskii Collection, Hoover Institution.

70. Letter, Zasulich to Plekhanov (undated; 1894), *Gruppa*, vol. 4, p. 283.

71. Letter, Zasulich to Plekhanov, January 1, 1895, *ibid.*, pp. 286–87.

72. *Ibid.*, p. 287.

73. Letter, Zasulich to Plekhanov, February 19, 1898, *Gruppa*, vol. 6, p. 196.

74. *Ibid.*

75. *Ibid.*

76. *Ibid.*, p. 197.

77. Zasulich [42], Zasulich [58], vol. 2, pp. 359–60.

78. Letter, Zasulich to Plekhanov (undated; 1896), *Gruppa*, vol. 5, p. 176. Her biographical essay, entitled *Zhan-Zhak Russo*, is reprinted in Zasulich [58], vol. 1, pp. 1–144.

79. Letter, Zasulich to Plekhanov (undated; 1895), *Gruppa*, vol. 4, p. 306.

80. Zasulich [31], in Zasulich [58], vol. 1, p. 108.

81. *Ibid.*, p. 109.

82. Letter, Lenin to Potresov, April 27, 1899, V. I. Lenin, *Sochineniia*, 3d ed. (Moscow, 1932), vol. 28, pp. 32–33.

83. Letter, Zasulich to Plekhanov (undated; 1896), *Gruppa*, vol. 5, pp. 166–67.

84. L. G. Deich, editorial note, *ibid.*, vol. 4, p. 247.

85. Letter, Zasulich to Plekhanov (undated; 1895), *ibid.*, vol. 5, p. 152.

86. Letter, Zasulich to Plekhanov (undated; 1896), *ibid.*, p. 159.

87. Letter, Zasulich to Axelrod (undated; 1896), *ibid.*, vol. 4, pp. 168–69.

88. Letter, Zasulich to Plekhanov (undated; 1896), *ibid.*, vol. 5, pp. 163–64.

89. Letter, Zasulich to Axelrod (undated; 1896), *ibid.*, p. 168.

90. Letter, Zasulich to Plekhanov (undated; 1896), *ibid.*, p. 181.

91. Editorial note in *Perepiska G. V. Plekhanova i P. B. Aksel'roda*, vol. 2, p. 157; Letter, Zasulich to Plekhanov and Blumenfeld (undated; 1896), *ibid.*, p. 171.

92. Letter, Zasulich to Plekhanov, February 20, 1897, *Gruppa*, vol. 5, pp. 187–88; Letter, Zasulich to Plekhanov, March 10, 1897, *ibid.*, pp. 188–89.

93. Quoted in Theodore Von Laue, "Problems of Industrialization," in Theofanis George Stavrou, ed., *Russia under the Last Tsar* (Minneapolis, 1971), p. 128.

94. Von Laue, *Sergei Witte*, pp. 265–68.

95. *Ibid.*, p. 269.

96. Michael Florinsky, *Russia: A History and an Interpretation* (New York, 1958), vol. 2, p. 1159.

97. Lionel Kochan, *Russia in Revolution, 1890–1918* (New York, 1966), pp. 23–27.

Chapter Five

1. Wildman, pp. xx, 89–90.

2. See, for example, V. Akimov, *Materialy dlia kharakteristiki razvitiia rossiskoi sotsial-demokraticheskoi rabochei partii* (Geneva, 1905), and Garvi, especially pp. 3–107, which describe this change in tactics in Odessa around the turn of the century.

3. See Jeremiah Schneiderman, *Sergei Zubatov and Revolutionary Marxism: The Struggle for the Working Class in Russia* (Ithaca, 1976). The failure of *Zubatovshchina* was probably not rooted in the views of any single individual, even one as powerful as Witte, but lay in the inability of Russian autocracy to alter its self-image to include a kind of "corporate absolutism" based on an alliance between the lower classes and the Tsar.

4. Wildman, pp. 116–17.

5. P. B. Aksel'rod, Introduction to *Bor'ba sotsialisticheskikh*, pp. I–V.

6. See, for example, her previously cited remarks in 1901 on proletarian consciousness (or rather its absence), reprinted in "Lenin. Zamechaniia na proekt programmy," *Leninskii sbornik*, vol. 2, p. 67.

7. Plekhanov's views are described in Baron, pp. 231–44. With respect to Axelrod one thinks especially of his repeated calls in 1904 for a "zemstvo campaign" including all forces opposed to autocracy. Ascher, *Pavel Axelrod*, pp. 135–38, 219–23.

8. Garvi, p. 440.

9. Quoted in Aksel'rod, *Bor'ba sotsialisticheskikh*, p. 67.

10. To be sure, this interpretation emphasizing the weakness of Russian socialism prior to 1917 is not shared universally. Soviet historians, as one might expect, consider the October Revolution a culmination of many years of Bolshevik agitation, and the question of Bolshevik influence upon the Russian working class is generally incorporated in Soviet accounts into a larger mythology which places Russian Marxists at the forefront of every revolutionary action, leading every strike, writing every pamphlet, planning every street demonstration. See, for example, A. L. Sidorov, ed., *Ocherki po istorii SSSR, 1907–mart 1917* (Moscow, 1954). Such views can be safely characterized as hagiography rather than history. But even Western accounts of Russian labor unrest which seek to demonstrate that World War I did not create but only intensified instability in Russian society do not refute the thesis presented here that Social Democrats exerted relatively little influence in Russia after 1900 and that their failure to do so triggered recriminations which reduced their political power even further. Leopold Haimson, for example, argues that Bolshevik influence increased only in the relatively brief period 1912–14, that the Bolsheviks were often incapable of controlling labor unrest after helping to initiate it, and that Menshevik attempts to create a Western-style labor movement bent on reformist and trade-unionist activities were easily thwarted by the government (which considered such activities subversive) and by an influx into the labor force of peasants (recently "emancipated" by Stolypin) who considered such activities incapable of satisfying their needs. See Leopold Haimson, "The Problem of Social Stability in Urban Russia," *Slavic Review*, vol. 23, no. 4 (December 1964), pp. 619–42; vol. 24, no. 2 (March 1965), pp. 1–22. David Lane, another "revisionist" on this question of socialist influence prior to 1917, amasses enormous amounts of data to prove that the Bolsheviks had a good deal of success in gaining working class support and that this support began to grow fairly soon after the Revolution of 1905. But Lane's statistics do not yield the conclusions that he extracts from them because he confuses composition for support, claiming, in effect, that the working class supported the Bolsheviks because the majority of the Bolsheviks' supporters were workers. David Lane, *The Roots of Russian Communism: A Social and Historical Study of Russian Social Democracy, 1898–1907* (Assen, 1968).

11. The establishment of the Union also made it possible for Plekhanov, Axelrod, and Zasulich to attend the London Congress of the Socialist International in 1896 as representatives of workers' organizations inside Russia that were affiliated with the Union. *Perepiska G. V. Plekhanova i P. B. Aksel'roda*, vol. 1, p. 141.

12. Frankel, pp. 22–24.

13. A cogent account of this conflict can be found in Ascher, *Pavel Axelrod*, pp. 117–67.

14. Iu. O. Martov, "Zapiski sotsial-demokrata," *Letopis' revoliutsii*, no. 4 (1922), p. 224.

15. Martov's early years in the Vil'na region have been described in detail in Israel Getzler's *Martov: A Political Biography of a Social Democrat*, pp. 26–35. See also Martov's autobiographical *Zapiski sotsial-demokrata*.

16. *Perepiska G. V. Plekhanova i P. B. Aksel'roda*, vol. 2, p. 81.

17. Quoted in V. I. Lenin, *Sochineniia*, 4th ed., vol. 4, p. 155.

18. Reprinted in Plekhanov, *Sochineniia*, vol. 12, pp. 25, 33, 41.

19. Letter, Zasulich to Axelrod, April 13, 1893, Axelrod Archives, International Institute of Social History, Amsterdam.

20. Letter, Zasulich to Plekhanov (undated; 1897), reprinted in Deich, ed., *Gruppa 'Osvobozhdenie Truda,'* vol. 6, p. 177; Letter, Zasulich to Plekhanov (undated; 1898), *ibid.*, p. 213.

21. Letter, Zasulich to Deich (undated; September 1899), *ibid.*, vol. 4, p. 263; Letter, Zasulich to Plekhanov (undated; 1897), *ibid.*, vol. 6, p. 180.

22. Letter, Zasulich to Plekhanov (undated; 1898), *ibid.*, vol. 6, p. 222; Letter, Zasulich to Plekhanov (undated; 1897), *ibid.*, p. 174.

23. Letter, Kuskova to Grishin (undated; 1899), "Materialy k istorii pervogo s"ezda," *Proletarskaia revoliutsiia*, no. 74 (March 1928), p. 160.

24. Letter, Zasulich to Deich, May 16, 1899, *Gruppa*, vol. 4, p. 261.

25. Letter, Axelrod to Plekhanov, June 1, 1898, *Perepiska G. V. Plekhanova i P. B. Aksel'roda*, vol. 2, p. 33.

26. Letter, Zasulich to Plekhanov, May 12, 1898, *Gruppa*, vol. 6, p. 205.

27. Frankel, pp. 32–34.

28. *Perepiska G. V. Plekhanova i P. B. Aksel'roda*, vol. 2, p. 39.

29. Letter, Zasulich to Plekhanov, May 12, 1898, *Gruppa*, vol. 6, pp. 204–5.

30. Letter, Zasulich to Plekhanov (undated; 1897), *ibid.*, p. 180.

31. Letter, Zasulich to Plekhanov, May 25, 1898, *ibid.*, pp. 207–8.

32. Letter, Zasulich to Plekhanov (undated; 1898), *ibid.*, p. 218; Letter, Zasulich to Plekhanov (undated; 1898), *ibid.*, p. 232.

33. Letter, Zasulich to Plekhanov (undated; 1898), *ibid.*, p. 233; *Perepiska G. V. Plekhanova i P. B. Aksel'roda*, vol. 2, p. 28.

34. Frankel, p. 36.

35. *Programma periodicheskogo organa Soiuza Rossiiskikh Sotsialdemokratov 'Rabochee delo'* (Geneva, 1899), p. 7.

36. Deich, editorial note in *Gruppa*, vol. 6, pp. 244–45.

37. Letter, Zasulich to Plekhanov, February 2, 1898, *ibid.*, p. 194.

38. Letter, Zasulich to Plekhanov (undated; 1898), *ibid.*, p. 222.

39. Zasulich [27], *Desiateletie Morozovskoi stachki*.

40. *Ibid.*, p. 35.

41. Quoted in Haimson, *The Russian Marxists*, p. 82. This pamphlet

was written by Arkady Kremer and edited by Iulii Martov. Many who read it immediately after its publication misconstrued it to imply that the objective of economist agitation was merely the granting of concessions by the government. Some readers concluded that this objective was worth pursuing, others that it was not. But both conclusions were based upon a misconception of exactly what the pamphlet advocated. One of the few who read *Ob agitatsii* and understood its tactical subtlety was Garvi, who indicates in his *Vospominaniia*, p. 26, that he realized economist agitation was meant only as a first step toward avowedly political struggle. This entire matter is treated very well in Wildman, pp. 46–47.

42. Nikolaevskii and Potresov, eds., p. 355; Georges Haupt and Jean-Jacques Marie, eds., *Makers of the Russian Revolution* (Ithaca, 1974), p. 390. I have been unable to discover the fate or the whereabouts of Zasulich's mother after Vera's arrest in 1869 or even to determine whether she was still alive when Zasulich returned to Russia in 1899. Alexandra Uspenskaia returned to European Russia from Siberian exile in 1882 and died in Moscow in 1924. There is no evidence that the two sisters were reunited in 1899.

43. Letter, Zasulich to Plekhanov (undated; spring 1900), *Gruppa*, vol. 6, p. 250; quoted in Nikolaevskii and Potresov, p. 11.

44. See, for example, Lenin's "Ot kakogo nasledstva my otkazyvaemsia?" reprinted in his *Sochineniia*, 4th ed., vol. 2, p. 489.

45. See the letter to his mother, April 6, 1900, quoted in Kovnator's notes to Zasulich [77], p. 297; Krupskaia, p. 55; Lenin quoted in Kovnator, p. 15.

46. Letter, Zasulich to Plekhanov (undated; 1900), vol. 6, p. 250.

47. Accounts of this episode can be found in Baron, pp. 209–18, and in Wolfe, pp. 147–52.

48. V. I. Lenin, "Kak chut' ne potukhla 'Iskra,'" reprinted in Lenin, *Sochineniia*, 4th ed., vol. 2, p. 316.

49. Letter, Zasulich to Deich (undated; September 1899), *Gruppa*, vol. 4, p. 264.

50. Lenin, "Kak chut' ne potukhla 'Iskra,'" p. 318.

51. Baron, p. 231.

52. Wildman, p. 230.

53. V. I. Zasulich [37], "Po povodu sovremennykh sobytii," reprinted as "Vystrel Karpovicha" in Zasulich [58], vol. 2, pp. 389–400.

54. *Ibid.*, p. 399.

55. Zasulich [39], reprinted in Zasulich [58], vol. 2, pp. 401–10.

56. Kelly, p. 221; *Perepiska G. V. Plekhanova i P. B. Aksel'roda*, vol. 2, pp. 139–43; *Leninskii sbornik*, vol. 1, pp. 72–75.

57. P. N. (pseudonym of Lenin), "Goniteli zemstva i annibaly liberalizma," *Zaria*, nos. 2–3 (December 1901), pp. 60–100.

58. Letter, Zasulich to Potresov (undated; May 1900), Nikolaevskii and Potresov, pp. 63–64, and editorial note, p. 357; Peter Struve, "My

Contacts and Conflicts with Lenin," *Slavonic and East European Review,* vol. 12, no. 36 (April 1934), p. 591.

59. Zasulich [32], reprinted in Zasulich [58], vol. 2, pp. 221–301; Zasulich [38], reprinted in Russian in *Katorga i ssylka,* no. 6(55), (1929), pp. 41–43.

60. For an exhaustive treatment of this issue see Stites, especially pp. 29–63, 89–154.

61. Zasulich [38], p. 42.

62. *Ibid.*

63. *Ibid.,* pp. 42–43.

64. Barbara Clements, *Bolshevik Feminist: The Life of Aleksandra Kollontai* (Bloomington, 1979), pp. 55–81.

65. Beatrice Brodsky Farnsworth, "Bolshevism, the Woman Question, and Aleksandra Kollontai," *American Historical Review,* vol. 81, no. 2 (April 1976), p. 294.

66. Stites, pp. 233–77; Alfred G. Meyer, "Marxism and the Women's Movement," in Atkinson, Dallin, and Lapidus, eds., p. 112.

67. Zasulich [32], in Zasulich [58], vol. 2, pp. 238–39.

68. *Ibid.,* p. 249.

69. Pisarev quoted in *ibid.,* pp. 228–29.

70. *Ibid.,* p. 255.

71. *Ibid.,* p. 249–50.

72. Kovnator, p. 30.

73. Zasulich [42], reprinted in Zasulich [58], vol. 2, pp. 313–71; the Struve quote is on p. 324.

74. Zasulich found especially objectionable Berdiaev's *Sub"ektivizm i individualizm v obshchestvennoi filosofii* (St. Petersburg, 1901) and "Bor'ba za idealizm," *Mir bozhii,* no. 6 (June 1901), from both of which she quoted extensively in her essay.

75. Zasulich, "Elementy idealizma v sotsializme," pp. 332–33.

76. *Ibid.,* p. 352.

77. *Ibid.,* p. 340.

78. Zasulich [31], in Zasulich [58], vol. 1, p. 82.

79. Zasulich, "Elementy idealizma v sotsializme," pp. 349–50.

80. *Ibid.,* p. 350.

81. *Ibid.,* p. 344.

82. *Ibid.*

83. *Ibid.,* p. 346.

84. Zasulich [70], "Sotsializm Smol'nogo."

85. Adam Ulam, *The Bolsheviks* (New York, 1965), p. 171.

86. Trotsky, *My Life,* p. 144.

87. Dan, p. 61.

88. V. I. Lenin, "Zamechaniia na vtoroi proekt programmy Plekhanova," reprinted in Lenin, *Sochineniia,* 4th ed., vol. 6, p. 21.

89. Plekhanov's drafts and Lenin's proposed revisions can be found in *Leninskii sbornik,* vol. 2, pp. 57–87.

90. Lenin, "Zamechaniia na vtoroi proekt programmy Plekhanova," pp. 78–80.

91. *Ibid.*

92. *Pis'ma P. B. Aksel'roda i Iu. O. Martova*, pp. 58–59.

93. This compromise program was reprinted in its entirety in *Zaria*, no. 4 (August 1902), pp. 3–10.

94. *Pis'ma P. B. Aksel'roda i Iu. O. Martova*, p. 59.

95. V. I. Lenin, "Agrarnaia programma Russkoi Sotsial-Demokratii," reprinted in Lenin, *Sochineniia*, 4th ed., vol. 6, pp. 91–130.

96. Letter, Axelrod to the Munich editors of *Iskra*, May 5, 1901, *Leninskii sbornik*, vol. 3, p. 169.

97. *Ibid.*, p. 371.

98. *Leninskii sbornik*, vol. 2, p. 83.

99. *Ibid.*

100. Baron, pp. 226–27.

101. *Leninskii sbornik*, vol. 3, pp. 429–30, 433.

102. Baron, p. 227.

103. Letter, Zasulich to Martov (undated; June 1902), Nikolaevskii and Potresov, pp. 92–93.

104. Letter, Zasulich to Potresov (undated; June 1902), *ibid.*, pp. 93–94.

105. *Ibid.*, pp. 95–96.

106. Wolfe, p. 231.

107. Zasulich [43], pp. 2–4.

108. Zasulich [46], pp. 3–4.

109. Zasulich [47], p. 4–10.

110. Reliable accounts can be found in English in Baron, pp. 231–41; Haimson, pp. 171–81; Getzler, pp. 75–83; Wolfe, pp. 230–48; and Schapiro, pp. 48–54. A reliable account of Zasulich's role in the Congress can be found in Kelly, pp. 245–84.

111. Wolfe, p. 240.

112. Zasulich [45], *Die Neue Zeit*, no. 11 (December 6, 1902), p. 329.

113. Kelly, pp. 282–84.

114. *Protokoly i stenograficheskie otchety s"ezdov i konferentsii Kommunisticheskoi Partii Sovetskogo Soiuza*, pp. 296–97, 332–34, 372, 382, 409–12.

115. Baron, p. 241.

116. Zasulich [53], p. 2; "K istorii II s"ezda RSDRP," *Katorga i ssylka*, nos. 7–8 (28–29), (1926), pp. 128–130; Kelly, pp. 254–57.

117. Zasulich [53], p. 2.

118. *Konferentsii Kommunisticheskoi Partii Sovetskogo Soiuza*, p. 359.

119. Krupskaia, p. 57.

120. Trotsky, *Lenin*, p. 44.

121. Gusev, p. 52.

122. *Ibid.*

123. Philip Pomper's recent biography of Nechaev, for example, argues that Nechaev's political choices and behavior—which, if nothing else, were far more self-destructive than Zasulich's—were motivated by

a subconscious desire for martyrdom. See Pomper, pp. 131–32, 216–19.

124. Baron, pp. 245–46.

125. Zasulich [52], pp. 4–6.

126. Axelrod's critique of Leninism, "Ob"edinenie rossiiskoi sotsial-demokratii i eia zadachi," appeared in *Iskra* in two issues in December 1903 and January 1904. Plekhanov's critique, entitled "Rabochii klass i sotsial-demokraticheskaia intelligentsiia," is reprinted in his *Sochineniia*, vol. 13, pp. 116–40.

127. Zasulich [52], p. 6. See also Zasulich [53], pp. 2–3.

128. Zasulich [52], p. 5.

129. *Ibid.*

130. *Ibid.*

131. Letter, Zasulich to Martov (undated; October 1905), Niko-laevskii and Potresov, p. 163.

132. *Ibid.*

133. Keep, p. 166.

134. Letter, Potresov to Axelrod, November 1, 1905, Nikolaevskii and Potresov, p. 164; Letter, Zasulich to Axelrod, November 1, 1905, *ibid.*, pp. 164–65.

135. Report from the Vice-Director, Department of Police, St. Petersburg, Archives of the Hoover Institution, Stanford; editorial note, Nikolaevskii and Potresov, pp. 380–81.

Chapter Six

1. Editorial note in *Pis'ma P. B. Aksel'roda i Iu. O. Martova*, p. 243.

2. Editorial note in Nikolaevskii and Potresov, eds., p. 383.

3. Letter, Zasulich to Potresov, July 8, 1910, *ibid.*, p. 205.

4. Editorial note in *ibid.*, p. 387.

5. Zasulich [57], in Zasulich [58], vol. 2, pp. 60–62.

6. Letter, Zasulich to Martov (undated; March-April 1908), Niko-laevskii and Potresov, pp. 179–81.

7. Letter, Zasulich to Axelrod, April 15, 1912, *ibid.*, p. 220.

8. Letter, Zasulich to Potresov (undated; September 1909), *ibid.*, p. 189.

9. Letter, Zasulich to Axelrod, May 21, 1912, *ibid.*, p. 223.

10. G. V. Plekhanov, "Prilozhenie vtoroe k No. 15 'Dnevnika sotsial-demokrata,' " reprinted in Plekhanov, *Sochineniia*, vol. 19, pp. 376–88.

11. Dan, Martov, and Martynov, p. 7.

12. Letter, Zasulich to Axelrod, May 21, 1912, Nikolaevskii and Po-tresov, p. 223.

13. G. V. Plekhanov, "Pis'mo k odinnadtsati 'perevodym' rabochim," *Pravda*, no. 83 (April 10, 1913), reprinted in his *Sochineniia*, vol. 19, pp. 464–67.

14. Zasulich [60], p. 1.

15. G. V. Plekhanov, "V. I. Zasulich, likvidatory i raskol'nichii fanatizm," *Pravda*, nos. 129 (June 7, 1913) and 130 (June 8, 1913),

reprinted in his *Sochineniia*, vol. 19, pp. 464–67; Zasulich [62]; V. I. Lenin, "Kak V. I. Zasulich ubivaet likvidatorstvo," *Prosveshchenie*, no. 9 (September 1913), reprinted in Lenin, *Sochineniia*, 4th ed., vol. 19, pp. 354–74.

16. For example, in his excellent biography of Stalin, Ulam maintains—incorrectly, in my opinion—that "as one looks at the two branches of Russian Marxism until the fateful days of 1917, one finds a striking similarity of views and, for the most part, of tactics." Adam Ulam, *Stalin* (New York, 1973), p. 51.

17. Zasulich [62], pp. 2–3.

18. Richard Pipes, *Russia under the Old Regime* (New York, 1974), pp. 281–318.

19. Zasulich [59], "Togda i teper'."

20. Baron, p. 286; Police Report, November 27, 1914, Archives of the Hoover Institution, Stanford; Brailovskii, p. 14.

21. Zasulich [64], pp. 3–6.

22. Letter, Zasulich to Potresov, August 22, 1917, Arkhiv P. B. Aksel'roda, Nikolaevskii Collection, Hoover Institution.

23. Zasulich [64], pp. 7–12.

24. For example, Zasulich [65], pp. 2–4.

25. Editorial note, *Pis'ma P. B. Aksel'roda i Iu. O. Martova*, p. 356.

26. Zasulich [67], pp. 3–7.

27. Leopold Haimson, ed., *The Mensheviks* (Chicago, 1974), pp. 100–101; Letter, Zasulich to Potresov, August 22, 1917, Arkhiv P. B. Aksel'roda, Nikolaevskii Collection, Hoover Institution.

28. Pares, pp. 448–49, 452.

29. George Woodcock and Ivan Avakumovic, *The Anarchist Prince: A Biography of Peter Kropotkin* (London, 1950), p. 399.

30. Zasulich [66], p. 1.

31. Zasulich [70], p. 286.

32. Telegram, Lenin to Zinoviev, February 18, 1919, *Leninskii sbornik*, vol. 24, p. 170.

33. Deich, "Vera Ivanovna Zasulich," pp. 13–14.

34. N. L. Meshcherniakov, "Vera Ivanovna Zasulich," *Pravda*, no. 99 (May 10, 1919), p. 1.

35. Vladimir Bonch-Bruevich, "Pamiati Very Ivanovny Zasulich," *Izvestiia*, no. 100 (May 11, 1919), p. 1.

36. Kovnator, p. 18.

37. Letter of L. G. Deich, May 24, 1924, p. 11, Arkhiv V. M. Zenzinova, Bakhmetoff Collection, Columbia University.

38. Letter, Zasulich to Deich (undated; 1900), in Deich, ed., *Gruppa 'Osvobozhdenie Truda,'* vol. 4, p. 267.

39. Trotsky, *Lenin*, p. 12.

40. An excellent study of German Social Democracy emphasizing its political continuity and ideological heterogeneity is Carl Schorske, *German Social Democracy, 1905–1917: The Development of the Great Schism* (New York, 1972).

Bibliography

Several archives and collections contain unpublished material concerning Zasulich. Foremost among these is the Nikolaevskii Collection in the Hoover Institution at Stanford, California. In the breadth and depth of its holdings, this collection, a lifelong project of the one-time Menshevik and Social Democratic bibliophile Boris I. Nikolaevskii, is probably the most comprehensive repository outside the Soviet Union of materials pertaining to Russian Marxism and Social Democracy. To be sure, it contains little material not already published (much of it by Nikolaevskii himself) which could be utilized directly in a biography of Zasulich. Within the Archive of P. B. Axelrod one finds a single box entitled "From the Papers of V. I. Zasulich." This box contains correspondence between Zasulich and Struve, Engels, Eleanor Aveling, Ivanshin, Blumenfeld, and Potresov as well as manuscripts of articles that were eventually published. In addition, one finds in various other sections of the collection isolated documents relevant to Zasulich: material on Krasnyi Krest, letters to the populist and Socialist Revolutionary, N. V Chaikovskii, and memoranda indicating Zasulich's presence at the London Congress of the Second International in 1896. The few references to Zasulich in the extensive Okhrana Archive deal with the establishment of Edinstvo in 1914 and her return to Russia in the fall of 1905.

The International Institute of Social History in Amsterdam, like the Nikolaevskii Collection, contains little that pertains directly to Zasulich, though the voluminous Axelrod Archives include a few letters from Zasulich which do not appear in the numerous published volumes containing her private correspondence. The Institute does have a superb collection of journals and newspapers published by Russian revolutionaries, including some which, to the best of my knowledge, cannot be found anywhere else in the world. Those directly relevant to Zasulich are *Luch*, *Zhivaia zhizn'*, and *La Commune*.

Finally, the Bakhmetoff Collection at Columbia University in New York City contains documents, letters, and memorabilia pertaining to the last years of Zasulich's life; included in this collection are Zasulich's address book, an unpublished letter of Deich, written in 1924 and incorporated in the "Arkhiv V. M. Zenzinova," and the unpublished musings of A. E. Damanskaia, which enlighten the reader about Zasulich's life in the Writers' Home.

Soviet sources are correct in the impression they give that the material on Zasulich that remains in the Dom Plekhanova in Leningrad is really too sketchy and is duplicated in far too many other, more accessible, places to warrant an extensive investigation.

The principal published works consulted in the preparation of this study are listed below.

Aksel'rod, L. I. *Etiudy i vospominaniia.* Leningrad, 1925.

Aksel'rod, P. B. *Bor'ba sotsialisticheskikh burzhuaznykh tendentsii v russkom revoliutsionnom dvizhenii.* 2d ed. St. Petersburg, 1907.

———. "Ob"edinenie rossiiskoi sotsial-demokratii i eia zadachi," *Iskra*, no. 55, December 15, 1903, and no. 57, January 15, 1904.

———. *Perezhitoe i peredumannoe*, Book I. Berlin, 1923.

Aptekman, O. V. *Obshchestvo 'Zemlia i Volia' 70-kh godov.* Leningrad, 1924.

Ascher, Abraham. "Pavel Axelrod: A Conflict between Jewish Loyalty and Revolutionary Dedication," *Russian Review*, vol. 24, July 1965.

———. *Pavel Axelrod and the Development of Menshevism.* Cambridge, Mass., 1972.

Atkinson, Dorothy; Dallin, Alexander; and Lapidus, Gail, eds. *Women in Russia.* Stanford, 1977.

Aveling, Edward. "Interview with Vera Ivanovna Zasulich," *The Clarion* (London), February 23, 1895.

Baron, Samuel H. *Plekhanov: The Father of Russian Marxism.* Stanford, 1963.

Bezobrazova, Elizaveta. "Contemporary Life and Thought in Russia," *Contemporary Review*, vol. 32, 1878.

Brailovskii, A. "V. I. Zasulich," *Zaria: Organ sotsial-demokraticheskoi mysli*, vol. 1, April 15, 1922.

Dan, F.; Martov, Iu.; and Martynov, A. *Otkrytoe pis'mo k P. B. Aksel'rodu i V. I. Zasulich.* Paris, 1912.

Dan, Lydia. "Okolo redaktsii 'Iskry,'" *Protiv techeniia*, vol. 2, 1954.

Debagorii-Mokrievich, V. *Vospominaniia.* Paris, 1894.

Deich, L. G. "Iuzhnye buntari," *Golos minuvshago*, no. 9, 1920–21.

———. "K vozniknoveniiu gruppy 'Osvobozhdenie Truda,'" *Proletarskaia revoliutsiia*, no. 4/16, 1923.

———. "Pamiati ushedshikh: Vera Ivanovna Zasulich," *Golos minuvshago*, no. 5/12, 1920–21.

———. "Vera Ivanovna Zasulich." Introduction to V. I. Zasulich, *Revoliutsionery iz burzhuaznoi sredy*, Petrograd, 1921.

———. *Za polveka.* 2 vols. Berlin, 1923.

———, ed. *Gruppa 'Osvobozhdenie Truda': Iz arkhivov G. V. Plekhanova, V. I. Zasulich i L. G. Deicha.* 6 vols. Moscow-Leningrad, 1923–28.

"Dokumenty dlia istorii Obshchestva Krasnago Kresta partii Narodnoi Voli," *Byloe*, no. 3, 1906.

Dragomanov, M. "Za chto starika obideli," *Obshchina*, April 23, 1878.

Engel's, F. *Razvitie nauchnogo sotsializma*. Translated with an introduction by V. I. Zasulich. Geneva, 1884.

Ertel, A. E. "Pis'mo ob ubiistve Sidoratskogo 31 marta goda," *Krasnyi arkhiv*, vol. 14, 1926.

Frankel, Jonathan. *Vladimir Akimov on the Dilemmas of Russian Marxism*. Cambridge, England, 1969.

Frolenko, M. F. "Iz vospominaniia o Vere Ivanovne Zasulich," *Katorga i ssylka*, vol. 10, 1924.

Gallinin, F. A. *Protsess Very Zasulich: sud i posle suda*. St. Petersburg, n.d.

Garvi, P. A. *Vospominaniia sotsialdemokrata*. New York, 1946.

Gay, Peter. *The Dilemma of Democratic Socialism: Eduard Bernstein's Challenge to Marx*. New York, 1962.

Geierhos, Wolfgang. *Vera Zasulič und die russische revolutionäre Bewegung*. Munich, 1977.

Gertsenshtein, A. M. "Tridsat' let tomu nazad," *Byloe*, no. 6, 1907.

Getzler, Israel. *Martov: A Political Biography of a Social Democrat*. Cambridge, England, 1967.

Glagol, M. N. "Protsess pervoi russkoi terroristki," *Golos minuvshago*, nos. 7–9, July–September 1918.

Gradovskii, G. K. *Itogi*. Kiev, 1908.

Gusev, S. "II s"ezd (vospominaniia)," *Proletarskaia revoliutsiia*, no. 6/77, June–July 1928.

Haimson, Leopold. *The Russian Marxists and the Origins of Bolshevism*. Cambridge, Mass., 1955.

Iakimova, A. "Pamiati Marii Aleksandrovny Kolenkinoi-Bogorodskoi," *Katorga i ssylka*, no. 2(31), 1927.

Iz arkhiva P. B. Aksel'roda. Edited by B. I. Nikolaevskii, P. A. Berlin, and V. I. Voitinskii. Berlin, 1924.

Kantor, R. "K protsessy V. I. Zasulich," *Byloe*, no. 21, 1923.

Keep, John. *The Rise of Social Democracy in Russia*. New York, 1963.

Kelly, Rita Mae Cawley. "The Role of Vera Ivanovna Zasulich in the Development of the Russian Revolutionary Movement." Unpublished Ph.D. dissertation, Indiana University, 1967.

Koni, A. F. *Sobranie sochinenii: vospominaniia o dele Very Zasulich*. Moscow, 1966.

Kovnator, R. A. "V. I. Zasulich: k istorii russkoi kritiki." Introduction to V. I. Zasulich, *Stat'i o russkoi literature*. Moscow, 1960.

Kravchinskii, Sergei. *Underground Russia*. London, 1883.

Krupskaia, Nadezhda. *Reminiscences of Lenin*. Moscow, 1959.

Kucherov, Samuel. "The Case of Vera Zasulich," *Russian Review*, vol. 11, no. 2, April 1952.

———. *Courts, Lawyers, and Trials under the Last Three Tsars*. New York, 1953.

Kudelli, P. "Final dela o Vere Zasulich," *Krasnaia letopis'*, no. 2, 1926.

Kunkl', A. A. "Meloch' proshlogo," *Katorga i ssylka*, no. 38, 1928.
————. "Vokrug dela Very Zasulich," *Katorga i ssylka*, no. 38, 1928.
Lenin, V. I. *Sochineniia*. 4th ed., 35 vols. Moscow, 1941–50.
Leninskii sbornik. 24 vols. Edited by L. Kamenev. Moscow, 1924–38.
Marks, K., and Engel's, F. *Izbrannye pis'ma*. Moscow, 1947.
Martov, Iu. O. *Zapiski sotsial-demokrata*. Moscow, 1924.
Narishkin-Kurakin, Elizaveta. *Under Three Tsars: The Memoirs of a Lady-in-Waiting*. New York, 1931.
Nevskii, V. I., ed. *Istoriko-revoliutsionnyi sbornik*, vol. 2. Leningrad, 1924.
Nikolaevskii, B. I., and Potresov, A. N., eds. *Sotsial-demokraticheskoe dvizhenie v Rossii: materialy*. Moscow and Leningrad, 1928.
Pares, Bernard. *My Russian Memoirs*. London, 1931.
Perepiska G. V. Plekhanova i P. B. Aksel'roda. Edited and annotated by P. A. Berlin, V. S. Voitinskii, and B. I. Nikolaevskii. 2 vols. Moscow, 1925.
"Perepiska G. V. Plekhanova, P. B. Aksel'roda i V. I. Zasulich s L. Iogichesem, 1891–1892," *Proletarskaia revoliutsiia*, nos. 11–12 (82–83), November–December 1928.
Perepiska K. Marksa i F. Engel'sa s russkimi politicheskimi deiateliami. Moscow, 1947.
Pipes, Richard. *Struve: Liberal on the Left, 1870–1905*. Cambridge, Mass., 1970.
Pis'ma P. B. Aksel'roda i Iu. O. Martova. Edited by F. Dan, B. Nikolaevskii, and L. Tsederbaum-Dan. The Hague, 1967.
Plekhanov, G. V. *Literaturnoe nasledie G. V. Plekhanova*. 8 vols. Moscow, 1934–40.
————. "K russkomu obshchestvu," *Obshchina*, April 1, 1878.
————. *Sochineniia*. 24 vols. Moscow, 1923–27.
Polevoi, Iu. Z. *Zarozhdenie Marksizma v Rossii*. Moscow, 1959.
Pomper, Philip. *Sergei Nechaev*. New Brunswick, 1979.
Protokoly i stenograficheskie otchety s"ezdov i konferentsii Kommunisticheskoi Partii Sovetskogo Soiuza. Moscow, 1959.
Revoliutsionnoe narodnichestvo 70-kh godov XIX veka, vol. 2. Edited by S. S. Volk. Moscow, 1965.
Rochefort, Henri. *The Adventures of My Life*. 2 vols. New York, 1965.
————. "Vera Zasulich i narodovol'tsy," *Golos minuvshago*, no. 5/12, 1920–21.
Schapiro, Leonard. *The Communist Party of the Soviet Union*. New York, 1960.
Stites, Richard. *The Women's Liberation Movement in Russia*. Princeton, 1978.
Trotsky, Leon. *Lenin: Notes for a Biographer*. New York, 1971.
————. *My Life*. New York, 1970.
Ulam, Adam. *In the Name of the People*. New York, 1977.
Uspenskaia, Aleksandra. "Vospominaniia shestidesiatnitsy," *Byloe*, no. 18, 1922.
Venturi, Franco. *Roots of Revolution: A History of the Populist and Socialist*

Movements in Nineteenth Century Russia. Universal Library edition. New York, 1966.

Volk, S. S. *Narodnaia Volia: 1879–1882.* Moscow and Leningrad, 1966.

Von Laue, Theodore. *Sergei Witte and the Industrialization of Russia.* New York, 1969.

Wildman, Allan. *The Making of a Workers' Revolution: Russian Social Democracy, 1891–1903.* Chicago, 1967.

Wolfe, Bertram. *Three Who Made a Revolution.* New York, 1948.

Wortman, Richard. *The Crisis of Russian Populism.* Chicago, 1967.

Yarmolinsky, Avrahm. *Road to Revolution: A Century of Russian Radicalism.* New York, 1962.

Zasulich, V. I. [1]. "Otkrytoe pis'mo," *Obshchina*, nos. 8–9, October 20, 1878. Written with Deich, Kravchinskii, and Stefanovich.

———— [2]. "Le Mouvement Révolutionnaire en Russie," *La Commune*, 1880, nos. 26, 27, 43, 45.

———— [3]. "Irlandskoe delo," *Delo*, no. 8, 1881.

———— [4]. "Otkrytoe pis'mo M. Dragomanovu," *Kalendar 'Narodnoi Voli,'* 1883. Written with Plekhanov, Deich, Axelrod, and Bokhanovskii.

———— [5]. "Nekrolog Karla Marksa," *Kalendar 'Narodnoi Voli,'* 1883.

———— [6]. "Adressen an den Kopenhagener Kongress der deutschen Sozial-demokratie," *Sozial-Demokrat*, no. 19, May 3, 1883.

———— [7]. "Pis'mo v redaktsiiu," *Obshchee delo*, no. 54, July 6, 1883.

———— [8]. *Predislovie k broshiure F. Engel'sa: Razvitie nauchnogo sotsializma.* Geneva, 1884.

———— [9]. "Pis'ma emigrantov," *Samoupravlenie*, no. 1, 1887. Written with Plekhanov and Axelrod.

———— [10]. *Ocherk istorii mezhdunarodnogo obshchestva rabochikh.* Geneva, 1889. Reprinted in Zasulich [58], vol. 1, pp. 245–318.

———— [11]. "Pis'mo v redaktsiiu," *Svobodnaia Rossiia*, no. 3, May 1889.

———— [12]. *Ob izdanii rabochei biblioteki: piat' let tomu nazad gruppa 'O. T.,' Rabochaia biblioteka.* London, September 22, 1889.

———— [13]. "K russkim druz'iam politicheskoi svobody," *Znamia*, no. 6, 1890.

———— [14]. "Revoliutsionery iz burzhuaznoi sredy," *Sotsial-demokrat*, no. 1, 1890. Reprinted in Zasulich [58], vol. 2, pp. 1–54. Also reprinted as a separate volume with an Introduction by L. G. Deich, Petrograd, 1921.

———— [15]. "Literaturnye zametki: nashi 'sovremennye' literaturnye protivorechiia," *Sotsial-demokrat*, no. 3, 1890. Reprinted in Zasulich [58], vol. 2, pp. 65–108, and in Zasulich [77], pp. 43–83.

———— [16]. *Varlen pered sudom ispravitel'noi politsii.* Geneva, 1890.

———— [17]. "Der Terrorismus in Russland und in Europa," *Sozial-Demokrat*, Book III, December 1890.

———— [18]. *Rapport, présenté par la rédaction de la revue démocrate-socialiste au congrès international ouvrier socialiste à Bruxelles au mois d'aôut 1891.* Geneva, 1891. Written with Plekhanov.

———— [19]. "Kar'era nigilista," *Sotsial-demokrat*, no. 4, 1892. Reprinted in Zasulich [58], vol. 2, pp. 111–47, and in Zasulich [77], pp. 84–120.

———— [20]. "Privetstvie russkikh sotsial-demokratov desiatomu natsional'nomu Kongressu frantsuzskoi rabochei partii v Marsele," *S rodiny na rodinu*. Geneva, 1893.

———— [21]. *K Londonskim rabochim.* Geneva, 1893. Written with Plekhanov.

———— [22]. *Vol'ter, ego zhizn' i literaturnaia deiatel'nost'.* Geneva, 1893. Reprinted in Zasulich [58], vol. 1, pp. 145–243.

———— [23]. "S. M. Kravchinskii (nekrolog)," *Rabotnik*, nos. 1–2, 1896. Reprinted in Zasulich [58], vol. 2, pp. 153–63, and in Zasulich [76], pp. 83–93, and Zasulich [77], pp. 125–35.

———— [24]. "Strikes in Russia," *Justice*, vol. 14, no. 677, January 2, 1897.

———— [25]. "International Notes. Russia," *Justice*, vol. 14, no. 677, January 2, 1897.

———— [26]. "Pis'mo v gazetu 'Justice' ot avg. 1896," *Narodovolets*, no. 1, 1897.

———— [27]. *Predislovie k broshiure: Desiateletie Morozovskoi stachki.* Geneva, 1897.

———— [28]. "Krepostnaia podkladka 'progressivnykh' rechei," *Novoe slovo*, no. 9, June 1897. Reprinted in Zasulich [58], vol. 2, pp. 165–93, and in Zasulich [77], pp. 136–61.

———— [29]. "Bibliografiia," *Listok rabotnika*, no. 7, 1897.

———— [30]. "Plokhaia vydumka," *Novoe slovo*, no. 12, September 1897. Reprinted in Zasulich [58], vol. 2, pp. 195–219, and in Zasulich [77], pp. 162–84.

———— [31]. *Zhan-Zhak Russo.* St. Petersburg, 1898. Reprinted in Zasulich [58], vol. 1, pp. 1–144.

———— [32]. "D. I. Pisarev," *Nauchnoe obozrenie*, nos. 3, 4, 6, 7, 1900. Reprinted in Zasulich [58], vol. 2, pp. 221–301, and in Zasulich [77], pp. 185–259.

———— [33]. "Zametki chitatelia po povodu 'uprazdneniia' gg. Tuganom Baranovskim i Struve ucheniia Marksa o pribyli," *Nauchnoe obozrenie*, nos. 10 and 11, 1900. Reprinted in Zasulich [58], vol. 1, pp. 1–33.

———— [34]. "Bor'ba v tiur'me," *Zaria*, no. 1, April 1901. Reprinted in Zasulich [58], vol. 2, pp. 375–87.

———— [35]. "Shtundist Pavel Rudenko," *Iskra*, no. 1, April 1901. Reprinted in Zasulich [58], vol. 2, pp. 148–52, and in Zasulich [77], pp. 121–24.

———— [36]. "Vestnik russkoi revoliutsii," *Zaria*, no. 1, April 1901.

———— [37]. "Po povodu sovremennykh sobytii," *Zaria,* no. 3, April 1901. Reprinted as "Vystrel Karpovicha" in Zasulich [58], vol. 2, pp. 389–400.

———— [38]. "Die Frauen in der russischen Arbeiterbewegung," *Gleichheit*, no. 9, April 1901. Reprinted in Russian in *Katorga i ssylka*, no. 6 (55), 1929.

————— [39]. "Pokhval'noe slovo 'Moskovskim Vedomostiam,'" *Iskra*, no. 6, July 1901. Reprinted in Zasulich [58], vol. 2, pp. 401–10.

————— [40]."N. A. Dobroliubov," *Iskra*, no. 13, December 20, 1901. Reprinted in Zasulich [58], vol. 2, pp. 302–11, and in Zasulich [77], pp. 260–69.

————— [41]. "Vozrozhdenie revoliutsionizma v Rossii. Izdanie revoliutsionno-sotsialisticheskoi gruppy 'Svoboda'—'Svoboda' zhurnal dlia rabochikh izdanie toi zhe gruppy," *Zaria*, nos. 2–3, December 1901.

————— [42]. "Elementy idealizma v sotsializme," *Zaria*, nos. 2–3, December 1901, and no. 4, August 1902. Reprinted in Zasulich [58], vol. 2, pp. 313–71.

————— [43]. "Vozmutitel'nyi po svoei derzosti sluchai," *Iskra*, no. 22, July 1902.

————— [44]. "Mertvyi khvataet zhivogo," *Iskra*, no. 28, November 15, 1902.

————— [45]. "Die terroristische Strömung in Russland," *Die Neue Zeit*, no. 11, December 6, 1902, and no. 12, December 20, 1902.

————— [46]. "Znakomye rechi," *Iskra*, no. 31, January 1, 1903.

————— [47]. "Kishinevskie sobytiia," *Iskra*, no. 39, May 1, 1903.

————— [48]. "Po povodu odnoi tsitaty," *Iskra*, no. 42, June 15, 1903.

————— [49]. "O chem govoriat nam iiul'skie dni," *Iskra*, no. 53, November 28, 1903. Reprinted in Zasulich [58], vol. 2, pp. 411–26.

————— [50]. "Revoliutsionnoe studenchestvo," *Iskra*, no. 59, February 10, 1904. Reprinted in Zasulich [58], vol. 2, pp. 427–38.

————— [51]. "N. K. Mikhailovskii," *Iskra*, no. 60, February 25, 1904. Reprinted in Zasulich [58], vol. 2, pp. 439–45.

————— [52]. "Organizatsiia, partiia, dvizhenie," *Iskra*, no. 70, July 25, 1904.

————— [53]. "K istorii vtorogo s"ezda," *Voprosy partiinoi zhizni, otdel'noe prilozhenie k Iskra*, no. 77, November 5, 1904.

————— [54]. *Predislovie k broshiure Zh. Longe: Sotsializm v Iaponii*. Geneva, 1904.

————— [55]. "Krovavaia lozh' fariseev sinoda," *Sotsial-demokrat*, no. 4, January–February 1905.

————— [56]. "Tsivilizovannomu miru," *Iskra*, no. 84, 1905. Written with Plekhanov, Axelrod, Deich, and N. Vtorov.

————— [57]. "Cherez 16 let." Addendum to "Revoliutsionery iz burzhuaznoi sredy." First published in Zasulich [58], vol. 2, pp. 55–64.

————— [58]. *Sbornik statei*. 2 vols. St. Petersburg, 1907. All references in the Notes to works of Zasulich reprinted in *Sbornik statei* are cited from this edition.

————— [59]. "Togda i teper'," *Luch*, no. 14, January 18, 1913.

————— [60]. "G. V. Plekhanov i 'likvidatory,'" *Luch*, no. 88, April 18, 1913.

————— [61]. "Vol'noe slovo i emigratsiia," *Sovremennik*, no. 6, 1913. Reprinted in Zasulich [76], pp. 99–112.

———— [62]. "Po povodu odnogo voprosa," *Zhivaia zhizn'*, no. 8, July 19, 1913.

———— [63]. "D. A. Klements," *Nasha zaria*, no. 2, 1914. Reprinted in Zasulich [76], pp. 71–82.

———— [64]. "Posle voiny," *Delo*, no. 3, 1916.

———— [65]. "O voine," *Samozashchita: marksistskii sbornik*, vol. 1. Petrograd, 1916.

———— [66]. "Sil'naia taktika," *Edinstvo*, no. 26, April 29, 1917.

———— [67]. *Vernost' soiuznikam*. Petrograd, 1917.

———— [68]. "Slova ne ybit'," *Gazeta-protest*, November 26, 1917.

———— [69]. "V zashchitu zvaniia soldata," *Den'*, December 8, 1917.

———— [70]. "Sotsializm Smol'nogo," *Nasha zhizn'*, no. 4, February 1918. Reprinted in *Zaria*, no. 9–10, 1922.

———— [71]. "Pravdivyi issledovatel' stariny," *Byloe*, no. 13, 1918.

———— [72]. "Vospominaniia," *Byloe*, no. 14, 1919. Reprinted in Zasulich [76], pp. 9–16, 58–70, 93–98.

———— [73]. "Nechaevskoe delo." In L. G. Deich, ed., *Gruppa 'Osvobozhdenie Truda': Iz arkhivov G. V. Plekhanova, V. I. Zasulich i L. G. Deicha*, vol. 2, Moscow-Leningrad, 1924. Reprinted in Zasulich [76], pp. 17–57.

———— [74]. "K nemetskim sotsialistam, sobravshimsia v Tsiurikhe 5 fevralia," *Katorga i ssylka*, no. 6(55), 1929.

———— [75]. "Predislovie k 'Nadgrobnomu slovu Aleksandru II,'" *Katorga i ssylka*, no. 6(55), 1929.

———— [76]. *Vospominaniia*. Edited with notes by B. P. Koz'min. Moscow, 1931. All references in the Notes to works of Zasulich reprinted in *Vospominaniia* are cited from this volume.

———— [77]. *Stat'i o russkoi literature*. Edited with an Introduction by R. A. Kovnator. Moscow, 1960.

Index

Index